Superstitions
of the Sea

Superstitions of the Sea

BY JAMES CLARY

Maritime History in Art
St. Clair, Michigan

Library of Congress Catalog Card Number: 94-76334
ISBN Number: 0-916637-00-X
Copyright, © 1994 by James Clary

Published in the United States by:
Maritime History in Art
201 N. Riverside
St. Clair, Michigan 48079

Limited Edition, signed and numbered collector prints of the J. Clary
paintings and original sketches by B. Clary in this book can be obtained
by contacting:

Cap'n Jim's Gallery
201 N. Riverside
St. Clair, MI 48079
810-329-7744

Inspiration from a dream
of dreams.

To Ann and our
children Pam, Donnie,
Todd, Jimmy, and Robin.

Gather 'round mates, I've somthin' to share,
Lend me 'n ear, listen if ye dare.
I'll tell ye a yarn, I ca' not explain,
But happen it did, jest like the rain.

Contents

Preface

It is no wonder that the most popular books of most libraries are those in the "superstition" section. We are all superstitious. We may not throw salt over our shoulder when upsetting the shaker, feel uneasy when a black cat crosses our path, or take extra special care on Friday the thirteenth, but weaved throughout our daily work or leisure routines are hundreds of superstitions that we voluntarily or involuntarily adhere to. They may have been handed down in an old-fashioned family tradition or custom, because "that's the way we've always done it." They may be integrated with old religious beliefs or they may be remnants of the superstitious ways of ancient mariners, the source of most superstitions.

One sailor said that he couldn't think of any superstitions involved in his work, but during our prompted conversation he recalled that it would bring on the wind if one whistled on the bridge, and quickly added, "But that's not a superstition, it's something you just don't do."

During the research for my paintings, I pigeonholed tidbits of superstitious stories, strange legends, unusual customs, and mysterious maritime incidents discovered during my main study. *Superstitions of the Sea* began long ago through the collection of interesting material many years before my other books.

Grateful acknowledgment is made to the following persons and institutions for their assistance in the authentication of the *Superstitions of the Sea* paintings and historical text: Lloyd's Maritime Information Services, London, England; United States Coast Guard Public Affairs, New London, Connecticut; United States Navy Public Affairs, Washington, D.C.; United States Naval Academy, Annapolis, Maryland; American Steamship Company, Buffalo, New York; Sailor's International Union, Camp Springs, Maryland; General Dynamics, Electric Boat Division, Groton, Connecticut; Maine

Maritime Museum, Bath, Maine; *The Queen Mary*, Long Beach, California; Cunard Line Limited, Southampton, United Kingdom; Bermuda Archives, Hamilton, Bermuda; Texas Maritime Museum; Carriacou Boat Builders, Grenada, West Indies; Society of Navy Ship Sponsors, Arlington, Virginia; Bay Shipbuilding, Sturgeon Bay Wisconsin; Quincy Historical Society, Quincy, Massachusetts; California Academy of Sciences, San Francisco, California; Chief of the Boat, Don Kultti, USSBN *Michigan*; Defense Mapping Agency, Fairfax, Virginia; Atholl Murray; Ted Richardson; Kristen Lee; Flo Normandin; Michael Cushman; the Charles Muer Family; Maryanne Golder; Bill Barr; Hap Rourke; Cliff Hock; Capt. Sherwood Anderson; Dan Duncan; Dorothy Evans; Capt. James Kelly; Capt. Patrick Stillman; Kelly Lane; Capt. H. Peter Gronwall; Tom Seller; Ben Clary; Jerome Clary; Nicole Krejniak; Dorothy Becker; Cecelia Matthys; and William Soboleski.

Superstitions
of the Sea

1. How Maritime Superstitions Began

Over nine thousand years ago the first seafarers began to explore the Aegean Sea. These early inhabitants of what is now Greece sailed south to the island of Melos, where they discovered the hard volcanic stone obsidian from which they made sharp knives and scrapers. Pieces of this glassy material dating from the eighth millennium B.C. were found in the Franchthi Cave of the Peloponnese. Discovered at the same time were large fish bones giving evidence that man was venturing to the sea. Little is known about the primitive craft of these first seafarers. Whether they were skin-covered boats, dugout canoes, or raft logs remains a mystery. We can only surmise that these early mariners in their fragile craft must surely have met with terror the sudden and violent storms common to the Aegean Sea. Our conception of the earliest boat comes from a clay model of the oldest known sailing vessel, found in a grave at Eridu in southern Mesopotamia, dating from the fourth millennium B.C. Probably a skin-covered craft, a round vertical socket near one end of the boat suggests that the vessel carried a stepped mast; holes in the gunwales gives evidence of the use of stays.

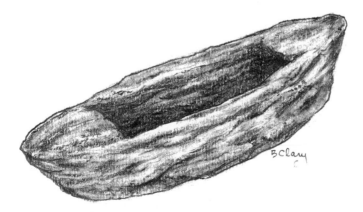

The first hint of the beginnings of superstitious beliefs among mariners is characterized by figures of fish on the prows of longboats used in the Cycladic Islands during the early Bronze Age.

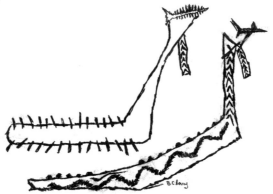

The fish ornaments were believed by historians to suggest the need for a boat to see its way. These embellishments, though part of the decoration of the vessels, announced the beginning of a ship's personality. From this theory it can be easily understood why the oculus, *or e*ye, appeared on each side of the bows of ancient Egyptian vessels. As a symbol and talisman the appearance of the eye appears to have been more in association with the all-seeing eye of Horus than the necessity of the boat to see its way along the Nile. Still, the repetitious appearance of bow ornaments on depictions of Egyptian vessels between 4000 and 3000 B.C. implied both the magical and religious importance of the bow of the ship and the belief that the vessel was a living entity.

Here, then, was the first indication of a belief in a symbol or superstition by the first seafarers. As these sailors ventured farther out to sea, they were not only vulnerable to the real dangers of freak weather phenomena in their fragile boats but they also sailed with the imaginary fears of sea monsters, fiends, devils, dragons, gods of monstrous shapes, fire-breathing bulls, terrific giants, enchanting sirens, dwarfed pygmies, man-eaters, seas of darkness, and rogue waves. The unknown bred fear. With this in mind it is easy to imagine how strange beliefs and superstitions began.

One has to wonder if Noah, the famous mariner who was spared from the great deluge in 2348 B.C., although steadfast in his obedience to and fear of God, was superstitious, for there is a legend that Satan entered and tried to sink the ark by cutting a hole in it.

The first charts the early navigators used included the depiction of reputed sea monsters, dragons, giants, and other aforementioned threats. Closer to their home ports, mariners of the time even feared the Red Sea because of its red color. It was further believed that the area beyond the Straits of Gibraltar was considered the end of the world, where no ship could navigate. An ancient Arab author wrote about a hundred-cubit-high pillar at Gibraltar embellished with a brass statue and an inscription to the effect that this area was considered the limit of navigation. Columbus was well aware of the alleged "sea of darkness" where devils dwelled and of the Sargasso Sea that devoured ships in the area we now know as the western Atlantic.[1]

An account in 1610 describing the Islands of the Bermudas as the Isle of Devils affording nothing but gusts, storms, and foul weather may have been the first dire description of the area later known as the Bermuda Triangle.

In their cruel environment of tempest seas and unknown weather phenomena, ancient mariners were often guided by strange beliefs that were nourished by the fears associated with their livelihood. From these ancient seamen came a multitude of warning omens, superstitions and other signs, and advice handed down and strictly followed through time.

In later years destitute wharf vagabonds, often impressed, drugged, and shanghaied for long voyages, easily made the better part of a ships crew. These illiterate and mistreated sailors, who barely existed through long, cold, and wet days, on little, usually advanced, pay and horrible diet, were highly vulnerable to the handed-down fears and superstitions that surrounded their harsh life. Ominous premonitions and beliefs that became part of their everyday experience were keenly observed, religiously followed, cultivated, and personally embellished. These beliefs fostered an array of taboo actions, customs, phrases, and deeds that encompassed and permeated the sailor's life. What seems to have been the norm was that a hundred good experiences could have resulted from some mysterious action, sign, omen, or dark deed, and the sailor would think nothing of it, but if a single bad experience or misfortune occurred, it was most assuredly blamed on the same circumstance.

Today, although it may not be clearly evident in the maze of our worldwide, high-tech maritime community, many of the age-old customs, traditions, and superstitions are still believed, observed, and reverently followed.

In the following chapters we will examine, in alphabetical order, everything superstitious in regard to mariners and the sea from the earliest accounts to the present. Care has been taken to relate only recorded facts. Selected myths and legends are identified to trace the origins of certain beliefs. Some topics, such as flogging, though not in the realm of superstition, are discussed to show the harsh and dreadful life of a sailor and how he was so vulnerable to fear and superstitious beliefs. Many of the stories and facts written herein were witnessed and recorded. As unexplained and unbelievable as some of these anecdotes may seem, it is not my purpose to debunk any of them, but to relate them as they were.

Notes

1. Bass, *A History of Seafaring*, 12.
2. Norton, *Ships' Figureheads*, 13.
3. Bassett, *Legends and Superstitions of the Sea and Sailors*, 12-13.

2. Animals

They read their signs, knew them well,
And feared the dangers of a wicked spell.
A witches' work, the devil's act,
Once a fable, now a fact.

There are thirteen animals that have had profound superstitious connections with the sea and with mariners. Because of their presumed bond with the supernatural, with witches, or the devil, their strange mannerisms, traits, and their reputed ability to forecast danger, the sagas of these unlucky thirteen can be traced hundreds and, in some cases, thousands of years.

Cats

With its legendary nine lives, mystical demeanor, and believed affiliation with the devil and the witch, more superstitions are connected with the cat than with any other animal. Associated with man for nearly four thousand years, the cat was honored as a goddess and scorned for its supposed satanic behavior.

Thought to have supernatural powers, the cat's ability to land safely on its feet when dropped, to see during the blackest of nights with eyes that glowed in the dark, and to emit static electricity from its fur when stroked were uncanny attributes that amazed ancient man. The Egyptians elevated the cat to the goddess Bast. From popular belief, this honor was bestowed because it rid the vast granaries of ancient Egypt of a plague of rats. Worshiped as a cat-headed idol with a human body the cat was also endowed with nine lives.[1]

Having the extraordinary agility of landing on its feet when dropped upside down from great heights, cats were

thought able to defy death. This phenomenon helped create the superstition that a cat had nine lives, and that if one killed a cat, nine years of bad luck was sure to follow.

The nine-lives superstition was further cultivated in Norse mythology. It is through this legend that the cat possibly attained its association with witches and Satan. Frigga, wife of Odin, the supreme god and creator in Norse mythology, was the goddess of married love. She traveled in a chariot drawn by a pair of cats. Odin bestowed Frigga with the power over Hel, the ninth world and domicile of the dead. When the Norse and Teuton peoples were converted to Christians, Frigga was sent to a mountain wilderness as a witch. Friday, her namesake day, was the day chosen for the weekly gatherings of the wicked witches. After seven years of service the cats that once drew the chariot of Frigga were transformed into the devil in the form of black steeds that carried the witches through the night. This myth is believed to have led to the superstition of impending bad luck, darkness, and danger that is feared when a black cat, in the disguise of the devil, crosses one's path.[2]

Thought of as taking the form of a witch because of their keen night vision, the cat was widely feared by old time mariners as a storm-raiser. The only exception were British sailors who thought one black cat brought good luck to their ships; two black cats aboard was unlucky. The wives of seamen in Scarborough, England, also kept black cats in their homes to assure their mate's safety at sea.

Sailors of old considered all cats feminine. Their every action, movement, or gesture was studied and thought to signify some deep or foreboding event. Cats were believed able to smell the wind and carry "a gale in their tail." If a cat howled or cried it was calling for witches to do their dastardly work. If a cat clawed a rug or furniture, or appeared generally uneasy, it was attempting to raise a wind. If one played with a string, lanyard, apron, or gown, rubbed its ears, licked its foot and passed it over one ear, or meowed at night, it was thought to be provoking a storm. If it licked its tail, its paws, or sneezed, it foretold of coming rain. If it stretched so that its paws touched each other or sat with its tail toward a fire, it was warning of bad weather to come. If it licked its fur the wrong way, it meant ill luck for the ship, and if it climbed the rigging, the ship was doomed! If a cat washed itself in the usual manner or slept with the back of its head down, calm weather could be expected.

In early times a cat was never to be a ship's mascot, and if a cat did happen to come aboard a ship it was always "someone's cat," never the ship's. It was, however, bad luck to display outright contempt for the animal or to harm it in any way. To provoke a cat or throw one overboard would surely raise a storm. To kick a cat brought certain bad luck and to drown one would bring a tempest.

A tragic incident in the days of our early navy was believed to have been caused by the killing of a cat. One man died and another man broke an arm after falling from the masthead. Discovering that a cat had been killed by a sailor the previous night, the crew was sure the accident happened because of the cruel act. The guilty sailor was flogged in an attempt to calm the crew but even after this punishment the men refused to mess with the man and he was so shunned that he had to be put off the ship.[3]

Though most seamen would not hurt a cat for fear of retribution, their obvious dislike of the animal was evident in the mariners' malevolent terminlogy in reference to the cat handed down over the years. The cat-o'-nine-tails was a most hated instrument of punishment, the cathead, catfall, catblock, and catdavit were various pieces of gear associated with the laborious task of raising anchor, the catlap referred to a watered-down, or weak drink, a catnap was an inadequate sleep, and a cat's paw was an insufficient breath of wind.

Seafaring cats most often received blame for any misfortune that came to their ship. A ship departing Gibraltar took aboard a beautiful black cat and was soon beseiged with endless light winds and doldrums. The crew was quick to affix the cause of their bad luck to the "Jonah" cat on board. After the cat turned up missing, an old sailor admitted that he "sank her to get a breeze."[4]

The veteran Capt. Jairus Allen of Cape Cod lost but one ship in his fifty-year career. The sailing vessel *Miss Church* had blown ashore on Long Island in an April snowstorm, and the loss was blamed on the ship's white cat, "a feline Jonah." The entire crew had been rescued, but the cat was believed lost. Crewmen rowed out to the wreck the next day to find only the topmast and a few rags of sail left above the raging sea. Unbelievably the shredded and wind-torn swatch of sail had formed a small hammock in which lay the ship's cat comfortably asleep. So, the cat was rescued too, but the crew quickly gave it away, thankful to be free of the Jonah they were sure had caused the wreck.[5]

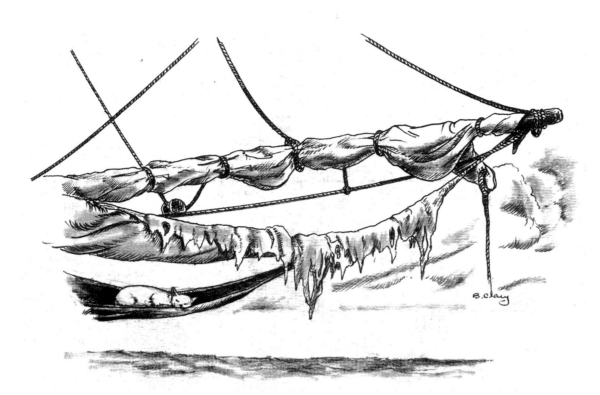

It is hard to say just when the cat became more of a friend than a foe to mariners. Scores of factual stories all but prove that the cat, feared and despised by some sailors, was truly the sailor's best friend. Sometimes a cat would "cross paths" with a nonsuperstitious ship's crew and live aboard in happy coexistence with the shipmates. Besides having the company of a pet aboard, many mariners sincerely believed that a cat was endowed with extrasensory perception and therefore able to foretell shipwrecks, sinkings, collisions, and so forth. One such incident took place as the New England paddle steamer *Portland* was making ready for departure from Boston on November 26, 1898. Passenger George Gott along with several others saw the ship's cat carry her litter of kittens off the vessel and into a nearby warehouse. Fearing something dreadful might happen to the vessel, Mr. Gott and those who witnessed the cat's exit did not embark. Their lives were spared, for the vessel sank in a hurricane that very night.[6] Was it coincidence, or did the cat somehow know of impending disaster?

One of the most mysterious incidents involving a ship's cat happened in 1955 on the *Joyita*, an interisland motor vessel out of Apia, Samoa. The ship's cook, especially fond and the

best friend of the big tomcat Ginger, the *Joyita*'s mascot, found the cat on the foredeck one day in extreme agitation. Darting to and fro, the cat, as if tormented and in great stress, rolled over and over crying out with fearful meows. Attempting to soothe the animal, the cook tried to stroke and calm the cat, but was hissed at and scratched by his close friend. The cat ran off the vessel and quickly vanished. Not wanting to depart without his companion, especially in its troubled state, the cook sent two hands ashore in search of Ginger but they only found someone who saw the cat racing away from the docks toward town. It appeared that their friend had deserted the ship for good. And so it was. *Joyita* departed but never reached her destination, a faraway island of the Samoan group. The vessel was found completely abandoned two months later north of Fiji. Although an exhaustive air-sea search of the area was undertaken, not a single trace of the *Joyita*"s crew or her passengers was ever found.[7]

During World War I, the *Remindo*, a British armed trawler, stood ready to sail from Portland, England, in service as a patrol vessel. Her duty was to guard and convoy vessels crossing the English Channel. She had just received word of a German submarine sighting in midchannel, and was fast making preparations for immediate departure. As if summoned by some supernatural voice, Victor, the ship's big gray tomcat, suddenly jumped from the vessel's foredeck to the dock and easily outran those who tried to catch him. Under orders for this emergency sortie, *Remindo* had to sail, but not before requesting that if the cat was found, it was to be confined until the vessel returned. *Remindo* had just barely cleared landfall when a massive explosion tore the ship apart. Rushing to the site, rescue vessels found nothing more than the obliterated remains of the crew floating amid the debris. It was never determined if the vessel hit a mine, had an internal explosion, or became the target of the target she was pursuing. Somehow, it appears, Victor's instinct told him of the upcoming tragedy.[8]

Another mysterious wartime incident involving a ship's cat and its danger warning ended with a bizaare twist. The British freighter *Tara* was on duty in the Mediterranean during

World War II making convoy runs to Malta. The scream of attacking aircraft, the deafening roar of antiaircraft guns, near-miss exploding bombs, and machine gun fire erupted constantly. Contrary to what most cats would do during this earsplitting chaos, Bertie, *Tara's* tomcat, appeared oblivious to the noise. Not only was he at ease and contented, he seemed to take interest in the battle by observing the engagements from his lofty post above *Tara's* bridge. After the clamor of war subsided and battle stations were secured, Bertie would descend from his position and retire to his galley quarters. *Tara's* crew was certain that they would be kept out of harm's way as long as Bertie was aboard as their good luck charm. Losing that good luck charm was a most serious threat, and you can be sure that great care was taken to assure that their mascot and friend was well looked after. One can imagine, then, the calamity that erupted one day when, just before a convoy departure, Bertie suddenly jumped overboard and began swimming to shore. A "cat overboard" alarm was sounded, and a lifeboat was quickly lowered and sent to retrieve the wet cat. Confined to a "friendly brig" until well offshore, Bertie was again safely aboard and the crew was again relaxed knowing their mascot was with them. With them to the end, for, two days later, *Tara* quickly sank after a torpedo hit by an Axis submarine. Among those lost was Bertie.

The cat, it seems, has a great advantage in times of impending peril at sea. Their extra sense not only informs them of when to flee, but when to stay, remain calm, and survive when shipmates who fail to heed its signs are lost.[9]

The U.S. Coast Guard cutter *Modoc* came upon the schooner *Melburne P. Smith* wallowing and completely dismasted by a northeaster some sixty miles east of Cape Fear in December 1923. A distress signal flew wildly from the stump of a mast. As well as could be determined from the tangled mess of cordage and spars on her decks, there was no sign of life aboard. A menace to navigation, the derelict had to be dealt with. She either had to be towed in and turned over to the authorities or destroyed with demolition charges. When coastguardsmen went over for closer examination, they were greeted by Tammy, the ship's friendly calico tabby. No one else was aboard and upon reading the last log entry, signed by the master, it was ascertained why. He had figured his best course was to abandon the ship in the midst of the storm. This was a poor decision because the holds of the vessel were filled with lumber, a buoyant cargo. Too bad, for none of the *Smith*"s crew was ever found. Tammy found a new life as a very grateful friend of the *Modoc*"s crew.[10]

The most famous seagoing cat was Fred Wunpound (he was purchased for one pound), who was "pressed into service" as a kitten aboard the HMS *Hecate* to become the "Leading Seacat" in 1971. Said to have sailed more than 250,000 miles, the shiny black mascot was known as the world's most traveled cat. Because he never quite attained his sea legs, he could usually be found in his wicker basket near the ship's gyro room, the most stable area on the vessel. A warrant was once issued for his arrest for "missing ship" and his service records provided for an allowance for "kit upkeep." He received regular promotions, two good conduct badges, and one disgraceful conduct citation. The latter was issued for behavior unbecoming of a ship's cat for an incident at a fish market. Fred "swallowed the anchor" in 1975 and lived at his retirement home ashore until he died in 1976.[11]

After a thousand years, the tradition of sailing cats aboard royal and merchant naval vessels came to an end in 1978 with the passage of strict antirabies legislation.

Rats

In ancient times to see a rat was a good omen. It was believed that as long as rats lived in a dwelling, it was safe from fire. Roman mystics derived both good and bad omens from the behavior and the squeaking of the rat. Hindus considered the rat sacred, believing that it could make itself invisible. Generally appearing to symbolize destruction, the rat was also thought to have superior wisdom because it always selected the choicest bread when seeking food.

Black rats, from their native land of the Orient, spread to every corner of the earth aboard ships. The first and great plague of rats in Europe in 1030 was said to have occurred after the arrival of a fleet of Asiatic vessels. It is further believed that the first black rat stowaways from India were transported on these ships. Another great invasion of Europe by black rats was in 1096, brought aboard the Palestinian crusade vessels. In the thirteenth century the brown and more vicious rat made its invasion from the Orient through Russia and into Europe. Settling in the bottoms of the first exploration vessels, rats, along with their surrounding superstitions, found their way to the New World.

Although rats were believed to be associated with the souls of men, though not having any direct connection with the underworld, mariners believed rats signified bad luck and dreadfully regarded the animal as a foreteller of disaster. It was thought that rats would never come aboard an ill-fated vessel and that they were capable of predicting disaster by deserting a ship. Dwelling in the bilge or bowels of a ship, rats were the first to know if a vessel was taking on water and therefore the first to make a hasty departure. If numerous rats were seen leaving their ships, early navigators attempted to kill the rats before they left, in hope of avoiding misfortune. If they could not kill the departing rats before they reached the shore, they were certain their ship was doomed.

An average population of this vermin aboard a given ship was staggering. So rat-infested were some ships that the scourge often caused a critical, end-of-voyage food shortage. A navy ship in 1800 was so infested with rats that the vessel was considered completely unusable until everything was taken off the ship to facilitate a thorough extermination of the rodents.[12] It was common in the days of the clipper ships to smoke a vessel before taking on cargo. This procedure involved making the vessel airtight by closing and sealing all cabin doors, skylights, portholes, and hatches. Huge charcoal and sulphur fires were then set atop the stone ballast beneath the hatches with big tubs of water nearby. To prevent a fire disaster, lookouts watched the fires by peering through holes in the hatch covers. Sealed up and smoking for twenty-four hours, the fires burned up all the oxygen in the air, luring all the rats to the fires and the water where they expired. After the air inside the vessel was again fresh, a search was made for the dead rats most of which had died around the fires. It was said that this smoking process killed a thousand rats on some ships.[13]

One cunning captain of a Welsh ship lying at Liverpool was said to have cleared his ship of rats by mooring alongside a neighboring ship that contained an enormous cargo of rich-smelling cheese. The hungry rodents quickly made their exit to the nearby feast. Nothing is known of the fate of the Welsh vessel or if ill luck came from the rats deserting it.

A rat departing a ship would not be the easiest thing to spot. After all they do not casually stroll down the gangplank; instead, they come aboard and exit by crawling on the mooring lines. To prevent this, many vessels today attach a circular metal apparatus to their hawsers, which has the appearance of a garbage can lid.

A single rat leaving a vessel struck terror enough in the minds of seafarers, but when they came off a ship in numbers it was cause for many sailors to desert and not look back. In July 1889, the riverboat *Paris C. Brown* was steaming on her regular run between Cincinnati, Ohio, and Plaquemine, Louisiana. Several crewmen noticed a number of rats leaving the ship, and they, in belief of the dreaded omen, ran off too. By doing so their lives were spared, for after the vessel departed, it was never heard from again, nor was any wreckage of the steamboat ever found.[14]

A similar and strange incident happened on the Great Lakes, November 13, 1872. An old sailor refused to ship on board a Lake Erie schooner because he had seen a rat swim ashore from the vessel. The schooner foundered the next night and all on board were lost.[15]

Two survivors of the *Titanic* disaster appear to have witnessed a danger sign in the form of rats running away from the bow of the ill-fated liner on the morning of April 13, 1912. Firemen John Podesta and W. Nutbean were chatting in one of the boiler rooms when they spotted half a dozen rats scurrying toward them. As the rats ran by, the men tried to kick at them, but they escaped and ran aft. Not much further thought was given the incident until after the disaster when the firemen realized that the rats had been running away from the starboard bow area, where collision with the iceberg occurred. Both Podesta and Nutbean made it into a lifeboat and were saved.[16]

Hares

Seafarers of old were wary of hares because they were thought to bring on storms. They were particularly circumspect of a dead hare on board ship. Exceptionally active in its spring mating season, hares seemed greatly affected by the weather, which fostered the proverb "as mad as a March hare." Rabbits attracted an equal measure of superstition, and both names were never to be mentioned at sea. As with the cat, hares or rabbits, as nocturnal animals with keen night vision, were thought to be associated with witches. By reciting the following verse three times, witches were said to turn themselves into hares:

I shall goe into an hare,
With sorrow and such and much care;
And I shall goe in the Devil's name
Until I come home again.[17]

An old Cornish belief was that a white hare appeared on the wharves before a storm. Fishermen in Berkshire, England, thought them to be devils or witches and were said to tremble at the mere sight of a dead hare, and in Scotland mentioning the animal's name was a sure way to bring a storm.[18]

Dogs

The most renowned superstition about the dog is that connected with the omen of approaching death when the animal howls. According to ancient beliefs, a howling dog signified a howling gale or the wind god, who was thought to bring the spirit of death. The superstition perhaps evolved from Aryan mythology in which spirits of the dead were believed carried away on howling night winds. Howling dogs or wolves characterized this deity. It is still believed by some that a dog's howling is caused by the coming spirit of death in a form that can be perceived or sensed only by animals, especially dogs. Seen only by the dog, the ghost supposedly appears just before death in the image of the living causing the dog to utter its mournful howls. In Greek mythology, Medes, the goddess of witchcraft, who roamed the earth at night, could be seen only by dogs, who, through their howling, warned of her approach.[19] So too, the dog, through a believed extra sense, could also foresee danger and death. Scottish fishermen believed a howling dog could predict a coming tempest. It was further thought that the wind would come from whatever direction the dog pointed its nose when howling.[20]

Many ship's crews became especially attached to dogs as a trusty friend and mascot, and considered them, as some considered cats, their most sacred good luck charm. Bombproof Bella, the dachshund mascot of the HMM *Sandown*, was believed to be the protector of the ship against bad luck during the heavy bombardment and divebomber attacks in the Dunkirk evacuation in 1940. The three-time decorated bulldog Peggy, who served as mascot of the HMS *Iron Duke* during the Battle of Jutland, was similarly adored by its shipmates. She slept in her own private hammock, knew all the boson's calls, and regularly fell in for physical training or football matches with the crew. She was buried at sea with full honors in 1923. Sport, the beloved mascot of the United States lighthouse tender *Hyacinth* spent twelve years on the Great Lakes vessel after being plucked from the Milwaukee River during a storm in 1914. Having the run of the ship, there seemed no operation of the ship or crew that he did not somehow participate in. No boat was ever seen leaving the ship without Sport aboard. When the old dog died in 1926, it was indeed a sad day for the crew. He was sewn up in canvas and buried at sea (Lake Michigan), off Ludington, Michigan, with kind and solemn words.[21]

The ancestors of the Belgian canal barge dogs, Schipperkes (Flemish for "little captain"), were bred especially for duty aboard low country barges. The frisky little dogs would swim to shore in the cold waters to bark at the heels of the slow-plodding tow horses. It was believed that they helped the barge captains navigate, and they were carefully trained to bark in the event someone fell overboard. Santos, the mascot of the ketch *Breath,* true to the characteristics of his breed, would bark long and loud whenever there was a sign of danger to his mates. He also proved to be a priceless navigator to his friends. After thirty-six hours of overcast, one dark night, with a storm approaching, the crew of the *Breath* could not estimate their position. They were attempting to reach the tiny island of Mayaguana in the Bahamas. As if seeking the attention of his crew, Santos suddenly began to whimper while pointing his nose into the wind. After sailing for nearly two hours on the bearing that Santo's nose pointed to, they safely gained the shelter of the island.[22]

Birds

Is there a curse placed on those who are cruel to animals? The poet Samuel Taylor Coleridge immortalized the albatross as a symbol of good luck and alludes to this belief in "the Rime of the Ancient Mariner":

> At length did cross an albatross,
> Through the fog it came;
> As if it had been a Christian soul,
> We hailed it in God's name.
>
> It ate the food it na'er did eat,
> And round and round it flew;

The ice did split with a thunder-fit,
The helmsman steer'd us through.

And a good south wind sprang up
behind;
The albatross did follow;
And every day, for food or play,
Came to the mariners' halloa!

In mist or cloud, or mast or shroud,
It perch'd for vespers nine,
While all the night, through fog-smoke
white,
Glimmer'd the pale moonshine.

" God save thee, Ancient Mariner,
From the fiends that plague thee thus;
Why look'st thou so?"—"With my
crossbow
I shot the albatross!"

And all averr'd I had kill'd the bird
That made the breeze to blow:
"Ah, wretch! " said they, "the bird to
slay,
That made the breeze to blow?"

Ancient mariners believed that the giant bird represented the souls of dead sailors. To kill one would certainly bring dark misfortunes, but to catch one with baited hook and drag it aboard to slaughter, in the mind of most sailors, was the most unlucky thing you could do, for a tempest would surely follow. It was thought that the only way to calm the ire of the air and sea spirits offended by the killing of the bird was to tie its carcass around the killer's neck and lash him to the mainmast without food or drink until the storm was over.

Obviously slapping the face of fate, some sailors killed them for food, for their plumage, or for prized tobacco pouches fashioned from the webbed feet of the giant bird. The meat being tough and foul smelling, it is hard to fathom anyone feasting on albatross. However, in want of better provisions it was edible when skinned, soaked in salt water for a day, boiled, and served with a strong sauce.[23] Once an albatross was caught and brought aboard a vessel, they were trapped within the maze of rigging, and it was near impossible for them to take flight again.

Examining the strange characteristics of the Great Wandering Albatross, the world's largest flying bird, it is easy to imagine how early seafarers might have perceived the bird to possess uncanny and supernatural powers. Hundreds of miles from land the albatross seemingly floated in midair for days on end. Because the bird barely moved its wings when gliding on the wind, it was believed that the bird never slept or slept on the wing. With a wingspan of up to ten feet and a weight of up to twenty-four pounds, they have been known to fly the raging winds of whole gales, soaring with ease and grace in confident harmony with their element. The latitudes of the Great Wandering Albatross are that of the southern oceans. Covering vast distances, they fly the donut belt of perpetual western winds that encircle the southern hemisphere from thirty degrees south to the edges of the Antarctic ice. They have been seen at a greater distance from land than any other bird. To see an albatross peacefully gliding along in the teeth of a howling tempest, which fearfully threatened his ship, might have led any mariner to believe the bird must be connected with the supernatural, and therefore not to be tampered with.

Other than their shipmates, the albatross was often the sailor's sole companion on long voyages. It was perhaps through this experience that the bond of superstitious friendship between the mariner and the albatross began. Although regarded as a companion or avoided through fear of repercussion by most seamen, sometimes its mere presence was believed to be a symbol of bad luck.

An albatross being transported to a German zoo aboard the *Calpean Star* in July 1959 was blamed for a series of misfortunes. The vessel was bound from South Georgia to Oslo and was docked at Liverpool with engine trouble after what was termed a disastrous voyage. Fifty crewmen went on strike after the albatross died in its cage from eating, it was said, a sausage roll. In 1960 the *Calpean Star* reportedly sank off Montevideo.[24]

Topman William Cammell was aloft furling the mainsail on the sailing ship *Speedwell* off Cape Horn in October 1718. Piercing westerly winds accompanied with sleet and snow encased the masts and rigging in glistening ice. Cammell cried out to his mates for help. His fingers and hands frozen, he lost his grip, fell overboard, and drowned before he could be reached. Dark clouds appeared more ominous with the sight of a black albatross hovering overhead. The scene seemed to emphasize more than ever the gloom that descended on the ship. Believing the albatross to be an ill omen, Mr. Hatley, one of the mates, in a fit of despair, shot the bird after many attempts. Shortly thereafter, Hatley was captured by the Spaniards and imprisoned, never to be seen again.[25]

Capt. James Cook, killed by natives in the Sandwich Islands in 1779, was thought to have fallen on that misfortune after he indulged in eating an albatross that his associate, Mr. Banks, had shot.[26]

Thought to embody the spirits of their dead mates, seamen at one time believed the souls of drowned men were reincarnated in sea gulls. Upset to see a gull harmed, mariners considered the act the same as killing one of their own, and were sure that if one was killed, evil would come. Retired Royal Navy Comdr A. B. Campbell, serving as an officer aboard a vessel carrying two marksmen passengers, was confronted by an alarmed bosun, who related that the two sharpshooters were on the boat deck shooting at sea gulls. The captain quickly addressed the situation by shouting, "How dare you shoot gulls from the deck of my ship!" They indignantly retorted that "Gulls don't belong to you." With that the captain declared that if they did not stop they would be put in irons, which abruptly put an end to the target practice. It was later discussed that the crew complained to the bosun that they believed the gulls were their drowned mates and if the shooting did not stop, there would be a mutiny.[27]

In old New England, gulls were believed to be the souls of unforgiving sailors that were to soar forever unless their sins were forgiven.

An old story relates how idle sailors devised a cruel game at the expense of sea gulls that were forever swooping and hovering about their ship. Three or four pieces of twine were cut in six-foot lengths and tied together at one end. To the other end of each line, a small morsel of fat was tightly attached and then thrown into the sea amid the gulls. Eyeing the feast, a gull would quickly grab one piece, and screech to other gulls that food was there for the taking. In the frenzy, other gulls would grab the other bits of food, until all was consumed. The group of gulls would then fly off attached to each other in this fashion until one or the other was forced to disgorge his portion.[28]

On coasts all over the world the sea gull has been a most highly regarded weather predictor. The general belief is that when the gulls fly toward land, a storm is approaching, or least it's a sure sign of rain. If they are seen flying low over the water or high over land, it means bad weather is sure to follow. If it was spotted sitting on the water near your vessel, it was thought to be an ill omen for that vessel. Three gulls flying together was a bad omen, and a lone gull flying in a straight line flight was thought to be tracing the drift of a corpse on the bottom of the sea. The chattering, chuckling, and fluttering of gulls or the sight of the birds cleaning their feathers in calms was also believed to be a sign of bad weather coming. In England in the late 1700s it was said that rain and stiff winds from the south-southeast always follow the appearance of sea gulls within twenty-four hours. An old Scotch verse says:

> Sea gull, sea gull, sit on the sand,
> It's never good weather when you're on the land.[29]

Perhaps the most famous sea bird is the black storm petrel also known as Mother Carey's chickens, alamottie, storm fish, or little Peter. Believed to appear before a storm as a warning to mariners, as its Latin name, *Procellaria* , infers, it did in fact warn sailors of a coming tempest by gathering under the stern of their ships. The severity of the storm was supposedly calculated by the number of birds sighted. The storm petrel commonly seen in great numbers in all seas of the world from coast to coast appeared as a close companion of the seafarer, as they were known to tirelessly follow ships to feed on the garbage thrown overboard. Still, early mariners saw the bird as a bad omen because of its black coat of feathers and, because it was often sighted hundreds of miles from land, seldom tiring, resting, or feeding. Its storm-foreboding character is described in this verse:

> Oh, stormy, stormy petrel!
> Thou art a bird of woe,
> Yet would I thou couldst tell me half
> Of the misery thou dost know.[30]

Although befriending man by warning him of approaching storms, man's unjustified contempt for the bird was exemplified in this verse:

> Thus doth the prophet of good or ill
> Meet hate from the creatures he serveth still;
> Yet he ne'er falters; so, petrel, spring
> Once more on the waves with thy stormy wing.[31]

Because they were always seen on the fly and rarely noticed on land, it was believed that the little bird hatched its eggs beneath its wings, and never rested.

> The bird of Thrace,
> Whose pinion knows no resting place.[32]

Mother Carey was the fabled wife of Davy Jones, the sea, both of whom were mythical maritime deities. To retire to "Davy Jones's locker" is the sea term for drowning. Storm petrels were often referred to as Mother Carey's chickens because they were believed to be the spirits of dead sailors.

Besides being able to swim, petrels possess the unique attribute of supporting themselves with flapping wings while rapidly striking the water with their webbed feet, which has given cause to them being compared to St. Peter walking on the water.

The crow and the raven, in very early times, served as a guide to mariners. A raven was the first bird released from Noah's Ark to search for dry land. Flok, a Norweigian navigator, was believed to have carried crows aboard as guides, before the use of the compass. When he thought he was near land, he discharged one of crows, who flew in that direction, thereby showing him the route. Ravens were also thought to be symbols of ill omen. In fact, any black animal or object, for fear of its connection with death, was generally avoided. An old Scotch verse relates how the crow looked upon the seafarer with ill will:

> As I sat on the deep sea sand,
> I saw a fair ship right at hand;
> I waved my wing, I beat my beak,
> The ship sank—and I heard a shriek.[33]

The raven's believed association with evil is related in another old ballad:

"Ah! well-a-day," the sailor said,
"Some danger doth impend;
Three ravens sit in yonder glade,
And evil will happen, I'm sore afraid,
Ere we reach our journey's end."

And what have the ravens with us to do?
Does thier sight betoken us evil?
To see one raven's lucky, 'tis true,
But it's certain misfortune to light upon two,
And meeting with three is the devil.[34]

To obtain fair winds, Chinese sailors of old offered crumbs of bread to crows that perched on their masts, and if the ravens along the Yangtze River were unsettled, sailors there feared disaster.

Similar feelings of forboding danger are attached to magpies. A master of a vessel in the Baltic trade once observed a single magpie enroute to his ship. When a friend asked why this was considered unlucky, the sailor replied, "I cannot tell you, but all the world agrees that one magpie bodes ill luck; two are not so bad; but three are the Evil One himself. I never saw three magpies but twice, and once I nearly lost my vessel, and afterwards, when I was on land, I fell from my horse and was much injured."[35]

Many other birds were believed to have sinister connections with the storm spirits. English Channel fishermen believed that the east wind was caused by the flight of the curlew or herringspear on dark nights. When they appeared overhead on a dark night, one could expect an accident. On one such occasion, the birds appeared with their dreaded song and struck fear into the fishermen, who wished to turn back. During the awful night there came a storm in which, sure enough, a boat was upset, and seven poor souls drowned[36]

Swallows, considered lucky on shore, were in ancient times unlucky at sea. Cleopatra was said to have aborted a voyage upon seeing a swallow at the masthead of her vessel.

The fish hawk, osprey gurnet, tern, swan, wren, dove, and kingfishers were all thought to bring good luck to mariners. The fish hawk and the gurnet were thought to bring especially good luck to English fishermen. The tern and the osprey were likewise favored as symbols of good luck. The sight of a swan peacefully floating was a sign of coming good weather. The wren was long esteemed as a sacred bird in England. An old tradition on the Isle of Man was to hunt the wren on a special day. Feathers acquired during this time were believed the best charm against shipwreck. Other fishermen would dare not venture out to sea without wren feathers with them to ward off disaster and storm.

The dove has a long history of being a good omen to sailors. Roman mariners would release a dove as their ship would leave port in the belief that its "homing" was a good sign of a speedy voyage. In 1590, Cortez's sailors thought the appearance of the dove was sent by God. At a time when they were out of fresh water and food to the point of starvation, they were looking for death in asking for God's mercy. At sunset on Good Friday a dove appeared and perched atop their vessel. They saw this as a sign of comfort, and, believing that land was near, steered their ship in the direction the dove flew.[37] The dove finally brought good tidings to Noah and has ever since been the sign of immortality to Christians. Truly the dove is an ancient favorable omen for mariners.

Like the dove, the kingfisher is looked upon by sailors and fishermen as a true comrade. According to Greek legend of Halcyone, the kingfisher is believed to bring fair weather. It was thought that if a sailor hung the feathers or part of the carcass of the bird somewhere on his ship, it would show them the direction the wind was blowing. English sailors believed that if a kingfisher was suspended to the mast by its beak, it would swing in the direction of the coming wind. It was common in those times to see the carcass of the bird hung somewhere on the ship, in the belief that its feathers would be renewed. The dead bird was also kept in sea chests to ward off moths.

Crowing hens, cormorants, owls, pigeons, and bluebirds. though there is little written record of lucky or unlucky incidents in connection with mariners, were also thought to be unlucky birds.

Pigs

The first reference to pigs having an association with the devil is traced back to the Bible: Matt. 8:31-32. The demons pleaded with him, "If you drive us out, send us into the herd of swine." And he said to them, "Go then!" They came out and entered the swine, and the whole herd rushed down the steep bank into the sea, where they drowned. With cloven hoofs, pigs were thought to have the "devil's mark" on their forefeet. This sign of the devil was the apparent reason why they were considered an unlucky animal. Scottish fishermen who would encounter a pig on the way to their boats would not venture out to sea that day. Mariners of old believed that pigs could see the wind and that tempests were brought on by the mere mention of the name *pig*. If a pig was seen running with a straw in its mouth, it was a sign of rain in the offing, and if one would squeal loudly, a storm was surely approaching. An old English proverb refers to them as a weather predictor:

> Grumphie smells the weather,
> An' Grumphie sees the wun';
> He kens when clouds will gather,
> And smoor the blinkin' sun.

Rather than use the word *pig*, sailors and fishermen would instead use the names "Curly-tail" "Gruff," "Little Fellah," or "cauld iron beastie." The Chinese call the pig "the long-nosed general." If the word *swine* or *pig* would accidentally enter a Scot's conversation, they would quickly touch "cold iron," the age-old guard against the devil's work.

The *Passat,* one of the great windjammers sailing during the last grain race in June 1949, encountered what was referred to as a "pig storm" after the master, who had a taste for pork, butchered the first pig for dinner.[38]

Seals, Turtles, Weasels, Fox, Wolves, Chickens, and Horses

Irish fishermen of old would not kill a seal in the belief that they were the souls of those who drowned in the great deluge. Because of seals' humanlike tender eyes and childlike cry, early seafarers believed seals could shed their skins and assume a mermaid or near-human form. Herman Melville wrote of how sailors feared the cry of seals as a sign of disaster.

The turtle, or tortoise, was also thought to be a weather predictor. If its shell was wet on land, it was a sign of rain. If a turtle was taken out of water and set face down on the ground, it was believed that a fog would lift. It was considered unlucky to kill a turtle if you did not eat it. Turtle bones carried in a sailor's pocket were thought to bring good luck. Old mariners of the Galapagos Islands believed that at death the officers of wrecked ships were transformed into tortoises.

If a weasel ran off to the left after crossing a sailor's path, it was a sure sign of ill fortune. Weasels were feared because they were thought to take the form of a witch; to hear one squeak meant that death was near. A white weasel was doubly feared as its form was compared to that of a ghost.

The fox and the wolf, also believed to appear in the form of a witch or the devil, was a definite sign of bad luck for fishermen who crossed their paths. The belief was so strong that rival fishermen would sometimes hang a dead fox near their competitor's boat as a sure way to prevent them from going out on that day.

A crowing rooster or cackling hen if heard before a voyage began meant ill luck was sure to follow. Though few superstitions connected with horses are documented, horses were also, like any four-footed animals, considered unlucky to have aboard ships.

Notes

1. De Lys, *A Treasury of American Superstition,* 97
2. Ibid., 98.
3. Roscoe and Freeman, *Picture History of the U. S. Navy,* item 448.
4. Bassett, *Legends and Superstitions of the Sea and of Sailors,* 123.
5. Baker, *The Folklore of the Sea,* 92.
6. Ibid., 84.
7. Waters, *"Tiger Afloat,"* 34.
8. bid., 35.
9. Ibid.
10. Ibid.
11. Baker, *The Folklore of the Sea,* 86-87.
12. Thrower, *Life at Sea in the Age of Sail,* 101.
13. Snyder, *Life Under Sail,* 22-23.
14. Ashley, *The Amazing World of Superstition, Prophecy, Luck, Magic & Witchcraft,* 34.
15. *Toronto Globe,* November 13, 1872.
16. Behe, *Titanic,* 37.
17. Brown, *A Book of Superstitions,* 95.
18. Bassett, *Legends and Superstitions,* 122.
19. De Lys, *A Treasury of American Superstition,* 101.
20. Bassett, *Legends and Superstitions,* 125.
21. Baker, *The Folklore of the Sea,* 86-87.
22. Muilenburg, *Saga of a Seagoing Dog,* 93-95.
23. Van Dervoort, *The Water World,* 295.
24. Baker, *Folklore of the Sea,* 149.
25. Riesenberg, *Cape Horn,* 172-74.

26. Ibid., 441.
27. Baker, *Folklore of the Sea,* 149.
28. Van Dervoort, *The Water World*, 290.
29. Bassett, *Legends and Superstitions of the Sea and Sailors,* 126-27.
30. Ibid., 128.
31. Van Dervoort, *The Water World*, 323.
32. Ibid., 294.
33. Bassett, *Legends and Superstitions of the Sea and Sailors*, 275.
34. Ibid., 275.
35. Van Dervoort, *The Water World*, 324.
36. Bassett, *Legends and Superstitions of the Sea and Sailors,* 126.
37. Ibid., 278.
38. Baker, *The Folklore of the Sea,* 95.

3. Beginning a Voyage

Bells, Boasting, Building a Vessel, and Burial

Build with luck, board with care,
Carefully sail from the devil's snare.
Hear the bells, never boast,
Bury right to rest the ghost.

Beginning a Voyage

The renowned maritime superstition of not beginning a voyage on a Friday is, with some variation, still alive in today's shipping industry. Most contemporary sailors will not ship out on a Friday; one minute after midnight that day, but never on a Friday. From Norse mythology, Friday was believed the day the wicked witches held their weekly gatherings. It was wiser to "put things off" till tomorrow so as not to offend the spirits. Friday has long been thought to be the unluckiest day of the week, as this seventeenth-century verse relates:

> Now Friday came, you old wives say,
> Of all the week's the unluckiest day.[1]

The origin of the fear of Fridays, however, dates to the Friday that Christ was crucified. The mariners' superstitious regard for the day may have gained more notoriety because of an attempt by the British admiralty to debunk the Friday superstition. As the story goes, one Captain Friday broke tradition by not allowing a gold coin, for good luck, to be placed beneath the mast of his new ship named *Friday*. Evading another traditional good luck practice, he refused to attach a red ribbon to the first spike used in construction of the vessel, and he went out of his way to assure that the building of the ship commenced on a Friday. The vessel was then launched on a Friday, and later departed on a Friday on its maiden voyage. Captain Friday, along with the ship *Friday*, was never heard from again.

Mariners could expect a double jinx if they were foolish enough to set sail on Friday the thirteenth—doubly unlucky because there were thirteen present at Christ's last supper.

This excerpt from the poem "The 13th Crossing" by Flo Normandin reflects well the ominous regard for that unlucky day.

They never saw that ship again,
but 'membered well the captain's cry,
"I'll sail her on the thirteenth, lads,
or damn it, I shall die!"

He proved one thing to everyone,
his thoughts were not a lie,
But what he proved to one and all,
was "Damn it, I shall die!"

The 13th Crossing

To ward off ill luck for this most unlucky day, about $130 million a year is spent on good luck charms in the United States, and another $275 million in business is lost because of absenteeism on Friday the thirteenth.

When a vessel was departing, certain actions by those aboard or on the wharf were considered extremely unlucky. One must not have written the name of the port of a ship's destination in the log before a vessel reached that port. Those seeing a vessel off dared not point at the ship, call after anyone aboard, or watch the ship sail out of sight, for fear it would never be seen again. It was also unlucky for those aboard to look back at anyone seeing a ship off. It was considered highly unlucky to step aboard a vessel with your left foot. It was even more unlucky for mariners to have a landlubber, often contemptuously referred to as one with "hayseed still in his hair," attempt to walk up the gangplank of their vessel with a pet animal cradled in his arms. If a sailor was lucky enough to depart without any of these unlucky actions taking place and then discover that he was sailing with a man who had unpaid bills, that was very unlucky too.

Bells

Few items of ship's gear were associated with superstition. One of these few was the ship's bell. An old belief was that a ship's bell would automatically toll if the ship sank, even if the striker was lashed in place. A jinx supposedly was created when a ship's bell was struck by mistake. The only way to eliminate the jinx was to strike the bell backward. Bad luck was also sure to follow if nine bells were inadvertently struck at sea.

A sequence of striking a ship's bell sixteen times to ring in the new year was customary in the old navy. At midnight on December 31, the oldest seaman aboard, regardless of rank, would strike eight bells, followed immediately by the youngest lad striking another eight bells.

One of the most mysterious incidents with regard to a ship's bell was said to have occurred on May 9, 1912, aboard the steamer *Montmagny* during its search for bodies from the *Titanic* disaster. The *Montmagny* was proceeding slowly through an area of debris to the location where the famous ship had sunk. Once over the believed site, the ship's bell on the *Montmagny* began tolling automatically! The Reverend S. H. Prince, a chaplain from the Church of England, later related the uncanny occurrence: "It seemed as if the elements had been purposely aroused to peal this sorrowful dirge. Strange to relate, not more that fifteen minutes after the ship passed over the spot where the great liner foundered, the ringing was not heard again. The incident was so remarkable that all on board commented on it."[2]

Boasting

If you can beleive it, one of the most unlucky traits of a sailor was to boast or brag about himself or his ship. A famous story of misfortune resulting from a boast is that of the first frigate action of the War of 1812 between the USS *Constitution* and the HMS *Guerriere*. The captain of the *Guerriere*, James

Richard Dacres, went into the battle bent on avenging the defeat of the British sloop *Little Belt* by the frigate USS *President* in a mismatched engagement some years before the war. The British captain was so determined to rectify the previous embarrassment that he had his topsails painted with a bold message: THIS IS NOT THE LITTLE BELT. In the ensuing battle, the *Constitution* so completely ravaged and dismasted the proud vessel that after only a short thirty-minute skirmish, the valiant British Captain Dacres reluctantly and sheepishly lowered his colors from the stump of his mizzenmast.[3]

Building a Vessel

Just as serious as the mariners were about their superstitions were the shipbuilders, whose work in most cases, was carefully watched over by the masters who would later sail in the vessels being built. Religious attention was given to customs and beliefs to absolutely assure that a vessel was looked upon with favor by the spirits, from the very first spike laid home to the completion of the work. Moreover, all the superstitious do's and don'ts routinely followed by the mariner at sea were likewise practiced in the building of the ships. For example, any animals or people that were considered unlucky aboard a ship were also viewed as unlucky around the shipbuilding yard.

In the early days of shipbuilding, if sparks flew when the very first blow of the workman's hammer was struck to begin work on the keel of a wooden vessel, it was believed that the ship would either be wrecked on its maiden voyage or be destroyed by fire. If a shipwright were to alter the design of a fishing boat once the keel was laid, it was considered grossly unlucky. If stolen wood was fabricated into the keel of a ship being built, it was thought that the vessel would sail much faster at night. A French shipbuilding ceremony dictated that the "ship's health" had to be drunk to before any construction could begin. Other shipbuilders would be sure to hammer the first nail in the keel in place through a horseshoe, for good luck. To signify the beginning of a favored construction, in 1921 the governor general of Canada, the Duke of Devonshire, was on hand to hammer into the keel a red-ribbonned, gold spike of the renowned Nova Scotian fishing schooner *Bluenose*. In 1963, the same ceremony was repeated at the keel-laying of the replica *Bluenose II*.

If through some accident blood flowed during the building of a vessel, it was believed that the vessel would be a death ship. Workmen were strictly cautioned to refrain from swearing in the presence of a keel for fear that if they did, nothing would go right in the building.

Certain woods, such as ash, rowan, or dogwood used in the keels of ships were thought to bring good luck, for they were supposedly despised by witches. The use of walnut was avoided by early American shipyards because of the belief that this wood attracted lightning.

Age-old superstitious ceremonies and customs in conjunction with shipbuilding are held and practiced in many shipyards today. At Ingalis Shipbuilding in Pascagoula, Mississippi, four 1993 silver dollars along with a small box of notes were recently placed beneath the foremast of an LHD-4 amphibious assault vessel for good luck. And in January 1993, the son of congressional Medal of Honor recipient and World War II hero Admiral "Red" Ramage participated in keel-laying ceremonies by inscribing his father's nickname "Red" in red pencil on the keel of the DDG-61 destroyer *Ramage* to symbolize good luck for the beginning of construction of that vessel.

Burial

Although nothing evoked more solemnity into the heart of a mariner than a burial at sea, the ritual was so filled with superstition and mysterious beliefs that any slight deviation from custom was sure to strike fear into the mariner as well. Committing one's remains to the deep is believed to be the oldest ceremony in maritime history. In the days of ancient Greece and Rome, pagan burial ceremonies held at sea consisted of appeasing the gods by placing coins in the mouths of the deceased for payment of fare to Charon to cross over the River Styx.

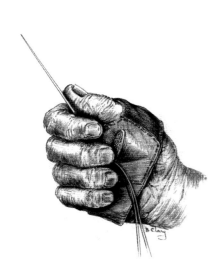

In accordance with a very old navy custom in preparing the deceased for burial at sea, the body would be placed in a canvas shroud or the poor soul's hammock, with a cannon ball or two placed at the feet of the corpse. The sailmaker would then sew the shroud with thirteen stitches, the last of which would go through the nose of the deceased. The stitch through the nose was to make sure that the corpse was truly dead, to keep the body within the shroud, and to prevent the ghost of the deceased from appearing on the decks. Careful attention was given to weighting the body for fear of it floating and following the ship. The macabre task of "sewing the corpse" usually fell to the sailmaker, who, by law, received for this work an extra fee paid from public funds. During the battle of Jutland, when the HMS *Castor* sustained twenty-three fatalities, twenty-three guineas was demanded and received by the rating who did the work.[4]

A decent burial would always take place from the starboard side of a vessel, during the daylight hours, never at night. If a decent burial was not made or was held after dark, it was thought that the dead would remain on board or return to where they were lost to haunt old shipmates. No rites of burial meant the sure return of the dead to the ship. The concern for a decent burial is related in the poem, "Burial Party," by John Masefield:[5]

'He's deader 'n nails,' the fo'cs'le said, "'n' gone to his
long sleep';
"N' about his corp,' said Tom to Dan, 'd'ye think his
corp'll keep
Till the day's done, 'n' the work's through, 'n' the ebb's
upon the neap?'

'He's deader 'n nails,' said Dan to Tom, 'n' I wish his
sperrit j'y;
He spat straight 'n' he steered true, but listen to me,
say I,
Take 'n' cover 'n' bury him now, 'n' I'll take 'n' tell
you why.

'It's rummy rig of a guffy's yarn, 'n' the jusice of a
rummy note,
But if you buries a corp at night, it takes 'n' keeps afloat,
For its bloody soul's afraid o' the dark 'n' sticks within
the throat.

"N' all the night the grey o' the dawn the dead 'un has
to swim
With a blue 'n' beastly Will o' the Wisp a burning' over
him,
With a herring, maybe, a-scoffin' a toe or a shark a chew-
in' a limb.

"N' all the night the shiverin' corp it has to swim the
sea,
With its shudderin' soul inside the throat (where a soul's
no right to be),
Till the sky's grey 'n' the dawn's clear, 'n' then the sperrit's
free.

'Now Joe was a man was right as rain. I'm sort of sore
for Joe,
'N' if we bury him durin' the day, his soul can take 'n'
go;
So we'll dump his corp when the bell strikes 'n' we can
get below.
'I'd fairly hate for him to swim in a blue 'n' beastly
light,
With his shudderin' soul inside of him a-feelin' the fishes
bite,
So over he goes at noon, say I, 'n' he shall sleep to-night.'

An improper burial at sea, at night, or during a storm brought about the worst forboding feelings among sailors. One such incident was related by Capt. Basil Hall of the Royal Navy. A much admired midshipman lost his life during the War of 1812, off the shores of the United States. Circumstances prevented the funeral during the day, so the burial took place after dark, when the ship was caught in a fierce gale. Lanterns provided dim and haunting light as the ship's crew gathered for the mournful service. The grating on which the corpse laid was nearly washed by the peaks of the raging waves. The tempest and the sea roared so violently that when the body was committed no one heard the usual splash made by the falling corpse. This predicament set fear into the crew, who believed that their beloved shipmate never touched the sea at all, but was carried away in the gale to his final resting place.[6]

A sailor said to have been murdered, hidden, and left unburied in a decomposed state aboard the *Wager* was believed to bring about a series of tempests that plagued the vessel. Once discovered the crew would not rest until the body was properly buried.[7]

Seventeenth- and early eighteenth-century French man-of-wars retained the remains of their dead in the holds of their ships until the vessel reached home port. The very disagreeable practice was for religious purposes so that the deceased could be buried on shore in consecrated soil.[8]

On an early U. S Navy ship when an officer died at sea a formal funeral ceremony was carried out. The carpenters built a plain coffin with holes bored in the upper end so that it would quickly sink to its grave. The deceased was placed in the coffin in full uniform, the lid was screwed down, and the coffin was covered with the union jack. At seven bells (half past eleven) all hands were called to bury the dead. Marines marched to the quarterdeck with arms reversed, the ensign was lowered to half-mast, the officers gathered aft with crape on their left arms, and all were hushed in silence. The band on the poopdeck played the sorrowful dirge, "The Dead March in Saul," while officer pallbearers bore the coffin to the gangway. The coffin was placed upon a wide plank, one end of which pointed overboard. With sails backed, the ship had been brought to, and the chaplain read the solemn funeral prayers. At the close of the service, eight bells were struck, and, with the words "we now commit this body to the deep," two quartermasters slowly raised the inboard end of the plank and the deceased shipmate went to his home beneath the waves. The marines then advanced to the gangway and fired a treble salute over the grave of the departed and the service was over. The boatswain "piped down," the main topsail was filled, and once again the ship was under way.[9]

The firing of muskets three times was to frighten away the devils, who it was thought could easily enter the hearts of the deceased which were vulnerable during that solemn and emotional time.

In contrast to the full ceremony devoted to the burial of officers, when poor Jack died he was sewn up in his hammock and brought to the gangway by his humble messmates, where only a part of the funeral service was read. The ship was not brought to unless a very strong breeze made it necessary.

Coffins always had to be placed at right angles to the ship's keel, and if the deceased was not buried at sea, the coffin would always be unloaded first before the living were allowed to disembark. Coffins aboard a ship always dispelled bad feelings among sailors of old. An incident during Nelson's time reflects these ill feelings. The commander had received a coffin as a gift from a fellow officer made from the mainmast of the French ship *L'Orient* to remind the famous hero that although he was surrounded in glory, he was still mortal. Nelson accepted the gift in good nature and had the coffin placed in his quarters on the *Vanguard*, but his crew could not stand the sight of the symbol of death, so it was accordingly stored below.[10]

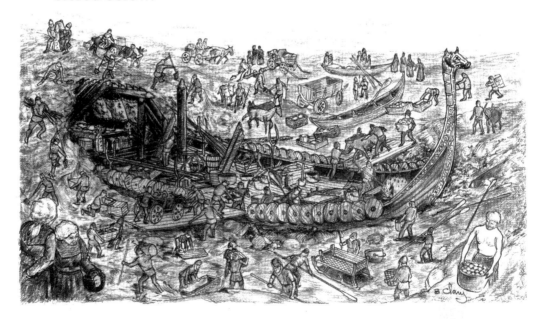

The elaborate burial ceremonies of the Vikings deserves mention. Even though great Viking chieftains would be buried on land, they were in fact buried in their longboats in an elaborate rite together with everything required for their life after death. First, a sixty-foot-long by fifty-foot-wide grave was dug near a fjord. The hero was placed in a burial chamber and surrounded with all the accoutrements for feasting and fighting. Weapons of war, chests of clothes, cooking pots, dishes, buckets of food, small boats, sleighs, and pony carts were loaded on the boat. A slave girl owned by the deceased was sacrificed and laid aboard to accompany her master. To signify high rank, a peacock was acquired through difficult trade from a distant land and sacrificed to join the dead. Horses were also sacrificed and laid in the boat to assist the chief in his future travels.

With the bow toward the sea, the boat was braced in an upright configuration and the entire grave was then filled with sand and blue clay.   Moss, twigs, and a final layer of peat were laid down to seal the grave. The mast was cut off at ground level and decorative memorial posts were situated on top. In this manner Vikings of renown were sent off on their long voyage to Valhalla, or Viking heaven.

A death of a sailor aboard a vessel in today's navy requires that the remains be stored until such time as the ship returns to its home port or until the body can be airlifted home. The old fears and foreboding feelings of sailors cognizant of the deceased stored aboard have largely vanished. A sailor who died of malaria aboard the missile cruiser USS *Worden* in 1987 was stored for a month in the ship's meat locker. Unbeknown to the two hundred-man crew for some time, when the word of the stored body did get around, nothing much was thought of the circumstance.

Notes

1. Lorie, *Superstitions*, 172.
2. Behe, *Titanic, Psychic Forwarnings of a Tragedy*, 46.
3. Gruppe, *The Frigates*, 83-89.
4. Baker, *The Folklore of the Sea*, 108.
5. Masefield, *Salt Water Poems and Ballads*, 13-14.
6. Baker, *The Folklore of the Sea*, 109.
7. Bassett, *Legends and Superstitions of the Sea and Sailors*, 474.
8. Lovette, *Naval Customs Traditions and Usage*, 41.
9. Nordhoff, *Sailor Life on Man of War and Merchant Vessel*, 219-21.
10. Van Dervoort, *The Water World*, 326.

4. Calming Storms

Cargo, Charms, Clothing, Coins, Colors, and Creatures of
the Sea

Some called on saints to still the wave,
Some trusted charms to make them brave,
Sea creatures, colors, and other fears,
Strange beliefs down through the years.

Calming Storms

Just as devils, witches, and certain animals and their actions were thought to produce storms, so too were actions, charms, sacrifices, conjurations, incantations, and oblations used to calm storms. An old-time, lascivious sailor's belief was that a storm would abate if a woman showed her nakedness to the sea. This seems a strange contradiction when it was believed extremely unlucky to have women aboard ships to begin with. Despite this fact, eloquent figures of bare-breasted women were often used for figureheads. On the prow of a vessel, the naked lady would be the first to meet and calm the ferocious seas. Long before it was called "mooning," Italian sailors sought to calm a storm by showing their bare bottoms to the wind.

A rosary cast into the sea with a string attached for retrieval was used to calm the seas by French fishermen until the 1930s. To quiet disturbed coastal waters of the Mediterranean, a glass of wine is still poured into the sea, and Eskimos pitch a bucket of fresh water into the rough seas for the same reason. Scottish fishermen believed a simple wave of the hand was enough to "kill" storm waves, and the Chinese would try to appease their storm gods by burning joss sticks in their honor.[1] Ancient mariners tried to calm the seas by throwing a coin into the water as a sacrifice to sea gods.

In life-threatening tempests, making sincere and near impossible-to-keep promises to the Virgin Mary or other patron saints was a common practice by old-time devout Catholic sailors. These mariners, who often beseeched the Holy Mother during storms, claimed to have had visions of her in the clouds or walking the tormented seas. They were convinced that she held more domain over the seas than all the saints in heaven. The Virgin Mother was claimed to have saved from shipwreck the Earl of Salisbury in 1220, England's Edward III and Edward IV, and Aethelsiga in the eleventh century.[2]

To be spared from an awful storm, one French sailor, it was said, went further than a mere promise to end his lustful ways. If he would only be saved, he vowed to find and marry the most immoral and ugly maiden upon his return home. With great effort to remain true to his word, after being saved from the storm, he found and married a girl just as he had promised.[3]

Many maritime patron saints were often evoked amid storms and shipwreck disasters. St. Nicholas, perhaps the most famous sailor's guardian, whom we will discuss in a later chapter, was often believed to have allayed stormy seas. St. Anne was believed a powerful aid to those in great danger; St. Peter, the maritime saint; St. Erasmus, St. Gonzales de Tuy, St. Ninian, St. Ringar, St. Helena, and St. Edmund were all claimed to have aided mariners in peril. St. Mark, patron of Venetian fishermen, was known to have calmed a stormy sea; St. Leonore, St. Germanus, and St. Thomas of Canterbury were all known to have saved sinking ships.

Mysterious Cargo

Sometimes the cargo or the ballast a ship carried was blamed for ill luck and dreaded misfortune. If the freight taken aboard was perceived by a ship's crew to be in any way connected with death or aligned with other mysterious omens, it was indeed blamed for whatever bad turn of luck might be encountered. When a ship carried little or no cargo, it would still carry ballast. Usually a heavy material, such as stone, iron, or gravel, it was placed low in a vessel's holds to provide increased stability and lower the center of gravity. In early times, if a ship carried white ballast stones or stones from a graveyard, it was deemed a bad omen.

A mysterious story about the so-called fatal ballast of the windjammer *Hinemoa* deserves mention. The sleek four-masted *Hinemoa* was built in 1890 and was fitted with refrigeration gear for the frozen-mutton trade from New Zealand. Although some considered her a good ship with an outstanding speed record, others openly declared that she was cursed, which deeply influenced her crews and her trade.

On her very first voyage four apprentices died from typhoid, which was believed caused by germs thought to be in her ballast. This "unlucky" rubble, it was said, came from an old London burial ground. During her outbound passage while running her easting down,[4] this ballast shifted to leeward, which laid the ship on her beam ends. After the *Hinemoa* reached her New Zealand destination, a lighter schooner came alongside to remove some of the ballast. Despite the grave warnings by crewmen of the *Hinemoa*, the schooner sailed off with enough of the "evil" material to later cause that ship to wind up on her beam ends from a similar shift of the same unlucky ballast. Other dark misfortunes, including the frequent breakdown of her freezing equipment, were all blamed on this ballast. One of her masters went insane, another was let go for a criminal act, one was a drunkard who caused a mutiny, one was found dead from an apparent suicide, one committed suicide after leaving the ship, and another was severely chastised for grounding the ship. Two hands were also washed overboard during a 1902 voyage. She would forever carry the stigma of the marked ship with the fatal ballast.

Charms

Probably the most unusual of all charms used by mariners for protection was the caul, or inner fetal membrane, which covers the face of the newborn at birth. The "holyhood," as it was called, was thought to protect a baby from drowning in the womb and thus became a favored charm against drowning and shipwreck. It was beleived that no ship that carried a caul would sink. It was common for a sailor to have a caul carefully sewn up in a special pocket in his trousers.

Much sought after by sailors, cauls were frequently advertised for sale in English papers. One such ad read: "To the gentlemen of the navy, and others going on long voyages, at sea. To be disposed of, a child's caul, worth twenty guineas." Or: "To persons going to sea, a child's caul, in a perfect state, to be sold cheap." Another advertiser in the *London Times*, May 8, 1848, offered a caul as "having been afloat with its late owner forty years, through all the perils of a seaman's life, and the owner died at last in his bed, at his place of birth." It was common in those days to hang a caul in the ship's cabin to protect the ship from sinking.[5]

During World War I, the captain of the HMS *Roebuck*, patrolling the English Channel, sent out a boat to investigate a derelict steamer. Among the documents retrieved from the abandoned ship was an envelope labeled "Our Little Darling's Caul." Sometime later, after the derelict's crew was found to have landed prematurely and safely ashore, the master of the vessel was most thankful to regain his valuable possession.[6]

What might be called "a long-term charm" to ensure luck is the tradition of placing coins in the step of the mast when a ship is being built. The practice, still alive today, dates to antiquity. In early times coins were thrown at the foot of the mast for the same reason. In 1910, during foundation excavation work on London's county hall, coins wrapped in canvas were found in the ribs of a Roman ship buried deep in a mud bank at the site.

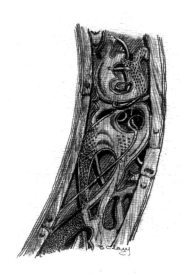

The Vikings used runes or charms in the form of various characters of their alphabet engraved on oars or rudders for protection against the storm spirits. Middle Ages ships carried tablets with engraved phrases attached to their poop decks like the name plates on modern vessels. Egyptian vessels carried painted emblems of the sacred vulture on their sails and figures of the sacred lotus and the eye on prows and rudders. The Chinese used strips of red cloth and paper affixed to rudders and sails for good luck. To catch spirits, sections of old fishing nets were hung about their ships. Eyes on the bows can still be seen on Chinese junks in the belief that these vessels must be allowed to see their way.

The cross was a most treasured charm at sea. Holy water, too, was favored, as St. Vincent was believed to have calmed an angry sea with it. Relics, bones, or pieces of dead bodies were thought to guard against shipwreck. Even though it was considered dreadfully unlucky to carry a corpse aboard a ship, human charms, such as a dead man's hand, were thought by some to be effective against shipwrecks.

Fish bones were also regarded as bringing special good luck. A sailor might have carried a bone from a haddock believed to be sacred because of the dark spots on either side of the fish long thought to be the fingerprints of St. Peter. Bones from a carp's head were also a good charm.

A piece of fish skin in a sailor's boot was thought to keep his feet warm, a bight of halyard was a good guard against witchcraft, seal skin guarded a vessel from bad weather, a gull wing was handy to bring a calm, and white-toed stockings protected one from the "little folk." Horseshoes, foxtails, and eagle's beaks were also favored against lightning. Wren's feathers were a useful guard against mermaids and sirens, and dirt from the graves of saints, hot cross buns, and cross stones were good against storms and shipwrecks. A piece of coal washed ashore from a high tide and sewn in a sailor's pocket was considered a good charm against being washed ashore.

The eyes of cuttlefish or whales, fish scales, skin of a seacalf, gold earrings, seashells, pincushions, pins from a church, amber, smooth stones with rings, white stones with holes, stones engraved with a ship or a fish, pebbles thrown up by the sea, ships in bottles, white woolen mittens, bones from a male horseshoe crab, horse chestnuts, knives, sharks' teeth set in gold, seal paws, otter skins, Brazilian malaga nuts, shoes, belts of seaweed, and a fished up right boot nailed to the mast were all thought to bring good luck.

Kings and others of prominent stature were considered living charms aboard a ship, for such royal personages were believed protected from shipwreck or other disasters. When Caesar was approached by his pilot fearing shipwreck, the emperor was said to have calmed him by saying, "Why fearest thou? Caesar thou carriest!"[7]

Although we will discuss many countercharms throughout the book, it is appropriate to discuss a few interesting ones here. A countercharm could be defined as an action performed in an attempt to eliminate or terminate a jinx or a spell of bad luck. Crossing one's fingers is an old, familiar countercharm. Spitting into the palm of your left hand or into your hat was thought to deter bad luck. Another jinx breaker was to wet the middle finger of the right hand, press it against the palm of the left hand, and then strike the left palm with the right fist. By breaking a small piece of wood with a snapping noise, old sailors produced what they believed "the lucky break." Touching cold iron was another countercharm action meant to scare the devil away.

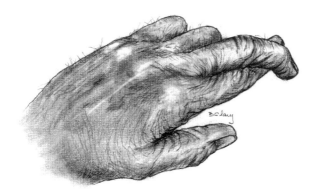

Clothing

More as tradition than superstition, the clothes, or uniform, of the sailor were designed for functionabilty, economics, and compatabilty. However, how some items of clothes were worn did have some superstitious connections.

Newly assigned noncommissioned officers, seamen, landsmen, or ships' boys in the man-of-war days of the U.S. Navy received in advance an amount equal to three months pay. This money defrayed the cost of clothing, bedding, and other supplies required by regulation. Green hands, not "knowing the ropes" and without the experience of a veteran in procuring items of clothing, were often suckered in by the "slop clothiers" who preyed upon them from their vantage-point shops on the wharves. Because there was no navy-issued clothing at the time, each man was responsible to outfit himself as best he could from the available, and often shady, sources at hand. The thieves provided inadequate essentials of clothing within the standard acceptable by the navy, which not only approved the misguided transactions but also in many cases, such as the following, allowed the cheating.

A lad of thirteen obtained the necessary permission and papers to enter service aboard the U.S. receiving ship *Experiment* as a first class ship's boy. Anxious to acquire the duds that would give him the appearance of a navy jack, the boy was easily taken in by a dockside swindler. For his first three months' pay of twenty-four dollars, the young seaman received a bag he believed contained the following quality items: one blue cloth mustering jacket, one pair of blue cloth mustering trousers, two white duck frocks (shirts) with blue collars, two pair white duck trousers, two blue flannel shirts, one peajacket, two pair cotton socks, two pair woolen socks, one pair pumps, one pair shoes, and one black tarpaulin hat.

Visualizing how becoming he would appear decked out in blue jacket, neat trousers, black silk neckerchief, and shining pumps, he instead discovered that he had bought a bag of near rags. The jacket and trousers were made out of a poor, rusty-looking material, looking as though you could "take a bull dog by the neck and fling him between any two threads of it. " Other trousers and frocks made of a cheap yellow bagging material "were so coarse they would scarcely hold peas." The neckerchief was a section of rusty bamboo rag, the shoes were made of varnished brown paper, which would surely vanish in one day of salt air and hot sun, and a tarpaulin hat of featherweight lacquered straw of equal poor quality.

These shabby clothes, probably not worth three dollars, were laid before the master-at-arms, who surveyed the quantity of the items, and oversaw the acceptance by the greenhorn's signature. Not "wanting to make waves," the poor ship's boy "touched the pen" (signed his name) and was dismissed with reassuring smiles from the cheat, who mentioned that he "was a regular brick and would no doubt become an admiral, if he lived that long."[8]

Procuring clothing in this manner did much to give the early navy men their ragtag look common in those days.

By 1830 American sailors were outfitted with a standard uniform. Bell-bottom trousers, which were around until 1970, could be easily rolled up for scrubbing decks or quick removal. Thought by many to represent the thirteen colonies or "thirteen chances to say no," the thirteen buttons on the fly of the drawers never had any official meaning. The black neckerchief was originally a sweat rag, and not in honor of Nelson's death, as was long believed. The "tar flap," or collar first buttoned on and later attached to the sailor's blouse, was derived out of cleanliness. The salts at the time wore their hair in pigtails or doubled up at the back of the neck. As a safety measure to guard against blows to the back of the neck and to keep hair out of one's eyes when working aloft, the pigtails were coated with tar. Hence the handle "jack-tar," and the collar that protected the blouse from being soiled with tar. Buttons on the sleeves of blouses have been traced to Nelson's time when three buttons were sewn on midshipmens' cuffs to prevent the homesick, sniffling, and snotty-nosed lads from wiping their noses on their sleeves. Hence the early nickname "snot-nosed kid" for a midshipman. The stars and stripes on collars and cuffs have no traceable meaning other than for decoration and because jack-tar liked to sew.

A sailor would never carry his sea boots over his shoulder, only under his arm. It was always imperative that a hat be worn properly. If a hat was worn cocked or backwards, it was believed to affect the winds. Some mariners believed that whoever was at the helm could influence the wind by pointing the bill of his cap toward a desired wind. To appear

on deck without a hat or to wear a hat in bed was also thought extremely unlucky.

I learned abruptly how unlucky it was to wear a hat in the galley of a ship. As part of the team on the 1983 *Titanic* search expedition, I walked into the galley of our research vessel, *Robert Conrad,* with my hat on. Instead of matter of factly being told of my bad luck action, I was yelled at by fearful hands from across the room. If you are superstitious, what better time to exercise your beliefs than on the search mission over the grave of the *Titanic.*

Welsh sailors believed a hat made from hazel twigs and leaves was especially lucky to wear.

It was thought unlucky to sew aboard a ship during bad weather, because of the danger of sewing on unfavorable winds and making them last.

Colors

Black, to the old mariners, was associated with the domain of darkness, the devil, and death. A black ship, black animals, or people in black clothes all held sinister and foreboding signs for the seafarer. Black patches in the sea were interpreted as "evil regions." Red hues in the water were a sign of impending disaster, while yellow tones in the sea meant that the area was the abode of treacherous spirits.

Ancient sailors believed that a blue sea was lucky and a green sea was unlucky. These beliefs no doubt were born out of the experiences of mariners who sailed with luck on a fair weather day in deep blue seas and those who feared the green hue of plankton in the dreaded Sargasso Sea.

Scottish sailors feared white as the color of bad luck and were careful to avoid having even white ballast stones aboard their vessels. The color red was used on ribbons and banners for keel-laying ceremonies as a guard against evil spirits. However, red-haired people were considered unlucky, which stemmed from the belief that Judas Iscariot was supposed to have had red hair.

Creatures of the Sea

No other creature of the deep has a more ancient or amorous relationship to man than the dolphin, or porpoise. Prehistoric South African engravings of man swimming with dolphins illustrate this age-old bond of friendship. Ancient Cretan images on vases also bear testimony to this bond, even though other peoples often feared and detested the gregarious creature. Historians have come to believe that the dolphin may have been first tamed by the Cretans, whose ancestors honored the dolphin as a god. Legend relates that Delphi, the most famed sanctuary in Greece, was so named because Apollo, the god of light, first appeared there in the form of a dolphin.

When compared with later-era recorded incidents of dolphins aiding drowning humans, one legend, it seems, was most likely based on fact. Ulysses was said to have always worn a ring engraved with an image of a dolphin after his son Telemachus fell into the water and was saved by a dolphin.

Mediterranean peoples believed for centuries that the presence of the dolphin around a ship was a good omen, and that the animal's departure foretold a storm. An accepted belief was that the dolphin would lead a lost vessel safely home.

Dolphins, or sea hogs as they were sometimes called, may have been looked upon as a bad omen by early mariners because the mouths of most varieties of porpoises resemble that of the swine. This perception may have offered substance to the belief that after the evil spirits entered the herd of swine at the lake of Genesaret,[9] and ran into the sea, they were transformed into porpoises.

As the years passed, the belief that the appearance of dolphins foretold tempests gradually subsided and was greatly overshadowed by the many ancient and contemporary recorded incidents of the dolphin's unusual friendliness and rescues of man.

The famous story of the dolphin "Opo," who captured the hearts of tourists at the resort of Opoponui in the 1950s, by allowing children to ride on her back, seemed to renew the long-lost bond of friendship with man.

An example of the sign of hope and good fortune the dolphin exemplified was witnessed by survivors of the *Britannia,* which sank twelve hundred miles off Brazil during World War II. The victims endured the long journey to safety beset by near starvation and lack of water in the overcrowded lifeboat number seven. Throughout the pitiful voyage they were accompanied by playful dolphins who seemed to continually encourage the periled group through their darkest hours. The dolphins offered such a sign of hope that when someone suggested killing one of the dolphins for food, no one could bring himself to destroy their symbol of luck.

An experience I had with dolphins was during the 1983 *Titanic* search. My job on the mission was to record everything in artwork supported by the mission photographs and those I took. When several members of the crew noticed my enormous telephoto lens, they commented that I would want to be sure to have the large lens handy when we encountered the dolphins, which would run with us en route to the *Titanic* site. If you have not seen dolphins cavorting and frisking through the sea, around, under, and pressed two or three abreast against the bow of your vessel, you cannot fully appreciate their friendly manner. Their svelte bodies glisten as they leap out of the sea and dart—I say dart because they swim so fast it appears your vessel is stationary—for hours in contented convoy with, it is obvious, their best friend—you.

For the two days or so it took to get to the area we wanted, I stood with camera ready at a moment's notice. I kept asking, "Where are the dolphins?" Each time I asked I was told, "Don't worry, they will be here, they always are." Well, the dolphins never were spotted. As the crew went into action to begin the great search, nothing more was thought about it. Nothing more, that is, until shortly after we left the *Titanic*'s grave, when many dolphins did appear. I believe that somehow the dolphins knew we were heading toward the *Titanic*'s grave and would have no part of us until we left.

Dolphin Trilogy - Don Clary

A story I often tell that gives me chills each time I tell it is about Steven Callahan, who survived seventy-six days on the Atlantic after the sailboat he was single-handedly sailing sank in a storm eight hundred miles west of the Canaries in 1982. Near exhaustion, he was sleeping below when he awoke to discover he was waist deep in a raging sea with his boat sinking beneath him! He desperately grabbed a knife, an emergency kit, and a few other meager items of gear, then miraculously made it into his fabric-bottom raft. Shortly

thereafter his boat was gone. For days on end he struggled to catch rainwater and what few fish he could spear. He was constantly hampered by the Dorados, large fish of the dolphin family, which agressively bumped the bottom of his raft. As the days passed, his weary attempts to spear the aggressive fish with a makeshift spear became ever more difficult. His weary eyes filled with tears at having to kill the fish for the food he so desperately needed. So feeble he could barely raise his arms, when he weakly threw his spear at the illusive targets they easily darted away. Toward the end of his ordeal, almost to the point of giving up, the Dorados, who had tried earlier to push him out of his raft to sure death, now turned their sides to him so that he could easily kill them in his weakest hour. It appears that these creatures somehow knew of the reluctance of this man to kill them and were therefore willing to sarcrifice themselves so that he could live. Several days later Callahan was rescued by three fishermen near Guadeloupe, much humbled but alive. This true story is undeniable proof that dolphins are truly loving friends of man.[10]

There seems to be a mysterious and far deeper meaning characterized by the prolific and repeated appearance of the dolphin in artwork of the early Cretans, Greeks, and Romans. In that these early peoples so revered the dolphin as a friend, helper, and savior of man, did they know something about this animal that we cannot comprehend? Is this creature of love a sign of hope and pleading for mankind to follow the divine course to salvation? Perhaps so, for Christ the Savior was often represented in the form of a dolphin.

Sharks

Mariners of old viewed sharks as their worst enemy. To see a shark following their ship was a dreaded ill omen, for it was long believed that these "villains of the sea" could scent death or those near death. To the sick aboard, it was even more of a fatal omen, for the appearance of the shark lurking or preying about was viewed as the feared prediction of inevitable death. An old story is told about the extreme jubilance of a man-of-war's crew who managed to harpoon a shark that had been hanging about when a sick man was aboard.[11] Several incidents are said to have occurred where an entire crew joined in to angrily and sadistically dismember a captured shark in crazed retribution for its believed evil ways.

An excerpt from the poem "Return of the Admiral" by Procter relates the grim shark superstition:

> That night a hurried whisper
> Fell on us where we lay,
> And we knew our fine old admiral
> Was changing into clay.
> And we heard the wash of waters,
> Though nothing could we see,
> And a whistle and a plunge
> Among the billows in our lea;
> Till dawn we watched the body
> In its dead and ghastly sleep;
> And next evening, at sunset,
> It was slung into the deep.
> And never from that moment,
> Save one shudder through the sea,
> Saw we or heard the shark
> That had followed in our lee.[12]

Another and equally feared threat mariners had of sharks was that of foundering, being caught helpless in the sea, and eaten alive by the dreaded monsters. One such sad and chilling incident occurred off Cuba when the small schooner *Magpie* in search of pirates encountered a freak squall and quickly sank. Twenty-two surviving crewmen were left floating in a sea that was again tranquil after the storm rushed past. The men spotted and swam a short distance to the ships' lifeboat, which had floated free. In a desperate attempt to board the small boat on one side, several men upset it to the point where it overturned and floated keel up. Hanging on for dear life, the men, clinging to whatever feeble hold they had on the overturned boat, were safe for the time being. Realizing that they could not remain in their predicament, they finally righted the boat so that several men could get aboard to bale out the water. While the boat was still half full, the fin of a shark was spotted and in the ensuing panic it was every man for himself.

Coming to grips with their fear, now four men frantically baled while the others splashed the water with their legs to ward off the shark. The water was nearly out of the boat when to their shock more than a dozen sharks swarmed in among them. Again the lifeboat was upset as panic seized the fear-stricken sailors, now at the mercy of the sharks. It appeared at first that the sharks were just playing as they swam around the men occasionally brushing against them; but suddenly a scream rang out from one of them—his leg was bitten off! A frenzy attack then occurred; shrieks uttered from one and another. Some were swiped from their hold on the boat; others sank into the sea either from being bitten or from outright fear. In the chaos, an officer somehow directed the others to right the boat and bale once again while he splashed the water with his legs. As he hung on the side of the boat, another shark bit off his legs above the knees. Unbelieveably, for a time he concealed his mortal wounds from his men, but soon, with a deep groan of pain, his hands slipped free and he began to sink. Two men then realized he had been bitten and dragged him into the boat. Several others still in the water then tried to get into the boat, upsetting it once again. Some of the remaining and bleeding crewmen pulled themselves onto the keel, but they soon began dropping into the sea.

It was estimated that the schooner *Magpie* sank at eight o'clock in the evening, and within one hour all the survivors except two were either eaten by sharks or drowned. The sharks still swam around and tried to upset the boat as the last two men continued baling. Finally, when the boat was almost free of water, the sharks, most likely gorged, at long last departed. Hungry, thirsty, and fatigued, the two slept through the night, awakened by a clear sky and burning sun. Shortly thereafter, a sail of a brig appeared, which seemed to be sailing directly toward them. As the brig hove in closer, the men desperately hailed the vessel, but were not noticed. In sheer desperation afraid of being left at sea after their calamity, one of the men decided to swim toward the brig, still about two and a half miles distant. With a prayer on his lips, he dove in and frantically swam, splashing his legs furiously as the sharks, out of nowhere, once again appeared. The brig, with a freshened wind, sailed closer to the swimmer, who screamed and waved his arms to be finally spotted by the passing ship. A boat was quickly sent out and the two survivors of the *Magpie* were saved to tell their grim story.[13]

One of the most shocking and shameful shark attacks on record took place after the sinking of the cruiser *Indianapolis* on July 30, 1945. After delivering a secret cargo of parts for the first atomic bomb to Tinian Island, the cruiser, en route to Leyte Gulf, was torpedoed by the Japanese submarine *I-58*. The loss would be recorded as the last major vessel sunk in World War II. Eight hundred of the twelve hundred-man crew spent over a hundred hours in the water awaiting rescue. Some of the men died of injuries sustained on the ship, others drowned, succumbing to exposure or the delirium of salt water intake. It is impossible to determine just how many were lost to the sharks. However, because 88 of the 316 men who lived through the tragedy were mutilated by sharks or other carnivorous fish, it is believed that this tragic incident was one of the largest mass shark attacks on record.

Of the approximately 250 known species of sharks, some 30 species are believed to be man killers. The most notorious among these are the mako, white-tipped, hammerhead, tiger, blue, and the great white shark. These killers have been primarily identified by the remains of victims found in their stomachs. However, because postattack, positive identification of sharks is made only in about one out of twenty-five cases, the exact number of killer species is not known. Researchers today estimate that there are twenty-five fatal shark attacks per year.[14]

The ferocity and outright tenacity of life in the shark is extraordinary. One shark was recorded as still being active in the sea for many hours after its head had been taken off. In other instances, a shark was known to have taken bait deep in the sea after its liver and entrails had been removed. In another instance the severed head of a shark bit off a sailor's finger!

A shark will not only devour those of its own species, but will bite chunks out of its own flesh. During one feeding frenzy, when many sharks were ripping apart the remains of a whale after flensing, a shark was said to have arched itself and torn out a large piece of its own body, leaving its own entrails dangling as it swam off.

The most feared of all the killers is the great white shark, or "swimming nose," the nickname defining its keen sense of smell. These deadly hunters have been known to be fiercely and quickly attracted to the smell of blood from hundreds of yards away. Omnivorous, sharks are scavengers that prefer fresh meat. On top of this threat, the feared great white displays an enormous and greedy appetite for human flesh. They have been known to attack everything within reach. To add to the stealthlike character of this killer, the white shark has no organs that produce sound and is an absolute silent swimmer.

Some sharks will select one victim out of a group and concentrate their attack on him with an awful steadfast determination to finish the kill. A grim example of this happened in 1952, when a young boy was attacked by a shark off the California coast. Five men, who had witnessed the attack, swam to the boy and began pushing him to shore on an inner tube. The shark circled the group and finally slipped through the men to attack the boy again, thereby completing the kill.[15]

The largest white shark on record was one taken off Cuba in the 1940s. This monster measured twenty-one feet and weighed 7,302 pounds, 1,005 pounds of which was liver alone. The range of this "pirate of the oceans" is worldwide, but can be found in greater numbers near the cool, temperate shores of North America, South Africa, and western and south Australia. Just how indiscriminate a shark's appetite can be is indicated in the following list which includes some unusual items found in various shark stomachs: The stomach of a shark caught in Australian waters contained a goat, a tomcat, three birds, four fish heads and other fish including one six foot in length; an

Adriatic sharks stomach contained a raincoat, three overcoats and an auto license plate; a shark caught off the Florida Keys was found to have ingested grass, tin cans, twelve cow vertebrae, and a cows head without horns; items found in the stomach of Philippine Island shark included seven leggings, forty-seven buttons, three leather belts and nine shoes.[16] In a shark captured off an Australian dock was found half of a ham, several legs of mutton, the hindquarters of a pig, the head and front legs of a bull dog, and pieces of horse flesh.[17] The hand and wrist of a man, a goat's head with nine inch horns, and a turtle's head was found in the stomach of a shark captured in Nassau harbor; and in the stomach of a shark taken off the island of St. Margaret was found the whole body of a horse.[18]

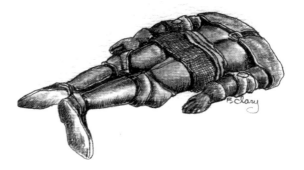

The most unusual find in the stomach of a shark has to be one recorded in Jerome Smith's 1833 Natural History of the Fishes of Massachusetts: "In the records of Aix, a seaport in France, in the Mediterranean Sea, is the account of a shark taken by the fishermen, twenty-two feet long, in whose stomach, among other undigested remains, was the headless body of a man, encased in complete armor."[19]

Although few superstitions were associated with whales, mariners nonetheless feared these giant creatures of the sea. Some fears were bona fide, others were entirely unfounded. For example, the highly misinterpreted name for *orca* is killer whale, but there is no record of it ever attacking man. Killer whales are one of the largest members of the dolphin family.

Orcas are believed to have been tagged "killer" because of the fierceness with which these so-called wolves of the ocean attack their prey. They have been known to terrify and destroy, in wolf-pack fashion, baleen whales many times their size and strength.

Whalers had every right to fear the quarry they sought, for there are many recorded accounts of provoked and unprovoked sperm whale attacks on their pursuers and even on their ships.

The most famous instance of a whale attacking a whale ship occurred on November 20, 1820. The Nantucket whale ship *Essex* was in Pacific waters some two thousand miles west of the Galapagos Islands a few miles from the equator. Having spotted a shoal of whales, two whaleboats were in pursuit while a third had returned to the ship for repairs. One whale lying near the vessel, suddenly increased its speed and headed directly for the ship. Familar with the docile character of the whale, those aboard did not even contemplate the possibility of an attack; still, the helmsman was ordered to sheer off to avoid the oncoming whale. This maneuver was in vain for the whale struck at full speed causing the ship to tremble from the impact. As the vessel was seriously staved in and shipping water, pumping had just begun when the whale struck again on the opposite side near the bow. Now with two serious wounds, the doomed ship soon went over on her beam ends, leaving twenty sailors in three whaleboats stranded in one of the least-frequented areas of the vast Pacific.

After traveling forty-five hundred miles and spending eighty-two days at sea in an open whaleboat, two survivors were rescued some three hundred miles from Chile. Their meager provisions devoured, the men resorted to cannibalism to survive. Three others, who chose to stay on a small island, were also rescued.

In 1851, the *Ann Alexander* was sunk off the coast of Peru after being struck by a sperm whale in an incident like that of the *Essex*. Also in 1851, whaleboats from the *Citizen*, on the Atlantic, were attacked by a sperm whale after it had been lanced. The infuriated whale, spouting blood, attacked and destroyed one boat and gave chase to another. In an attempt

to divert the attention of the crazed animal, another boat came to the area and was also chased by the whale. While running at this boat, the enraged whale spotted and charged the whale ship, fast coming to the aid of the threatened boats. Realizing that the whale was now coming after their ship, those on the vessel put the ship before the wind in an effort to outmaneuver the animal. After narrowly missing the stern of the ship, the whale finally went into its "flurry" (death throes) and "turned up."[20]

Although many accounts from the early days of whaling reported men being swallowed by whales, other than Jonah, who was spewed from the belly of a large fish,[21] there is but one verifiable incident of a man swallowed by a whale who lived to recount his horrifying experience.

Searching for sperm whales near the southern Falkland Islands in February 1891, a lookout on the English whaler *Star of the East* sighted a large sperm some three miles from the ship. Two whaleboats were dispatched and before long the whale was struck in the side with the first lance. As the creature began to sound, its twelve-foot-wide tail violently sprung out of the water and upset one of the boats, spilling the crew into the sea.

Those in the other whaleboat managed to kill the whale, which after a few hours was lying beside the *Star of the East,* ready to be flensed. All the whaleboat crewmen were accounted for except hardy young seaman James Bartley, who had been lost, and another man, who had drowned.

Not the time for mourning, the crew worked till after dark "cutting in" and "trying out" their prize. The next day, the whale's enormous stomach was removed and hoisted aboard to be cut up. As the stomach was laid on the deck, crewmen were sure they detected movement from within the giant paunch. Knowing that it was common for these leviathans to swallow large fish whole, the men anxiously cut open the stomach expecting perhaps to find a shark, one of their worst enemies. An incision near the movement was made. To their shock, there, in a curled up fetal position, laid the unconscious, but alive, James Bartley.

Several dousings with cold salt water brought him

around but not out of his incoherent state. Practically reduced to a babbling vegetable, the unclothed parts of his body were ghostly white and shriveled from exposure to the acid in the whale's stomach. It was doubtful that he would pull through. With kindness and attention from the entire crew, he convalesced and gradually regained his senses while locked in the captain's quarters. When well enough to talk, Bartley recalled that he had heard sounds of the whale moving through the water after being thrown into the sea. He was then engulfed in darkness and had the sensation of moving in a smooth passageway, which itself seemed to move as he was carried along. He soon discovered that he had more room. Groping about in pitch darkness, he felt the slimy walls of his confinement, and realized to his horror where he was. Although there seemed to be no lack of air, he felt extreme stifling heat, which quickly sapped his strength. The darkness, the intense heat, a most unusual dead quiet, and the thought of his entrapment overcame him. From then on he could remember nothing until coming to in the captain's cabin. After three weeks he had recovered from the shock and was strong enough to return to duty.

The captain and one other officer of the *Star of the East* both wrote detailed reports of the incident. After an investigation the reputable French scientist and editor of the *Paris Journal des De bats*, M. de Parville, thoroughly believed the incident took place as described. In 1914, de Parville published an account of the affair in the *Journal des De bats*, which ended with the statement: "I believe that the account given by the English captain and his crew is worthy of belief. There are many cases reported where whales, in the fury of their dying agony, have swallowed human beings, but this is the first modern case where the victim has come forth safe and sound. After this modern illustration, I end by believing that Jonah really did come out from the whale alive as the Bible records."[22]

Not a direct threat to man, the swordfish too was feared by the early mariners because of its deadly looking sword snout and occasional aggressive assaults on ships.

A swordfish reportedly attacked an East Indiaman with such a force that its sword was driven through the bottom of the ship. The fish thus died of its own violence. The vessel would have sustained a serious leak had not the animal's snout remained imbedded in the wood. A section of the vessel with the sword punched through it is said to be preserved in a British museum.[23]

A swordfish also attacked the research submarine *Alvin* in 1967. At a depth of twelve hundred feet off the Georgia coast, thirty-eight inches of the animal's sword pierced the outer fiberglass hull, forcing it to the surface.[24]

The aggressive tactics of the swordfish are described in this old verse:

> He summons to his instant aid
> The oft-tried prowess of his trusty blade;
> Selects some boat, and runs his puissant sword
> Full many an inch within the fatal board.[25]

Because of its black body and hideous appearance, early sailors had dire convictions of the manta ray, also known as the devilfish or sea devil. It was once believed that mantas attached themselves to anchor chains and dragged ships down to unknown dooms. It was also thought that unwary swimmers were caught and wrapped in their giant wings to be devoured. The manta has never attacked man, but the graceful swimming creature has been sighted bursting through the surface of the sea and leaping to fifteen-foot heights to evade a probable underwater enemy. An ancient belief was that the devil took the form of a manta with horns, accompanied by a white fish that often attacked it. Between the horns swam another small gray fish, called the pilot of the devil. The manta, or "devil," surely must have been the source of many unidentified sea monster (USM) myths.

It was considered extremely lucky for fishermen or sailors to catch a fiddlefish also known as the angelfish or monkfish. Having a body that resembles a violin, the nonedible fish was thought to bring good luck to the ship that netted it. A custom in practice as late as 1949 was to drag these fish on a line from the stern of the ship until they disappeared. To lend the monkfish's aroma to the fo'c'sle, sailors might have nailed a carcass of the fish near their bunks or on sea chests for more direct good luck.

Cuttlefish spotted on the surface of the water or sea urchins trying to bury themselves in the sand were thought to foretell a storm. The sight of the floating Portuguese man-of-war indicated calm weather.

Many superstitions about fish came about through old legends. The ancient name for the pilotfish was *naucratis* (ship guide); thus it was believed that fish would safely steer ships into port. Vessels would steer a course to follow the white foam tracks of the fish, considered the ship's companion.

There was also a legend about the echeneis, a fish of the sucker family. Known as the "ship stopper," it would affix itself to the sides or bottoms of ships, slowing their progress or stopping them altogether. Early mariners believed that just a few of these tiny fish could stop ships in midocean.

The little fish John Dory shares with the haddock the distinction of having St. Peter's fingerprints on its sides. Known as St. Peter's fish, its name was said to have been derived from *janitore* (doorkeeper), referring to St. Peter, the keeper of the gates of heaven. According to legend, a penny which paid the temple tax, was found in the fish's mouth, and the spots on each side of its mouth were from St. Peter's thumbs.

In Iceland, the flounder was called the "holy fish," and in Finland there was a belief that when the Virgin Mary laid her hand upon the fish, its sides turned white.

Ancient mariners also had their "fish" stories. One was about the barnacles that cling to a ship's bottom. The feathery tentacles, or arms, that inhabit its shell led some to believe that if the barnacle was broken off it would turn into a goose.

Notes

1. Baker, *The Folklore of the Sea*, 156.
2. Bassett, *Legends and Superstitions of the Sea and Sailors,* 76.
3. Rappoport, *Superstitions of Sailors*, 87.
4. A term defining the long sea route to New Zealand via the Cape of Good Hope.
5. Bassett, *Legends and Superstitions of the Sea and Sailors*, 460-61.
6. Baker, *The Folklore of the Sea*, 77-78.
7. Bassett, *Legends and Superstitions of the Sea and Sailors*, 428.
8. Nordhoff, *Sailor Life on Man of War and Merchant Vessel*, 35-37.
9. Matt. 8:31-32.
10. Callahan, *Adrift*, 310.
11. Bassett, *Legends and Superstitions of the Sea and Sailors*, 240.
12. Sharper, *The Origins of Popular Superstitions and Customs,* 183.
13. Van Dervoort, *The Water World*, 152-55.
14. Cousteau and Richards, *Cousteau's Great White Shark*, 16.
15. Engel, *The Sea*, 135.
16. Lineaweaver & Backus, *The Natural History of Sharks*, 30.
17. Engel, *The Sea*, 133.
18. Van Dervoort, *The Water World*, 146.
19. Lineweaver and Backus, *The Natural History of Sharks*, 30-31.
20. Scammon, *The Marine Mammals*, 78-79.
21. Jon. 2:1-11.
22. Gunston, *"The Man Who Lived in a Whale,"* 8-11.
23. Van Dervoort, *The Water World*, 259.
24. Cromie, *Secrets of the Sea*, 97.
25. Van Dervoort, *The Water World,* 259.

5. Days

Death, Deities, Devils, Disaster, Dreams, and Drowning

Days of darkness, the corpse of a mate,
The devil's form, a disastrous fate,
Ominous dreams, fiends of the deep,
All the fears a mariner will keep.

Days

Although Friday the thirteenth appears to be the most unlucky day of all, mariners regarded many other days as lucky or unlucky. Unlucky days for sailing were the first Monday in April, believed to be the birthday of Cain and the day he killed his brother Abel; the second Monday in August, the anniversary of the destruction of Sodom and Gomorrah; the thirty-first of December, the day Judas Iscariot hanged himself; and the second of February, Candlemas. The twenty-sixth of June, Saint Peter's Day, was deemed unlucky for fishermen. Although Swedish fishermen would not fish on Christmas, they would set their nets on that day for good luck. All Hallows' Eve and All Saints' Day were also considered unlucky days, and as recent as 1976 many Newfoundland fishermen, when ordered to, refused to fish on Easter Day.

Sunday was considered lucky for seamen and fishermen. Monday, except those previously mentioned, was a lucky day. Tuesday was thought a bad day to start a voyage. Spanish and Portuguese sailors would not go to sea, marry, or leave their wives on this day. Wednesday, a day consecrated to Odin, the chief deity of Viking mariners, was believed a lucky day. Thursday, a day dedicated to Thor, the eldest son of Odin, who protected man from evil spirits, was also figured a lucky day. Friday was strictly an all-around unlucky day. Along with the beliefs earlier mentioned, fishermen would not move to new fishing grounds or work on a new boat on Friday. Some sailors were careful not to end a voyage on a Friday, thinking the act would shore up bad luck for the next voyage. Spanish sailors, however, favored Friday because it was the day Columbus began his great voyages. Saturday had no significance either way.

The old mariners believed that the seventh of any month was a good day for fishing, the seventeenth or the twenty-ninth good days to begin long voyages, and the fourth a lucky day for launchings.

Death

Nothing cloaked the sailor's life with gloom more than the death of a shipmate. Aside from the superstitious beliefs that might have attended the demise, those who made their life at sea still had to suffer with the loss of a friendship likely born of adversity and often emphasized by the increased work load for those left behind. The smaller the crew the more acute the passing seemed.

During a voyage it was taboo to wear the clothes of a sailor who died at sea. To do so would present the threat of the wearer following the same fate as the deceased. Once ashore the same clothes could be worn without care.

So superstitious were mariners about the departed that they would take strict care in never mentioning the decease's' name without preceding the name with "poor" as "poor John." This was done so as not to offend the spirits. A death aboard a ship had to be reported to the captain immediately, day or night. Many seafarers believed that a ship could not make headway with a corpse aboard.

Anything related to death was thought to bring ill luck, such as black, a death dirge, or unused coffins. In 1847 officers on a man-of-war prevented the playing of a fife and drum death march because they thought that inevitable death would surely follow.[1] In another incident a vessel was lying at anchor in the bay of Gibraltar with a deceased crewman aboard in a coffin, who was to be buried ashore. When a violent storm came up, the vessel slipped her anchors and was driven out to sea. Consequently, the dead sailor had to be buried at sea. The men were so fearful and superstitious of the unused coffin that it had to be cut up in small pieces and thrown overboard.

When a sailor died he either "cut his painter," "slipped his cable," "went aloft," or "unraveled his lifeline." If a sailor was lost at sea through accident or violence, he was said to have "gone to Davy Jones's locker," a giant sea chest at the bottom of the sea that swallowed ships and men. Favored seamen and those shellbacks with fifty years of service could expect to go to Fiddler's Green when they died. Among the popular descriptions of this heaven, it is where a sailor goes to settle down in a paradise of endless free grog and tobacco. There are pubs on every corner, steaks at every meal, and the world's most beautiful women to fill the glasses and pipes of old sailors.

Deities

In antiquity there were countless imaginary, good, and evil deities who held dominion over the seas, to whom ancient mariners directed their fears, prayers, and hopes. Traces of these legends and beliefs persist in present-day seafaring jargon and tradition.[2]

The sparse records of the peoples who first settled in the plains between the Euphrates and Tigris rivers tell of the famous Babylonian deity Hea, or Hoa, also known as the "Deity of the Abyss." This ruler of Hades and the lower world had temples at Ur and in other ancient port cities. His spouse, Doakina, was goddess of the deep.

On, or Oannes, according to Assyrian accounts, a deity from the Erythraean Sea, was an animal endowed with reason. It had the body of a fish with two heads; one head was beneath the fish head, and human feet adjoined its fish tail. Six similar sea monsters were said to have come from the waters of the Persian Gulf. Other fables tell of a man known as Oes, who came out of the Erythrean Sea having a body of a fish and head, arms, and feet of a man. He was said to have spoken with humans in the daytime, educating them in astronomy, science, letters, and art. At sunset, the amphibious being returned to his abode in the deep. This legend is believed to be the origin of all the mermaid and mermen myths. Huge statues of gods with characteristics like those described above were said to have been found among the ruins of Nineveh and Babylon.

Derceto, or Atergatis, was another Babylonian maritime deity. The moon was her emblem. She sank into the sea to evade the evil gods.

Because the ancient Egyptians were not a seafaring people only a few maritime deities were related to them. The Egyptian moon goddess, Isis, spouse of the sun, was known as the patroness of navigation. She was worshiped also by the Romans, and the fifth of March was dedicated to her as the main festival of navigators. Num, the Egyptian lord of the water, appeared in the Nile as late as the sixth century, and was honored there by rivermen. Sacred vessels and festivals were dedicated to this god of the Nile.

Ancient Phoenician mariners worshiped many gods of the sea. The primary Sidonian goddess, known as Astarte, Ishtar, or Ashtaroth, was considered the Venus of Semitic lands and was highly esteemed by mariners. According to Syrian legend, the Cabiri were prolific gods of learning and the arts, who also invented navigation. They were believed by some to be direct descendants of Noah and therefore named as guardians of navigators. Figureheads, or *pataikoi,* on the prows of Phoenician vessels bore their resemblance.

Among ancient mariners the most prominent nation at sea was the Greeks, who had many maritime deities. Most famed of all was Poseidon, god of the sea (Mediterranean) and master of the water. Neptune was the Latin equivalent. He summoned clouds, created and calmed storms, yet provided safe voyages. All other gods were subordinate to him. Before beginning a voyage, during a calm, and upon a safe return, Greek, Roman, and Phoenician seafarers prayed and made sacrifices to him. He invented the ship, and on land, created the horse and the bull. He was portrayed as a grim old man who carried a trident, riding in a car drawn by horses or dolphins and accompanied by an entourage of Tritons, Nereids, and other sea monsters. This old verse characterizes this king of the sea:

"Where'er he glides
His finny coursers, and in triumph rides,
The waves unruffle, and the sea subsides,
His finny team Saturnian Neptune join'd,

Then adds the foamy bridle to their jaws,
And to the loosen'd rein permits the laws.
High on the waves his azure car he guides;
Its axles thunder and the sea subsides,
And the smooth ocean rolls her silent tides;
The tempests fly before their father's face,
Trains of inferior gods his triumphs grace,
And monster whales before their master play,
And choirs of Tritons crowd the wat'ry way."

Poseidon's fair spouse, Amphitrite, also reigned mightily at sea. Often seen with Poseidon, or sometimes riding a sea animal, the beautiful woman appeared with a net on her hair and claws of a crab on her forehead.

Another powerful sea monarch was Oceanus, who dwelt in the fabled ocean stream that encompassed the known world. His kingdom was far to the west in the setting sun. He symbolized and personified the sea, and ancient mariners made devout sacrifices to him in preparation for long voyages. He was depicted as an old man enthroned on the waves. The emissary of Oceanus was Hler, deity of the raging sea, whose turbulent water boiled in his kettle. His spouse was Ran, the northern Amphitrite; their daughters were the nine waves. Ran captured in her net those who drowned at sea, even lurking beneath the frozen waters for them. "Fara til Rana" (go to Ran) meant to drown.

Father of the Nereids, the fifty nymphs of the waves, was Nereus, a prophet god of the sea. Dwelling in a magnificent palace in the Aegean Sea, he was seen as an old man with long flowing hair. Figured the ancestors of the mermaids, the

Nereids, or ocean nymphs, represented the sea as half women and half fish. They were in the court of the higher gods, and were enthroned at altars on the seashore, where tribute was made to them. Pictured by the ancients as most beautiful, they emerged from their watery abodes as the waves arose.

Represented as the white sea foam and known as the guardian of the sea monsters, Phorcus was another maritime god, whose spouse was the whale.

The ancients also made sacrifices to Zeus, or Jupiter, the god of the heavens and the air. He sent storms and was considered more powerful than all the other gods of the land or the sea.

Worshiped by ancient Greek mariners, Minerva, or Athene, was the believed inventor of navigation and builder of the mystical ship *Argo*. A belligerent goddess, she was especially patronized by naval seamen.

Artemis, or Diana, goddess of the chase; Priapus, god of fertility; and Glaucus, son of Poseidon, were principally venerated by fishermen.

Mariners particularly honored Apollo, the great god of the Delphic temple, who was adored at many temples by the sea. It was said that his statue on Mount Actium, which could be seen from a great distance, served as a landmark for mariners. From legend, Apollo Delphinius, as a dolphin, led a ship full of sailors to his holy place, where they became his priests.

Romans adored Portumnus, the god of harbors. They dedicated a majestic temple to him at Ostia, where annual festivities were held on the seventh day of August.

Triton, a son of Poseidon, was a powerful sea deity who dwelt in the deep and was believed able to quiet the waves. He was pictured blowing a shell having an upper body of a man and the lower body of a fish. From this legend, the word *triton* was used to define the merman. The triton was described in an old account: "The hair of the head resembles the parsley that grows in marshes; the rest of their body is rough with small scales; they have fish-gills under their ears; their nostrils are those of a man, but their teeth are broader and like those of a wild beast; their eyes seem to me azure, and their hands, fingers and nails are of the form of the shells of a shell-fish; they have, instead of feet, fins under their breast and belly, like those of the porpoise."

Among the other ancestral Greek sea gods was Indra, god of the firmament and ruler of the storm. Chief god of the atmosphere, he ruled the weather and sent forth thunder, lightning, and rain. The god Rudra governed the winds, which were his children. Referred to as the "howler" or "terrible," he was a mighty god of storms. Varuna, the Indian Neptune, god of the seas and rivers, had a fish as his sign and the wind as his breath.

The Scandinavian sea god Odin was figured the almighty father and the most powerful, who sent storms and controlled the waves. Odin's son Thor, governed the tempest, thunder, and the clouds. Ruler and chief god of the ocean and the wind was Niord, the Nereus of the North. Mariners and coastal dwellers prayed and made sacrifices to him. His abode was in Noatun, "place of ships," and he also represented the mild sea of the coast. His children, Freyr and Freya, also powerful at sea, were adored by mariners.

Ancient sailors feared the German goddess Holda, who rode on the waves. Nav, god of the waters, was an old British deity. Neith was a Celtic water goddess. The Irish sea god was Man-a-nan. The Welsh god of the deep was Avaron. Shetland fishermen venerated the water god Shony. The son of Neptune, Albion, was a patron sea god of Britain, who, legend states, introduced shipbuilding in Great Britain.

Greenland Eskimo tribes worshiped the giant sea god Kayaker, and the storm-raising gods Kayarissat, Mitgh, and Tongarsuk. The goddess Arnar Kuasak, mother of Tongarsuk, reigned from her seal-guarded palace beneath the sea.

Among the Indian sea deities was Unktahee, the Dakota first god of the water. The Arizona Kaibalit tribe worshiped Tilcompa Masoits, the grandmother goddess of the sea. The Ojibways also honored a water god, a toad. Cipactli and Tlaloc were old Mexican water gods; Opochtli was their god of fishing, and Chalcihuitlicue, a goddess of the water, created storms and sank canoes. An ancient Mexican proverb stated: "We are all of us children of "Chal" (water goddess).

Among the renowned South Pacific sea deities were Tawhiri-matea, Taaruatai, and Ruhahatu, sea gods of Society Island tribes. Akaenga, lord of the lower waters, washed souls about in his net, and the Maori sea god Tangaroa had fish and reptiles as his children.

Famous among Australian sea gods was Nguk Wonga, the spirit of the waters, and Vatea, lord of the ocean, who became a whirlpool. He was represented as having a half-man and half-shark body along with other fish and human organs. As the great lord of the ocean, he originated nets and fishing, the legend says.

Fishermen on Mangaia and Ranatonga considered the cocoanut leaf their god. A frond of the tree was wrapped with sennit and carried on the prows of their boats to ward off storms. These adornments were called Mokoiros, and the fishermen there would never go to sea without them. One of the Sandwich Islands sea gods was Mooarii, a shark. Temples were built in his honor, and the first fish caught was offered to him. The Hawaiian god Kunra and the goddess Hina were worshiped by fishermen because they believed these deities drove shoals of fish to them.

Tin-hau, the goddess of the sea, queen of heaven, holy mother, and protector of the boat people has been worshiped by Chinese junk mariners since antiquity. Worshipers paid homage to the god whose image was glass-enclosed or engraved on wooden plaques within little shrines on the port side of the vessels. Today, the annual Tin Hau day of thanksgiving and worship in honor of this god is the biggest Chinese festival of the year.

Devils

Aside from the dead, mariners feared most the devil and the many forms they believed the devil assumed.[3]

The origin of the devil's association with the sea is believed traced to an Egyptian representation of him as Typhon, the lord of the deep, or as Apophis, a serpent of the lower world. A multitude of legends followed that connected the devil to the deep; his powers caused the storms at sea. Thus came the belief of the devil as a typhoon. Whirlwinds caused by developing low-pressure systems over deserts are still referred to as "dust devils."

According to a Hindu legend, Panchayana was the devil who dwelled in the deep as a conch shell.

In ancient Persian writings the demon was represented as a fish. Middle-age myths figured him both a demon in female disguise and a sea monster. Satan as a sea monster was also found in Norse legends. St. Nicholas perceived him at sea bearing a sword. Lake demons in Austria and Hungary were thought to appear as a frog, and in Bohemia water demons were believed to float on the sea in the form of a red flower. A storm at Bongay, England, in 1597 was thought to have been caused by Satan, who appeared as a dog. An alligator with a dog's head was the water demon in an old Philippine Islands myth. Other legends had him appearing with half the body of a fish, a shark, or a ship.

Greenlanders believed that water demons appeared as enormous sea gulls, seals, or bears. To ward them off, the eldest man drank water first. A Miskito Indian legend told of the demon Wihwin, who as a horse rose from the depths to slay men. The demons in the lakes and rivers of Norway were believed able to change into a creature with half a body of a horse or as a horse with its hoofs turned backward. Pomeranian mariners believed that Satan appeared as a burning barrel of tar floating on the ocean waves.

Satan was also thought to appear as a cat, a pig, and the devilfish, or manta ray. In the human image, he was believed to take the form of a dark, grim, shrouded figure; a young man with a red beard; or an impeccably dressed businessman in a trim black suit with a fine black leather attaché case. The only departure from a normal businessman was his sharply pointed ears.

Seafarers of old believed that they could beat the devil out of their ship by going aloft at sunset to beat the sheaves

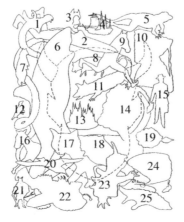

Believed forms the devil assumed

(1) Serpent; (2) half fish - half man; (3) devil wind; (4) ship; (5) frog; (6) shark; (7) bear; (8) pig; (9) half horse - half man; (10) shrouded figure; (11) half dog - half alligator; (12) seal; (13) burning barrel of tar; (14) beautiful woman; (15) businessman; (16) horse with hoofs backward; (17) cat; (18) conch shell; (19) red flower on sea; (20) sea gull; (21) devil with sword; (22) devilfish; (23) sea monster; (24) typhoon; (25) manta ray.

and pins of the blocks. In ancient times Babylonians cast off the devil by placing figures of the demons in small boats, chanting a magic phrase to make the boat capsize, and casting them off to the open water.

Topmen furling sail in stiff gusty winds believed they were being tugged at by the devil trying to make them lose their footing. An old Icelandic oarsman's concern was that if one left part of an oar handle exposed, the devil would surely use it.

As absurdly superstitious as mariners were, one would surely expect when naming a vessel that a name the extreme opposite of the devil would naturally be chosen. However, when a rakish little topsail schooner was launched at Preston, England, in 1868 and christened *The Devil*, her reckless and daring owners seemed only to be inviting disaster. One story suggests that the name was taken from a machine in a factory run by the owners, which was nicknamed "the devil." Another version was that one of the owners in arguing over a name vehemently exclaimed: "Call her the *Devil* if you like." And so, even though the underwriters pleaded otherwise, the name stuck, but not without ill fortune. Curiously the invitation for bad luck did not stop there, for the owners had placed on the prow a life-size figurehead of the devil himself, complete with horns, cloven hoofs, and forked tail. Every inch of the vessel was painted solid black and in large gold letters on the bows and stern, the feared name *Devil* gleamed brightly, keeping even the most daring redneck a good distance away from her at the wharf. Although she was said to have made a record Atlantic crossing driven by the devil himself, bad luck indeed followed the ill-named and weather-breeding schooner throughout her career.[4]

Disaster

Disaster at sea seems always to be enshrouded in mystery. Collisions, shipwrecks, and founderings are often accompanied by unexplained, coincidental, uncanny, or at the least unbelievable circumstances.

What is chronicled as the most mysterious shipwreck ever occured when the five-masted schooner Carroll A. Deering was driven on Diamond Shoals near Ocracoke, North Carolina, on the stormy night of January 31, 1921. The superstitious would say there were three unlucky strikes against the vessel. First, the Deering was launched on Friday, April 4, 1919, the taboo day of the week for launchings. Second, she was christened with a cascade of roses and carnations rather than with the customary smash of a champagne bottle across the prow. Third, the ship carried two cats, who turned out to be the only survivors.

On that morning, ocean-shore dwellers were shocked to see the big schooner hard aground on the distant shoal with all her sails set. Examined only with binoculars because the sea was still raging, she was stripped of her lifeboats, a ladder hung over her side, and no sign of life was aboard. Four days later, the wreckers were able to board the vessel to find food set on the table and on the stove in the galley. Eerily, the only sign of life left aboard were the ship's two cats. Theories of mutiny, piracy, and abandonment in connection with the loss persisted for many years, but the strange mystery was never solved. None of the crew's bodies were ever found nor did a single shred of evidence ever shed light on the mystery of this "Ghostship of the Diamond."

Courtesy Maine Maritime Museum, Bath Maine

Living through the tortures of a storm and shipwreck was still no guarantee of survival. Mariners in fact feared the mooncussers more than the peril of going on the rocks in some latitudes. Moonlight helped a vessel stay clear of threatening shoals and hampered the devious work of treacherous shore pirates, thus the name "mooncussers."

Shipwreck!

The citizens of Lizard Point, a tiny town near the mouth of the English Channel, requested the government in 1619 to *not* build a lighthouse on the hazardous point to facilitate their profitable wrecking. Nearby, at Wolf Rock, wreckers muffled a howling blowhole created by the crashing surf that warned ships away from that dangerous area. When a ship was in peril and there was "wreckers weather" (a savage sea and a shattering wind, the cliffs before and the gale behind), thousands of poor townsfolk would follow a troubled ship for days with all the tools necessary to strip the vessel clean of its needed goods. No care was given to stranded survivors, who either drowned, were totally ignored, or murdered by the merciless vultures. It was said that inhabitants along the western coast of the British Isles were so destitute that the children there were taught to pray for wrecks. This verse about one of the ships that came ashore exemplified the plight of the desperate wreckers:

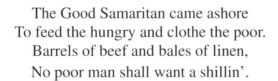

The Good Samaritan came ashore
To feed the hungry and clothe the poor.
Barrels of beef and bales of linen,
No poor man shall want a shillin'.

A prayer written on the Scilly Islands was more direct in beseeching the help of Providence: "We pray Thee, O Lord, not that wrecks should happen, but if any wreck should happen, Thou wilt guide them into the Scilly Isles for the benefit of the inhabitants."[5]

Fake lighthouse lights, made to look like a vessel at anchor, were called "Judas lanterns," and were used by the mooncussers to deceive captains to steer their ships on the rocks. Nags Head, North Carolina, was believed named after the horses used to carry lanterns along the beaches simulating ship lights that lured the unwary vessel aground. Cape Cod wreckers, imitating a ship at anchor, gently swayed lanterns to lure ships into their lairs. Mooncussers in Bahama walked horses in circles with lanterns tied to them to simulate a lighthouse beacon.

For a percentage of the salvage, legitimate Key West, Florida, wreckers were said to have stripped an average of one ship per week in the early 1800s.[6]

Out on the vast, endless abyss of the oceans, where a vessel could steam for days or weeks without sighting another ship, it would seem nearly impossible for two vessels to collide. Thus it was indeed a mysterious coincidence how the *Eleanor A. Percy* and the *George W. Wells*, the first two six-masters built and the only two operating at the time, collided on the Atlantic in 1904, each captain unaware of the other's position or route.

According to Lloyds of London, from 1950 to 1956, there were 6,110 collisions involving some twelve thousand ships registering over five hundred gross tons, most of which had radar. The famous collision of the Italian liner *Andrea Doria* and the Swedish liner *Stockholm* off Nantucket Island in 1956 happened even though those in command watched each other on the radar screens!

If you totaled the loss of life from all the major maritime disasters including the *Titanic* (1,525), *Lusitania* (1,198), *Empress of Ireland* (1,027), and the *Eastland* (812, Chicago, 1915), you would still not surpass the losses from the sinking of the *Wilhelm Gustloff*, the worst sea disaster in maritime history. It was bound for Kiel, Germany, with refugee passengers and German military personnel; an estimated 8,050 lives were lost when the Soviet submarine S-13 torpedoed and sank the *Gustloff* in the Baltic Sea on January 30, 1945.

The sinking of the RMS *Titanic* at 2:20 a.m. (Atlantic time), on April 15, 1912, is the most renowned sea disaster of all time. The tragedy is so famous and so widely publicized that one would have great difficulty in finding any corner of the world unaware of the event. Yet there remains an all but hidden incident, an unbelievable but true incident that fateful night, which, had it not occurred, could very possibly have saved the lives of the 1,525 souls who were lost.

Titanic That Night No.1

There is substantial and documented proof that after the *Titanic* hit the iceberg and stopped, she started up again and ran for an undetermined length of time, perhaps as long as thirty minutes! In doing so, she undoubtedly hastened the intake of sea water through her wounded hull to greatly reduce the precious time she had left before foundering. The time from when the *Titanic* struck the iceberg at 11:40 p.m. until she sank at 2:20 a.m. was only two hours and forty minutes. The Cunard liner *Carpathia*, fifty-eight miles away, racing through ice floes at 17-1/2 knots, would reach the stricken *Titanic* just one hour and fifty minutes after the sinking.

The proof that the *Titanic* steamed on again comes primarily through an analysis written by *Titanic* passenger and science teacher Lawrence Beesley, whose version is recognized as one of the most credible accounts of the disaster.

Beesley, in his berth reading, noticed the engines slow and then stop a few moments after the collision, which he estimated was at 11:45. He relates that because of the location of his stateroom, when the liner was steaming along he could feel engine vibration when he placed his bare feet on the floor or when he placed his hands on the metal sides of his bathtub. Beesley went to the top deck, talked with another passenger, descended to the deck below, talked with others in the smoking room, and then returned to his cabin for some time to read again. Hearing people in the corridor, he went up on deck again to discover that "the ship had now resumed her course, moving very slowly through the water with a little white line of foam on each side. I think we were all glad to see this: it seemed better than standing still." Allowing for his movements and conversation, the time was now about 12:30.

Titanic That Night No.2

Although noticing a lifeboat being uncovered without any undue alarm, he decided to go below again. Upon doing so he noticed an ever so slight downward tilt at the bow. On the way to his stateroom, he met two ladies concerned about why the *Titanic* had stopped: "Oh! Why have we stopped?" they said. "We did stop but we are now going on again," Beesley answered. The ladies were not convinced of this so Beesley took them along the corridor to a bathroom and showed them how to feel the vibrations of the engines: "They were much reassured to feel the engines throbbing down below and to know we were making some headway." Entering his gangway, Beesley met a man who asked if anything was new. "Not much," he replied, "We are going ahead slowly and she is down a little at the bows, but I don't think it is anything serious."

In an article written by *Titanic* survivor Miss Caroline Bonnell for the *Columbus Citizen* newspaper, April 19, 1912, Miss Bonnell related that upon returning from an upper deck, accompanied by her cousin, Nathalie Wick, they were told by an officer to "go below and put on your lifebelts—you may need them later." On the way to their stateroom, the two girls told Miss Bonnell's aunt and uncle, Mr. and Mrs. George Wick, what they had been told to do. Uncle George just laughed at them and said, "Why, that's nonsense girls, this boat is all right. She's going along finely. She just got a glancing blow I guess."[7]

Retiring to his cabin once more, Beesley read for about ten more minutes, when he finally heard the call: "All passengers on deck with lifebelts on."

On the way to the top deck, he met other passengers none of which appeared alarmed except for one lady who amused him by frightfully squeezing his arm as she asked him for help in finding her lifebelt. Kindly locating a steward who

Titanic That Night No.3

found the lifebelts, he eventually reached the top deck to find many passengers assembled there. Feeling the chilled air, he noticed that "even the breeze caused by the ship's motion had died entirely away, for the engines had stopped again and the *Titanic* lay peacefully on the surface of the sea." Time now was about 1:10.

1:40 A.M. Titanic Time, April 15, 1912

The time spent by Beesley in his stateroom, ascending and descending stairs, talking with and assisting passengers after he noticed the *Titanic* had resumed headway (about 12:30), until he was on deck the third time to realize the vessel had again stopped (about 1:10), was about forty minutes. It seems quite logical then that the *Titanic* steamed on during this interval of forty minutes for at least twenty minutes.

The Stockholm - Andrea Doria Collision

The Italian liner *Andrea Doria*, which sank in 1956 after collision with the Swedish liner *Stockholm*, although sustaining a vertical wound far worse than the *Titanic*'s wound, did not steam on again and remained afloat for nearly twelve hours, even though that vessel went into a severe list a short while after impact. If in fact the *Titanic* steamed on after collision, the action could have been the reason she stayed afloat for only two hours and forty minutes.

Why did veteran mariner Captain Smith of the *Titanic* start up again? Why did this not appear in the *Titanic*'s log or come out during the inquiries? Captain Smith most likely felt that he had to try to reach landfall, to get his vessel in shallow water or beach her, though he was some 380 miles from Cape Race, Newfoundland. In the interim he had the vessel sounded and made preparations for abandoning ship. After it was determined that his vessel was soon going to sink, he then stopped and began lowering lifeboats.

Smith knew at once his shortage of lifeboats and the appalling consequences that would soon follow. These circumstances, combined with the embarrassment of losing the "unsinkable" ship, were perhaps considered by him as incrimination enough without advertising his actions in the log, if there was even time to do so. As such an entry was not in the ship's log, it would not be an issue in the inquiries. Questions in this direction were probably not even asked and the supposed incriminatory information was certainly not offered.[8]

Titanic That Night No.4

Everyone aboard could easily have been saved as well by utilizing some of the thousands of deck chairs or other floatable material and lashing mattresses to fashion makeshift rafts. The ship had an enormous and well-stocked repair shop, which could have easily provided the required items. The sea was absolutely calm—crudely designed rafts could easily have taken and supported those without lifeboat space until the *Carpathia* reached them.

To the very end, it seems, most of those who were lost honestly believed that the unsinkable *Titanic* would not sink.

Dreams

To the superstitious mariner, dreams or objects in dreams were seriously regarded as sure ways to foretell events and predict good or ill fortune. If Scottish sailors dreamed of swine or blood, it was a warning of death. If they dreamed of sheep, it was a sign of good luck. Whalemen on the island of Bequia in the Lesser Antilles believed that the number of sheep seen in a dream would be the number of whales they would encounter that season. Dreams of anything green meant good luck. To dream of corn meant you would receive money. Dreams of a white child swimming in the sea meant good luck; however, dreaming of a black child, black people, or of eggs meant misfortune was coming. Dreams of muddy water, were warnings of ill luck or approaching death. Dreams of lice foretold that a member of one's family would fall sick. Dreams about snakes meant that you had an enemy, and killing the snake in the dream meant that you would outsmart your foe. It was a sign of hope when a sailor dreamed of an anchor. To dream of wading or bathing was a sign of coming joy; to dream of drowning meant good luck; dreams of fish meant coming rain; dreams of a rough sea or a tempest foretold of an unprofitable voyage; and dreams of dolphins meant the loss of one's lady love. Vague or confusing dreams suggested a coming event, and any dream related before breakfast brought bad luck.

When the *Isidore* sailed out of Kennebunkport, Maine, in 1847, it departed without its new crewman, Thomas King. He did not ship out, because in a dream he envisioned his ship wrecked and seven dead crewmen lying on its deck. King's dream became reality when the wreck of the *Isidore* was found with the corpses of seven crewmen on her deck.

The sailing ship *Lara* was bound from Liverpool to San Francisco in 1881, when a fire forced the captain and crew into three lifeboats some fifteen hundred miles off the west coast of Mexico. From exposure, thirst, and exhaustion, in a few days seven of the thirty-six survivors were unconscious. Capt. Neil Curry later reported: "We dreamed. . .and in the midst of one of our dreams, we imagined the water beneath us had turned from the blue of the sea to green. . .I managed to muster up strength to let out a container. I tasted the water and it was fresh."

After the dream the boats mysteriously entered an area distinctly different from the surrounding blue sea. It appeared as a strange but defined green oasis in the middle of the vast sea. They found the water fresh and lifesaving. After twenty-three days in the lifeboats, the captain, his family, and all the crew made it safely to landfall.[9]

Drowning

Perhaps the most cruel and inhumane maritime superstition was that which led to the widespread practice of not lending aid to a drowning victim. In antiquity, to drown was the most detested way to die. The souls of purgatory and the devil dwelt in the bottom of the sea, which in later times came to be known as Davy Jones's locker. Demons, water spirits, mermen, and mermaids were thought to seize the unwary or lure them to the depths. Therefore, to have helped a drowning person and thereby foil the devil's grasp of that person meant that a vengeful curse would be placed on those who dared thwart the devil's quest. At the very least, to save one from drowning, depriving the sea of its victim, resulted in making the sea a lifelong enemy. It was thought wrong to cheat fate out of a life.

Scottish fishermen and sailors even feared retrieving the body of a beached drowning victim, believing they would meet their end in the same way. A boat from which someone had drowned would not be used.

An old story tells about a man who fell overboard and was not given the slightest aid by his shipmates. Although he desperately struggled at length in the rough sea, those aboard shouted, "Jack! Give in! Dost thou not see that it pleases God!"

Chinese mariners also refused to help one drowning, believing the sea was the purgatory of the deep, which would release a victim only if another took his place.

Superstitious English, Russian, and Malaysian mariners also refused aid to the drowning.[10]

Notes

1. Bassett, *Legends and Superstitions of the Sea and of Sailors*, 438.
2. Information about deities in this section is from Bassett, *Legends and Superstitions of the Sea and of Sailors*, 54-75.
3. Information about devils in this section is from Bassett, *Legends and Superstitions of the Sea and of Sailors,* 86-97.
4. Lubbock, *The Last of the Windjammers*, 343-44, 428.
5. Fowles, *Shipwreck.*
6. DeWire, *Wreckers and Mooncussers*, 28-31.
7. *Columbus Citizen,* April 19, 1912.
8. Beesley, *The Loss of the S. S. Titanic: Its Story and Its Lessons*, 27-32.
9. Reader's Digest Assoc., *Mysteries of the Unexplained*, 267-68.
10. Bassett, *Legends and Superstitions of the Sea and of Sailors*, 466-69.

6. Equator Crossing

and Evil Eyes

Those who sailed o'er the mighty deep,
Honored Neptune while in his keep.
Peering from the darkness there,
Those evil eyes, that dreaded stare.

It is possible that the origin of equator-crossing ceremonies began with the Vikings, who were known to have performed rituals and services upon crossing certain parallels. Other ancient rites were also known to have taken place when ships crossed the thirtieth parallel or upon going through the Straits of Gibraltar. Phoenician mariners were said to have made sacrifices at the Pillars of Hercules upon entering the sea of darkness (Atlantic), and ancient Greek sailors paid similar homage when nearing major capes.

As far back as the Middle Ages, ceremonies were held on vessels upon their arrival in the tropics, crossing the Arctic Circle, or passing major points of land. These ceremonies were believed to be the first to include an impersonation of Neptune, the mythological god of the sea, by a ship's officer, who presided over the event. It was the custom then for all seafaring apprentices who sailed into areas where they had never been before to undergo the rude baptism of a ducking in the sea. On Dutch ships in the seventeenth century, a roll call muster was held to learn who had not passed that way before. Those who had not could either pay a fine or be hoisted to the main yardarm and dipped into the sea three times. Young boys were doused with buckets of water as they sat beneath a basket. Leniency could sometimes be bought by giving money to those in charge. A regular seaman would be penalized fifteen sols, and officers thirty sols. Passengers were charged as much as

they could pay. No one was exempt. Even admirals and those of high civilian stature had to pay the fines or be doused.

In many cases the ceremony served more as a severe test of human endurance. Some of these early rituals helped determine if first-cruise greenhorns could withstand the rigors of sea life by enduring rough initiations designed by the veteran crew members.

Even during wartime the event took place. In 1805, when Lord Nelson was in pursuit of the French to the West Indies, the usual routine was interrupted so that Crossing the Line ceremonies could be carried out.

Sometimes the frolic turned to near mutiny. On the Royal Navy vessel Acteon in 1857, when those who had not crossed the line greatly outnumbered those who had, near chaos erupted in the attempt to observe the custom.

In later years the dousing baptism ceased but a longer ceremony was adopted, which included other crude initiation pranks.

A typical line-crossing ceremony might have consisted of the following activities and players: Neptune's court, composed of veteran shellbacks aboard including his majesty Neptunus Rex; his assistant, Davy Jones; the Royal Scribe; the Royal Doctor; or others to accommodate the whims of the crew.

The night before crossing the equator, Davy Jones would be received by the captain to advise him when the vessel was to be hove to in order to greet the royal party. At this time Davy Jones served the captain with a summons for the persons whom he wanted to appear before him. The next day, when the navigator reported the ship was "on the line," the royal party was greeted by the captain, who turned his command over to Neptune and the initiation ceremonies began.

Repulsive foods were prepared far in advance of the ceremony. Chicken and pig droppings were made into a sickening lather for shaving the new recruits, who would be shaved with dull razors and "cleaned up" by a slosh in the face with a white wash brush dipped in slimy bilge water. Blindfolded candidates would approach the enthroned Neptune on hands and knees, receiving paddle spankings along the way.

The novitiates were made to eat putrid foods especially made for the event. The initiation menu for a line-crossing ceremony on the U.S. Navy submarine Wahoo in 1942 included a doughlike substance containing Tabasco sauce, chili powder, iodine, castor oil, vinegar, and soap. To become a shellback, Wahoo recruits had to prove their loyalty by kissing the bare bottom of the royal baby, the fattest man aboard, who was part of Neptune's court on that boat.[1]

Some vessels presented a certificate to the new shellbacks, which testified that upon crossing the equator among all "Mermaids, Sea Serpents, Whales, Sharks, Porpoises, Dolphins, Skates, Eels, Suckers, Lobsters, Crabs, Pollywogs, and other living things of the sea, John Doe has been found worthy to be numbered as one of our trusty shellbacks, and has been gathered to our fold and duly initiated into the solemn mysteries of the ancient order of the deep."[2]

The new shellbacks, for the most part, withstood the rough initiations, knowing they would someday inflict the same punishment on other novices.

The beginners who balked at the antics or who would not go easily along with the program would get the worst treatment. An old story about a sailor who refused to go along with a crossing ceremony relates the consequences the mariner might have feared by avoiding the event.

The sail maker aboard the bark Sunderland had not crossed the line before. Of the twelve-man crew, he was a wicked man, whose every other word was foul or degrading. As the vessel neared the line, Sails openly stated that he would have no part of the foolishness planned at the crossing. On a Sunday just before the ship crossed the equator, the man swore vehemently that he would have Jemmy Squarefoot (the devil) carry him off to hell before submitting to the ritual. No sooner had he spoken these words than he was lifted bodily by some unseen force and carried away in a prone position, yelling and struggling as he went. Grabbing at everything within reach, he was taken overboard in this manner, disappearing in the grasp of the invisible power. Bellows and groans from the inflicted man could be heard for some time afterward. So shocked were the remaining members of the crew that when the captain heard of the strange incident he led the group in prayer from the good book. This presented a solemn and repentant mood that eliminated further swearing on the ship that day.

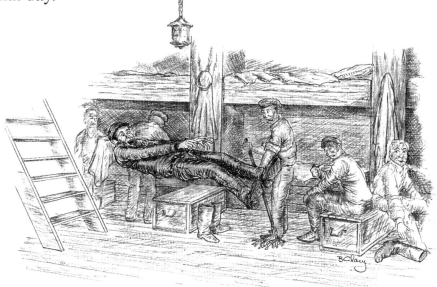

Was the devil listening and waiting to grant the wretch his wish? In a haunting atmosphere of gloom, each man went about his duties and tried his best to forget what had happened. One week from the day of the strange disappearance, the body of the sail maker was shockingly discovered on the foremast rigging, moaning and barely conscious.Most of the men refused to touch the man or even sleep in the same quarters with him. He was cared for reluctantly, nursed back to his feet, and was soon back to his duties.

Thereafter the old sail maker was a changed man. No further unkind word or curse did he utter, and his manner became gentle and quiet. When the ship reached her port of Buenos Aires, the crew vanished in haste from the ship they feared the devil had a hold on. The *Sunderland* acquired the reputation of a devil ship. As a result, it was a long while before the ship gained a crew, and when she finally did, she sailed for the West Indies never to be heard from again.[3]

Evil Eyes

When someone gives you a "dirty look" or "stares daggers at you," you might contemplate that "if looks could kill," you would have quickly died from the glance. These expressions evolved from the age-old fears of being watched by the "evil eye." Some ancient seafarers believed that the dreaded stare from the emerald eyes of sea monster dragons possessed the power to paralyze those who looked at them.  Other superstitious mariners believed that cat eyes or the eyes of other animals that gleamed in the dark would bring ill luck to those being watched. Although eyes on the prows of ancient ships served as good luck charms for a vessel to "see its way," when human or animal eyes stared at you, it was thought that an evil spell was being cast. During the sixteenth and seventeenth centuries, witches were believed to be closely associated with Satan and thus able to cast a spell with their eyes. If a witch was caught staring with malice at a person, the witch would have likely been burned at the stake.

Because a person's eyes were thought to be the windows of his or her soul, to be stared at was considered unlucky. The only ways to break the spell of the evil eye was to outstare the one who was staring at you, spit in your hat, cross your fingers. To be looked upon by someone with eyebrows that met or by someone with crossed or squinty eyes was very unlucky. A twitching eye or an itching left eye was also considered unlucky. An old belief was that the eyes of the dead had to be quickly closed so that the spirit might not capture another victim.

Always fearful of being watched, the superstitious sailor might have imagined evil eyes peering at him from the holes in a deadeye or from some dimly lit area perceived to have imaginary eyes. The beautifully carved figurehead of a little wooden sailor on the *N.B. Palmer* in 1851 had to be removed because frightened helmsmen believed that the eyes of the figurehead moved at night.[4]

Notes

1. Baker, *The Folklore of the Sea*, 114.
2. Lovette, *Naval Customs, Traditions, and Usage*, 45.
3. Nordhoff, *Sailor Life on Man of War and Merchant Vessel*, 132-37.
4. Baker, *The Folklore of the Sea*, 19.

7. Figureheads

Fishing, Flags, Food

Protect the figure that calms the wave,
Follow beliefs that fishermen gave.
Honor the flag to guard the ship,
Beware the food that'll jinx the trip.

Figureheads

Almost simultaneously with the time that man built the first primitive boat to sail upon the sea, he began to decorate and embellish his craft. The way in which ancient reed boats were lashed together to form an upturned prow provided a natural mount from which to affix ornaments or emblems.

Fish figures on the prows or eyes on the bows of these and other ancient vessels were put there by these first mariners to help the vessel see its way or hopefully endow the vessel

with an attribute of the figure it carried. Bullhead ornaments bore the symbol of strength; holy birds, stag antlers, or horses characterized swiftness; lions or boars' heads represented aggressiveness. From these archaic adornments came both the origin of the figurehead and the theory that a ship had its own personality.

Mostly for decoration at first, throughout history figureheads were placed on ships for many other reasons. As sentinels they were used to ward off evil spirits. As an adornment of sacrifice they were meant to appease the gods of the sea or to commemorate the spirit of the boat.

As a scare tactic, grotesque figures presented terror or a dreaded threat to enemies. Viking ships often carried intricately carved serpents' heads with gaping jaws to terrorize their foe. The figures could be removed so that friendly land spirits would not be offended or frightened when approaching shore. On the other side of the globe, a common figurehead carried on Maori war canoes was carvings of human figures with protruding tongues. The aggressive figures, poised as if ready to leap, signified a challenge or insult to their enemies.

Ship ornamentation reached its crescendo about 1700. A new era of naval architecture and the massive naval expansion of England, France, Spain, Holland, and Scandinavia led to a proliferation of the design and use of grandiose figureheads. The lion was adopted as a multinational emblem and was predominantly used in varied forms of figureheads by most navies until the mid-1700s. From this time until late in the eighteenth century, figurehead design ran rampant. Enormous figures of complex detail and embellishment, although masterful pieces of workmanship, were so excessively elaborate that their themes were nearly impossible to interpret. Intricate figurehead carvings of everything from kings to oxen and dashing horsemen to hovering cherubs with endless trim and convoluted garnish were state of the art.

In 1796, because of economics, an attempt to abolish ornate ship carving except for a simple billet (a small scroll-like carving used instead of a figurehead) proved highly unpopular with sailors who believed it was unlucky to sail behind a billet. Soon thereafter, custom-built, single-figure figureheads, characteristic of the ship's name, came into being. Vessels named after a famous person usually carried a figurehead of that celebrity. Greek warriors, lords, kings, maidens, sea gods, saints, and other classical figures began to dominate figurehead motif.[1]

The dramatic expansion of America's merchant fleet in the nineteenth century produced an array of renowned American figurehead carvings of superb quality and workmanship. The quest for speed in the clipper ship era, which began in the 1840s, inspired an additional provocative, imaginative, and romantic flair to figurehead designs and themes. A detail in the expression of many figureheads was the glaring eyes of the subject, derived from the oculi of ancient times.

Young daughters of captains and owners, no doubt the sweetheart's of many sailor's dreams, often posed as models for modest figurehead carvings. The most popular female figureheads, however, were those of bare-breasted ladies. Believed capable of calming angry seas, the near life-like figures probably became the secret love of many lonely seamen. After all, they were often the only image of a woman seen by sailors during very long voyages. Other matronly figures listened as homesick seafarers, having no one else to talk to, poured out their woes to them. An old story relates how lovesick sailors often confided in the motherly figurehead on a ship called the *Princess*. According to the captain, some members of the crew would sneak forward at night to tell their troubles to the lady who always listened intently.[2]

One matronly figurehead did more than just listen. When the Spanish barque Primos went on the rocks in July 1871, seaman Vincenzo Defelice was the only survivor. During his long ordeal in the water, Defelice clung to the matronly figure, which had broken free from the bow when the ship struck the rocks.[3]

The *Cutty Sark*, one of the most famous clippers, was named after the undergarment worn by her bare-breasted figurehead of the witch, Nannie. It was said that every sailor who served on the *Cutty Sark* spoke of the figurehead with great affection.[4]

As a guest for a week on the Coast Guard training barque *Eagle* in 1976, I decided one day to venture out to the tip of the bowsprit to photograph her majestic prow dashing through the sea while under near-full sail. Carefully edging forward with my feet on a thin cable, I was encouraged by my escort to step on the firm, broad, folded wing of the ship's eagle figurehead. My hesitation and look of disbelief was enough for the escort to assure me to "go ahead, everyone does it." I was surprised at the indifference to the old superstition about showing disrespect to a figurehead.

Reverently cared for, figureheads represented the lucky symbol of a ship. To desecrate, mock, or abuse a figurehead was tantamount to a deliberate attack on the spirit of the ship itself.

In the light of that old supersitition, it is incomprehensible why and how the most unusual figureheads of all would dare appear on any ship, for they could hardly be called lucky for the ships that carried them. At the very least they were terrifying and were surely a reckless provocation to the forces of evil. These figureheads were that of the devil on the topsail schooner *Devil* mentioned in chapter 5 and the figurehead of the female devil Sheitan, the Chinese goddess of evil, on the schooner *Sheitan*. Owned by P. Miller, the same owner of the Devil, the *Sheitan* was built in Preston, England, in 1869. Ill luck followed the *Devil* throughout her career, while the *Sheitan* somehow escaped misfortune.[5]

Another unusual work is the figure of the dancing *twin sisters*, an unidentified carving in the Mystic Seaport collection. In early nineteenth-century dress, two chubby girls appear about to begin a dance step, arms around each other's waist, hands clasped and pointing forward.

A figurehead on the Royal Navy sloop of war *Termagant* (1796-1819) included the unusual feature of a double-faced head, a man on one side and a woman on the other. On the female side, the woman, with a real broom, appears to be attacking the man, who, in full color, has a bloody nose.[6]

There have been some unusual incidents in connection with figureheads. During the 1833 restoration of the USS *Constitution*, the commandant of the Boston Navy Yard, Capt. Jesse D. Elliot, insisted that the billet be replaced with a life-size figure of the president of the United States, Andrew Jackson. Townsfolk of Boston, a Republican city, did not approve of the idea and voiced their heated dislike through threats in newspapers, handbills, and anonymous letters. Undeterred, Elliot had the figurehead carved and installed anyway. For peace of mind he stationed a marine sentry nearby to guard it and provided further protection by mooring the *Constitution* between two lines of battleships. Despite the precautions taken, on the night of July 2, 1834, Samuel W. Dewey of Falmouth, Massachusetts, was able to sneak aboard and saw off the head of Jackson during a thunderstorm, the clamor of which muffled the sounds of his sawing. Even though despised by Boston Republican citizens, the navy got its way and retained the figurehead of Andrew Jackson, an army man. The repaired figurehead remained on the *Constitution* until 1846, when it was replaced by a better figure of Jackson, which remained there until 1874, when that figure was finally replaced by a billet again.[7]

To prevent embarrassment to the figure and protect the spirit of the ship, when the HMS *Royal George* was in retreat of a larger Franco-Spanish force in 1778, a hammock was fastened over the figurehead of George II to prevent him/it from witnessing the withdrawal.[8]

Another safeguard of a ship's spirit took place in the French Revolutionary Wars during the Glorious First of June Battle of Ushant between British and French forces on June 1, 1794. The hat of the Duke of Brunswick's figurehead on the HMS *Brunswick* was shot away in an engagement with the *Vengeur du Peuple*. Representatives of the ship's crew quickly approached twice-wounded Captain Harvey of the *Brunswick* requesting his cocked hat for a replacement. In the heat of battle, the gold-laced hat was nailed in place and the *Brunswick*, her honor restored, fought on to sink the *Vengeur*. During the ensuing heavy fight, Harvey received a third and fatal wound.[9]

Old superstitious mates believed that misfortunes that occurred on the *Grand Duchess* were caused by the severing of an arm from the ship's figurehead during a careless towing incident on the St. Lawrence River in 1920.[10]

When the Allies appropriated the German liner *Imperator* as part of World War I reparations, her old crew members were quick to blame the humiliation on the loss of the eagle's wings from the ship's figurehead, which took place during a storm years before.[11]

Courtesy of United States
Naval Academy

Although figureheads are now a defunct tradition aboard ships, the respect for and admiration of their spirit lingers. Today, midshipmen at the United States Naval Academy in Annapolis, Maryland, throw pennies at the quiver on a bronze replica of the figurehead of the Indian chief Tecumseh, the original carving of which once adorned the bow of the seventy-four-gun, ship of the line USS *Delaware* (1817-61). According to legend, midshipmen will receive a passing (2.0) grade if their pennies, thrown on the way to an exam, land in the quiver of Tecumseh, also known as the god of 2.0. It is strongly pointed out to the mids that this is a legendary promise of Tecumseh and not that of the professor giving the exam.[12]

Fishing

It is said that among all seafarers, fishermen are the most superstitious. Perhaps so, for strange as it may seem, it is bad luck to wish a fisherman good luck. Many fishermen even believe it unlucky simply to be looked at by another person before setting out for the day.

The first fish caught by ancient fishermen was treated with great reverence and sacrificed to Poseidon, the god of the sea. Scottish fishermen threw their first catch back to the sea for good luck. Other fishermen, instead of returning the first

fish, gave it tender care and spoke kind words to it. In many fishing communities around the world, for good luck, fishermen would nail to the mast the first fish caught in the season. This fish also predicted a good or bad year. A female fish portended a good season, a male fish a poor one.

French fishermen believed that three days before bad weather set in, the fish would quickly take the bait, but on the day of the change in weather the fish would stay away from the lines. When big fish were sighted swimming near the surface of the sea, it was a definite sign of approaching winds. A jumping whale was also an old weather advisory. It was thought that severe weather agitated the whale to jump higher. The higher the animal jumped, the more intense the storm would be. Cod fishermen believed that when fish bit with fervor it meant a coming storm. If the cod ran early in the season a severe winter was on the way. This old wind advisory predicted when good or poor fishing could be expected:

> When the wind is in the East,
> Then the fishes bite the least;
> When the wind is in the West,
> Then the fishes bite the best;
> When the wind is in the North,
> Then the fishes do come forth;
> When the wind is in the South,
> It blows the bait in the fish's mouth.[13]

Contrary to the belief of other superstitious mariners, Shetland fishermen considered it lucky to meet a deformed or retarded person on the way to their boats. Hawaiian fishermen saw an omen of bad luck if a fish was hooked in its tail.

Fishermen of old sincerely believed that witchcraft caused meager catches. To keep witches away from their boats, Yorkshire, England, fisherfolk stuck pins into and burned the heart of a sheep to inflict pain on those who would cast a spell. Other English fishermen stuck a mackerel with pins and stowed it with their nets, believing it would "prick" any lingering sorcerer. Belgian fishermen, by burning straw in their holds, stamping it out, and throwing it overboard believed they could overcome with smoke, destroy by fire, trample to death, and drown the evil spirits. Japanese fishermen burned feathers on their boats for the same reasons.

A handful of salt carried in the pockets of many fishermen was believed the best deterrent against witches, who despised the mineral. It was thought that a witch had to count every grain of salt a person had before any evil spell would work. Fishermen also threw salt into the sea, or "salted" their nets, at the beginning of the fishing season. A shoe thrown at a departing fishing boat was thought to insure a good catch.

Although sailors and fishermen alike considered it taboo to spit into the sea, some fishermen would spit on their bait for good luck. Fishermen would never curse their nets. To cuss the most important tool of their trade invited disaster. Sportfishermen today consider it unlucky to bait a hook with the left hand, to switch fishing poles while fishing, or to tell the number of fish caught. It is also considered unlucky to sit on a bucket turned upside down or count your catch before unloading it.

Care was taken when cleaning the fishing boats to leave a few fish scales about at the end of a successful haul, for it was believed that fish, attracted to a fishy odor, would stay away from well-scrubbed boats. In the same regard, all the fish from a good catch were never sold, because it was believed that a few remaining fish strewn about assured the continuance of successful hauls.

Normandy fishermen affixed a bottle of brandy to the stern of their boats for good luck, and others inserted coins in the floats of their nets as an offering to the sea for a good catch.

The old fishermen's belief that fish were thought to be infested with fleas was perhaps the most absurd belief of all.

Flags

Representing the nation it hails from, a ship's flag is one of the most revered symbols of a ship's spirituality. During the great sea battles, when a defeated commander "struck his colors," or lowered his country's flag signifying surrender, it not only marked in part the defeat of that country, but also symbolized defeat, humiliation, and embarrassment for the spirit of the surrendering ship.

To lose, tear, or drop a flag into the sea was a sure sign of coming misfortune for the ship it was on. To hand a flag to another sailor through a porthole or through the rungs of a ladder or to repair a flag on the quarterdeck brought ill luck to those involved.

Newly assigned personnel coming aboard the Coast Guard barque Eagle climb the mainmast to kiss the commissioning pennant for good luck. The tradition also abruptly familiarizes the green recruits with the dizzying heights aloft.

When a ship flies a paying-off pendant, the tradition dates to the Napoleonic wars. A narrow strip of bunting equal in length to that of a ship's career is flown when the ship sails for home to "pay off." On the last Atlantic voyage of the RMS Queen Mary in 1967, a 310-foot pendant flew from her masthead representing ten feet of banner for each year of her service.[14]

The U.S. Navy has a similar tradition of flying a coming-home pendant equal to the number of sailors aboard or the number of days at sea. On June 1, 1945, when the aircraft carrier USS Enterprise, CV-6, the most decorated ship in the history of the navy, arrived at Pearl Harbor after 578 days of valiant Pacific action, she proudly flew a 578-foot pendant, one foot for every day the ship was at sea.

Courtesy Bill Barr

Food

Old-time mariners had many superstitions about food. Because eggs were used by witches, one would never mention them by name at sea. English fishermen believed that a ship would be lost for every loaf of bread turned upside down. As a guard against shipwreck, the wives of sailors would be sure their husbands sailed with hot cross buns baked on Good Friday. Rice, also known as "strike me blind," was not favored by sailors who believed that it caused blindness. Fishermen perceived fish as too ignorant to swim out of a net. They believed that "you are what you eat," and if one ate fish heads he too would become ignorant. Nowadays bananas are considered bad luck to have aboard on deep-sea fishing charters.

Because turtles live to be very old, it was believed that the eating of turtle flesh or keeping a piece of its shell with you was good insurance that you would have strength in your old age.

Pouring salt between the rocks at the seaside assured the wives of seafarers that their loved ones would be guarded from the dangers of the sea. For good luck, fishermen were often showered with salt before venturing out to sea. To accidentally overturn a salt shaker in Holland meant that a shipwreck would take place.

In some maritime communities, pieces of cake saved from special festivals were securely wrapped and carefully stored for absent seafarers. If the cake dried up during a storm it signified bad luck.

For a sailor to eat every last crumb of food given him meant that clear weather was ahead. To return food to the galley invited bad luck and forthcoming hunger.

On Great Lakes freighters today some consider it a sign of bad luck if all the coffee mugs are not hung in the same direction.

Notes

1. Norton, *Ships' Figureheads,* 12-127.
2. Baker, *The Folklore of the Sea*, 20.
3. Norton, *Ships' Figureheads*, 117.
4. Ibid., 21.
5. Lubbock, *The Last of the Windjammers*, 344.
6. Cornwell, ed., *The Illustrated History of Ships*, 469.
7. Magoun, *The Frigate Constitution and Other Historic Ships*, 89-90.
8. Cornwell, ed., *The Illustrated History of Ships*, 469.
9. Ibid., 469.
10. Baker, *The Folklore of the Sea*, 19.
11. Ibid., 23.
12. Edsall, *A Place Called the Yard*, 33.
13. Lys, *A Treasury of American Superstition*, 81.
14. Baker, *The Folklore of the Sea*, 119.

8. Games

Ghosts, Grooming

Play with the devil 'n he'll own your heart,
Believe in all ghosts to play it smart.
Hail not the phantom, better look away,
Take care in grooming for a lucky day.

Games

What little idle time a sailor had aboard a ship during the age of sail was undoubtedly spent overcoming the ravages of exhaustion. If he could read, few ships had much of a library. Leisure time was more likely spent trading yarns, smoking a pipeful, or working on handicrafts, such as scrimshaw, wood carving, or rope work. Rough choruses of the popular songs or chanteys of the time, sung by shellbacks and greenhorns and accompanied by fiddle, harmonica, or concertina, helped warm the otherwise cold environment.

Dice, card, and other games of chance often brought bad consequences. Some sailors lost their entire pay and prize money earned on long voyages to gambling, and arrived home as penniless as when they departed.

The religious mariner believed that the devil played in every card game, and with the "devil's luck," he was sure to win the pay, the hearts of the men, and the ship to boot. Most probably these mates were advocates of the belief that if playing cards were torn up and cast overboard, fair winds would result.

French seamen, during fleet campaigns at Mitylene, were said to have seen a horned, hideous spirit descend into the sea at Zante, accompanied by one of their mates, who had defied the Virgin Mary during a dice game aboard their vessel.[1]

Because of the endless problem with vermin aboard ships, plenty of cockroaches were always available for use in games devised by severely bored crew members to break monotony. In a game called "weevil races," insects were placed inside a circle drawn on the deck with charcoal. The winning insect was the first one to crawl out of the circle.

One of the most bizarre incidents involving a card game was related in an issue of the *Atlantic Telegraph*. The anecdote, "Strange Adventure at Sea," is found in the handwritten booklet published aboard the *Great Eastern* Monday, July 24, 1865, during an Atlantic cable-laying expedition.

> The ship *Medisim* in Lat. 56.40 N, Long. 23.15 W. observed a raft with two men on it distant about one mile. On approaching the raft the men were found playing at Ecarte [French for discarding cards]. They presented a most miserable appearance. Their arms and legs looking as if pieces had been bitten out of them. On inquiry it was ascertained that the two men were the sole survivors of the crew of the French ship "*La Floire.*" Ten days past she struck against an iceberg and the boats being crushed, the crew, twenty in all, made a raft and succeeded in getting clear of the ship. They had some water on board but no provisions, so it was agreed that they should play at Ecarte,

the victor in each game having the privilege of biting out a piece of his opponent's flesh. In this way the whole of the crew had been disposed of excepting the two found on the raft and it is conjectured, owing to their skill being en equal, and but for the timely arrival of the *Medisim* no one would have been left to tell the tale.

Ghosts

"Do you believe in ghosts?" asked the ship's boy. The crusty old sail maker's warm presence suddenly turned cold. "I didn't, till I saw one," he faintly replied.

Ghost sightings aboard ships have been reported since ancient times. The Virgin, saints, and other ethereal spirits, appearing during tempests, calmed storms after receiving homage or promises to keep holy certain feasts. According to legend, the Holy Mother appeared on ships in the Middle Ages. St. Thomas of Canterbury, St. Edmund, and St. Nicholas were said to have visited one of the ships of the crusading fleet sailing to the Holy Land in 1190. Also in the twelfth century there was record of the appearance of Notre Dame de la Garde who took the helm of a ship in peril and aided fishermen in a storm.

Ghosts of the violently killed or murdered, unable to rest, often returned to haunt the scene.

According to navy crewmen aboard the USS *Constitution*, at the Charlestown, Massachusetts, Naval Yard, ghosts from the War of 1812 often appear on board the venerable old vessel.

In their attempts to verify these apparitions, newly assigned navy personnel are not told about the ghosts until they themselves relate a ghost sighting. Time and again, it is said, the new men offer their own, unprompted ghost story.

Often seen around the cannon, where violent deaths would have occurred, the ghosts, in early naval uniforms, appear in a mist from the waist up. Locked doors found ajar, mysterious noises, and bloodcurdling battle screams are all attributed to what are believed to be the spirits of past heroes.

In the text of the 1981 *USS Constitution Turn Around Cruise* program, Engineman Fireman K. A. Bradford and Seaman B. W. Shugar wrote about these spirits: "At night you can come aboard and let your mind open to the ship and watch the life that looms and lurks about her decks and passageways. She holds the inner spirit of many unsung heroes, but if given the chance, these spirits tell their story. The bloody screams of her heroes' past are locked deep within her hull. At night the key is found and the screams pour out as illusions in front of our eyes offering us care and guidance."

While the old Cunard liner *Queen Mary* was undergoing conversion to a museum ship near the Long Beach Naval Shipyard, a security guard patrolling the ship was startled one night when his dog abruptly stopped and stared ahead. He was near watertight door number 13 in the shaft alley. Believing the dog sensed someone hiding there, he made a complete search of the area, but found no one. Resuming his patrol he found that the dog, although urged toward the doorway, refused to go through it. The incident was chilling enough for an investigation, which revealed that in 1966, during a routine watertight door drill, an eighteen-year-old crewman, John Pedder, was accidentally crushed to death by this doorway number 13. What is believed to be the ghost of John Pedder is said to be periodically seen in the area still at work wearing his blue engineer's coveralls. According to the Cunard Line fleet personnel department in Southampton, England, John Pedder was employed from March 31 to July 10, 1966. It is noted on his record that he died at sea.

Cries and screams were also said to have been heard by workmen in a forward area of the ship where damage was sustained in collision with the light cruiser HMS *Curacoa* in one of the best-kept secrets of World War II. Racing across the Atlantic at over twenty-eight knots, carrying 10,398 American troops bound for the Firth of Clyde, Scotland, the *Queen Mary* accidentally sliced in half the *Curacoa* at approximately 2:12 p.m. on Friday, October 2, 1942. The *Curacoa*, part of a six-destroyer escort in the area to guard the *Queen Mary*, inadvertently cut across her bow. The *Queen* steamed on and through the wreck, under strict and cold orders not to stop. The *Curacoa*, severed into two parts, sank almost immediately with 329 of her 430-man crew.

Many vessels, it is supposed, begin their career already haunted, plagued with misfortune and death during their construction before the jinxed ship even slips into her element. The turbulent sea of misfortune encountered by the German World War I submarine *UB-65* was believed responsible for one of the most astounding ghost visitations on record.

While under construction at the Vulkan shipyard in

Hamburg in 1917, a heavy steel girder fell from its sling and killed one workman and gravely injured another man, who later died from the accident. Deadly toxic fumes in the engine room claimed three more lives before the vessel was completed. Strange incidents that occurred during her sea trials certainly must have aroused further uneasy feelings about the already ill-fated sub. When a veteran crew member was sent forward to inspect the hull, he was mysteriously lured toward the sea and deliberately continued walking, without stopping, into the water, where he drowned. During her first dive the sub was made to descend to thirty feet. As if she had a will of her own, she continued to dive, to the very floor of the North Sea. Poisonous fumes circulated through the vessel when leaking water found her batteries. A gripping twelve hours passed in the would-be grave when miraculously the sub began to surface. Luckily no lives were lost to this misfortune. Ordered back to dry dock, the difficulties were rectified and the submarine was again ready for service. However, during the loading of torpedoes, without apparent cause, a warhead of one of the deadly fish exploded, instantly killing the second officer and five ratings. While the sub was ordered back to drydock for repairs, some of the crew, cognizant of the multiple deaths and other grave misfortunes, declared the vessel jinxed.

Finally clearing inspection, she set out on her first patrol; shortly thereafter, a petty officer of the watch dashed into the wardroom and passed out. When he came to, he said that "the dead man's come aboard," claiming that he had seen the ghost of the second officer killed by the torpedo explosion. Another man also identified the apparition as that of the fallen officer. The commander, suspecting a hoax, threatened arrest of anyone discussing the matter. When the sub returned to its base, one of the men who had seen the ghost deserted after confiding in a friend that he felt the ship and its men were doomed.

For a while on the next patrol, spirits (no pun) were lifted when the sub sank a British merchant ship off the coast of Kent. The cheered atmosphere soon turned grim when a lookout and the first officer sighted the ghost again. As before, the apparition stood on the bows staring at the conning tower with its arms folded. When the sub returned to the base at Bruges amid an air attack, a bomb blast decapitated the commander as he was leaving the sub, and seconds afterward the ghost once again appeared.

In an attempt to squash the jinx, a thorough inquiry was held, each crewman was carefully interviewed and sent home on leave. While the sub lay idle, a Lutheran chaplain was ordered aboard to perform a rite of exorcism.

A new hard-line veteran commanding officer took charge of the sub. He made it known that ghosts and all the associated foolishness would have no place on his boat. To the crew, engrossed in the activities of a hunter sub stalking an enemy, for a while on this first sortie after the exorcism, everything appeared normal. There were no reports of ghosts, and the sub had sunk several Allied ships. Deep in the minds of her crew, however, lurked the dreadful fears about the jinxed sub. In a letter, a chief petty officer related that "something about the boat was evil." He told of seeing the ghost come into his quarters and pass through a bulkhead to the torpedo room. He further revealed that the sub's former commander, despite openly stating his disbelief of the ghost, did believe that the boat was haunted.

On the next patrol, things returned to normal—normal for a haunted ship. The ghost of the second officer was sighted once again by a man who became so unnerved that he had to be given morphine. This man shortly thereafter committed suicide. Another man sighted the ghost, fell and broke his leg, and went into a high fever. Petty Officer Richard Meyer suddenly left the conning tower, descended to the deck, and jumped into the sea. He was last sighted swimming madly away from the sub as if chased by sharks. One other seaman, after sighting the ghost, went into a rage, and was shot at by the commander. Whether he was injured or killed is not known.

Because of the extreme low state of morale, the sub returned to base, and its commander, who defied the foolishness about the ghosts, admitted to his superiors that he too had twice seen the second officer's wraith. Although the sub was believed in good operational order, it went to dry dock once more, for no other apparent reason than to attempt to rectify the predicament.

The next recorded sighting of *UB-65* was through a U.S. Navy submarine's periscope. On July 10, 1918, off southeastern Ireland, the commander of the American submarine *L-2* observed *UB-65* rolling in a heavy swell with no sign of life aboard. Although she appeared to be a derelict, she would still have to be dealt with, so preparations were made for attack. No sooner had those activities begun when to the disbelief of the American commander the German sub erupted with a violent explosion from within. Baffled by the explosion, the American captain, peering through his scope, saw an officer standing motionless on the bow of the German sub with his arms folded, facing its conning tower. He was positive the man was not there when he first sighted the boat. All thirty-four officers and ratings on *UB-65* were lost. Fifteen other lives had been mysteriously lost during the short life of the sub. The ghost of one of these, returning to the sub many times, became known as the ghost of *UB-65*.[2]

Was it the ghost of a World War II German submarine that sent a note found in a small container washed ashore on a Danish beach in 1979? The message, written in German on wax-treated paper, read, "We have been hit by a bomb. Our submarine is resting on sea bottom, torpedo and engine rooms flooded. Five men besides me are still alive." The note was signed by Capt. Heinz Ratsch of the U-boat *U-583,* which sank in the Baltic Sea in November 1941.

Benevolent spirits have sometimes appeared to the unwary mariner to help, guide, or call him away from danger. During Joshua Slocum's solo (?) voyage around the world aboard the *Spray* in 1895, the pioneer mariner, accepted a large amount of white cheese and fruit given him by the natives of Fayal Island in the Azores. After his usual meager diet, the rich cheese and savory plums seemed like a king's feast. Not until severe stomach cramps took hold of him, did he realize how foolish he had been in his hunger. The sea had turned extremely rough, he was in agonizing pain, and his last ounce of strength was spent reefing sails. He somehow was able to lash the helm and make it to his cabin where he passed out.

He came to, realizing that his boat was being tossed about like a loose cannon. In his weak state he could hardly move, but he had to get on deck to steer his vessel in the storm. When he finally did so, he saw something that at first chilled him to the bone. At the helm was a tall stranger in strange garb.

The man tipped his large, red hat and smiled, assuring Slocum with his genteel manner that he was a friend. Introducing himself as the pilot of Columbus's *Pinta,* he said he was there to help until Slocum regained his strength. When Slocum asked the pilot if he would stay there during the night, he accepted the offer, stating that his vessel would be in good hands while Slocum recovered. He kindly offered that plums and cheese should not be eaten together, especially white cheese with unknown content.

Slocum retired to his cabin and awoke the next morning to find that the *Spray* had sailed ninety miles in the storm, was on course, and still driving as if she were bewitched. Sailing on alone, Slocum safely reached Gibraltar.[3]

A crewman on a fishing vessel off Georges Bank near Nova Scotia encountered a stranger writing at the chart table one stormy winter day. The man had disappeared when the startled crewman returned with the captain, but they found only a mysterious message written on the ship's slate: "Change your course to NNW and in a certain time you'll see a vessel turned on its side with the crew hanging to it." Knowing it was unlucky to change course in search of a wreck, the captain hesitatingly steered as advised to soon discover a wreck with sixteen men hanging on it, whom they rescued. One other man had been lost.[4] Did the ghost of this man seek and find help for his imperiled shipmates?

In one three-year interval, before 1900, ship captains worldwide sighted over sixteen hundred floating hulks. According to the 1991 *Lloyd's Register Casualty Return* records of ships lost that were over 100 gross tons, from 1941 to 1991, an average of 134 vessels per year either foundered, were lost because of fire or explosion, or were reported missing. In 1992, 94 vessels foundered, 35 were lost because of fire or explosion, and 3 were reported missing.

The largest vessel posted as missing by Lloyd's was the 965-foot, 91,655-ton British motor vessel *Derbyshire,* which was last reported about 230 miles east southeast of Okinawa on September 9, 1980. Believed to have sunk in a typhoon, the vessel and all aboard were lost without a trace.

Some of these vessels may have been abandoned because of severe weather, fire, collision (with icebergs or other vessels), explosion, piracy, or even murder. It is impossible to determine how many of these wrecks, instead of sinking, became floating derelicts that endangered other vessels. As ship-to-shore communication and sophisticated search technology came into use, their population thinned. However, the recorded encounters with derelicts, some of which sailed crewless for decades, would lead one to believe that their existence, even today, is quite possible. Even though most derelicts are found and dealt with through coast guard actions around the world, one could surmise that some unmanned phantoms still ply the seas.

When sighted in 1878, the *San Christobal*, a ship registered in Lisbon, Portugal, bound for the Americas from that port, appeared with her sails in tatters and no sign of life aboard. She was hailed by the captain of the *Elizabeth Watson* of Halifax, who received no response. Those that boarded her for investigation were shocked to find a death ship of unequaled renown. Dead passengers and crew were found in practically every area of the ship except the master's cabin and the hold. As the boarding party, stouthearted as they must have been, groped through the eerie setting for an explanation of the mass of dead, they found stuffed in the log several crudely written pages that supplied the answer.

A peculiar man named Alvar tried many times to court Manuelita de Pelflor, a beautiful Lisbon girl, who repeatedly turned down his advances. One of the girl's many suitors was the master of the *Christobal*, Capt. Diego Santas, who won her hand in marriage just before his ship sailed. The incensed Alvar, known to be a vicious man when crossed, signed on the *Christobal,* bent on getting even by murdering the newlyweds. When captain Santas invited passengers and crew to celebrate his marriage, Alvar, working in the galley, saw the chance for his evil deed. At first he just sprinkled poison on food meant for the captain and his wife, but evidently his hate overcame his senses when he spread the poison on all the food offered to everyone at the party. The portion used was enough to kill double the number of those aboard.

One by one they met their horrible end. He watched with indifference as the beautiful Manuelita, a mother still breast-feeding her child, praying nuns, and mere boys lay writing in their agony. Into the night, as the lanterns were dying, the last flickers of light danced in the staring eyes of the dead and made them appear alive again.

The scene must have chilled even Alvar before the lanterns burnt out. Then it was dark and he realized he was alone. Quickly filling a lantern, he went to the captain's quarters, away from the frightful glances of his victims, to write about his love for Manuelita and state his full confession. Alvar then jumped into the sea. Although the *Christobal* sailed on for just a short while, it carried what may have been the first mass murder episode on the seas.[5]

In 1923, a captain of a ship sailing off the tip of South America caught sight of what appeared to be an enormous green growth protruding from the green sea. Examination with binoculars revealed the strange image of a three-masted vessel cloaked in bright green, almost camouflaged by the surrounding sea. All the rigging, the tattered sails, the cabins, the hull, and every other speck of the ship were covered with brilliant green.

A boarding party sent to investigate found the rotting ship covered with algae, which had collected after years of unattended sailing. The decks, although covered with the same coating, were mushy with decay. Skeletons of the crew were still dressed in what was left of their slimy clothes. The ship was identified as the *Marlbourough,* which had sailed for Great Britain from New Zealand and was last reported near the Straits of Magellan twenty-four years earlier! The ghost apparently sailed through the notoriously rough "roaring forties" seas and onward, manned but by her ghostly crew. The mystery of the *Marlbourough* and the strange fate of all those aboard was never solved.[6]

The miles covered by some derelicts is astounding. Bound for Peru from British Columbia, the Canadian ship *Florence Edgett* was caught in a severe tempest in 1902. When the crew took to their lifeboats, the vessel was listing severely. However, the abandoned ship somehow managed to round Cape Horn and sail to the North Atlantic's Sargasso Sea, where she ended her trek ten years later.[7]

Another unusual derelict was the *Leon White,* which reportedly sailed across the Atlantic and back again in a seven thousand-mile voyage that lasted slightly longer than three hundred days.[8]

There is also the strange story of a derelict schooner found in the mid-Atlantic by the American vessel *Ellen Austin* in 1881. Because the abandoned vessel was in good condition, the captain of the *Austin* claimed the derelict, sent a crew aboard, and the two vessels made for port. Soon afterward the schooner and its new crew disappeared in a violent squall. As the weather cleared, the *Austin* found the schooner but shockingly discovered it deserted again. After a reluctant second crew was persuaded to take her in, the two vessels became engulfed in another squall, the derelict with her final crew vanished, and was never seen again.

What has to be the king of derelicts is the thirteen hundred-ton steamer *Baychimo*, which sailed as a fur carrier and supply ship in the treacherous waters of the Northwest Passage, the Bering Strait, and the western Arctic. With over a million dollars of furs in her holds, she became trapped in ice off the village of Barrow, Alaska, October 1931, during her last manned voyage from Vancouver.

Arrangements were made to rescue twenty-two of the crew by airplane over six hundred miles of the most barren country in the world. The captain and fourteen crewmen stayed with the ship, hoping the next summer's thaw would break her free. As a violent polar storm approached, those on the *Baychimo* decided they would best survive the fury in a shelter built with supplies from the ship. After the three-day storm abated, the men were bewildered to discover that their ship with its valuable cargo was gone. Nothing was found of the vessel after a wide search that lasted for weeks. Upon their return to Point Barrow, an Eskimo hunter there declared that he had found the *Baychimo* some forty-five miles from her first position. Most of the cargo was retrieved after many long and arduous trips, in blizzard conditions, between the ship and Barrow. Returning for the last of the furs, they found that once again the ship had vanished.

The wayward derelict was sighted in 1933, 1935, and 1939 by the captains of other vessels all of whom boarded the specter to find her in seaworthy condition and not taking water. Scores of other reported sightings by Eskimos continued to surface to testify that the ship still sailed on. One group of Eskimos, who had boarded the ghost, even spent ten days aboard her after being sent adrift in a storm. Is there truth in the report of her last sighting about 1973, or was it a desire to keep the mystical legend afloat? Regardless, the *Baychimo,* believed to have sailed unmanned for at least forty years, will long be known as the ghost ship of the Arctic.[9]

The most renowned maritime legend is that of the *Flying Dutchman.* This phantom ship, sighted for centuries by mariners worldwide, meant disaster and doom for those who viewed it. It was thought that sure death or at least blindness was in store for the one who first saw it. Some mariners believed that the only way to avoid the curse was to stay as close as possible to the ship's figurehead, the symbol of the spirit and soul of the ship. Others believed that a spell would be put on your ship if the phantom crossed its path. Consequently, a man of the cloth would then come aboard to unite all hands in prayer to drive the devil out.

According to the legend, the Dutch Captain Falkenberg in the ship *Vanderdecken* tried in vain to round stormy Cape Horn. Swearing to sail on until the day of doom if necessary, he laughed at his fearful crew throwing overboard some of those who tried to dissuade him. As the gale increased, he vowed to sell his soul to the devil, cursed God, and was thereafter condemned to navigate the stormy seas forever.

The Dutchman was sometimes seen just before the weather got dirty or in the teeth of a storm when the wind shrieked and vision was blurred by stinging rain or snow. With every stitch of sail bent, the ghost has been sighted amid the low clouds that announce a storm's approach or partly obscured as she crashed through storm-tossed seas in her hellish advance.

Sir Walter Scott writes of the phantom:

"The phantom ship whose form
Shoots like a meteor through the storm,
When the dark scud comes driving hard,
And lower'd is every topsail-yard,
And canvas wove in earthly looms
No more the brave the storm presumes!
Then 'mid the roar of sea and sky,
Top and top-gallant hoisted high,
Full spread and crowded every sail,
The demon frigate braves the gale,
And well the doom'd spectators know
The harbinger of wreck and woe."

An 1881 diary/log entry on the HMS *Bacchante* relates the sighting of the Dutchman: "At 4 A.M. the Flying Dutchman crossed our bows. A strange, red light, as of a phantom ship all aglow, in the midst of which light the masts, spars and sails of a brig two hundred yards distant stood out in strong relief as she came up. The look-out man on the forecastle reported her as close on the port bow, where also the officer of the watch from the bridge clearly saw her, as did also the quarter-deck midshipman, who was sent forward at once to the forecastle; but on arriving there no vestige of any sign whatever of any material ship was to be seen either near or right away to the horizon, the night being clear and the sea calm. Thirteen persons altogether saw her, but whether it was Van Diemen or the Flying Dutchman, or who, she must remain unknown. The *Tourmaline* and *Cleopatra*, who were sailing on our starboard bow, flashed to ask whether we had seen the strange red light."

The dreaded curse of the legend became reality. Soon after the phantom was sighted, the intelligent and responsible seaman who first hailed its approach fell to his death from the foretopmast. And later, as the fleet came into port, the commander, believed to have been in excellent health, suddenly took ill and died.

When any vessel is sighted then quickly disappears, it is automatically labeled a Flying Dutchman. Such was the case when several crewmen aboard an Argentine trading vessel sighted a five-masted phantom with all sails set running before the wind in a Pacific gale in July 1930. At that time there were no five-masted ships sailing in any fleet. About this same time a five-masted ship was sighted by fishermen off the coast of Chile by those on a vessel sailing off Easter Island and by passengers on a liner off the Peruvian coast. The sightings all closely matched the description of the five-masted Danish navy training vessel *Copenhagen*, believed lost after reporting an "all is well status" on December 22, 1928. No one can explain the mysterious sightings of the five-master some nineteen months after her disappearance in an area hundreds of miles from where she was presumed lost.[10]

In a report, the World War II German U-boat commander in chief Admiral Karl Doenitz relates a more recent sighting of the phantom: "Certain of my U-boat crews claimed they saw the *Flying Dutchman* or some other so-called phantom ship on their tours of duty east of Suez. When they returned to their base the men said they preferred facing the combined strength of Allied warships in the North Atlantic than know the terror a second time of being confronted by a phantom vessel."[11]

Between 1937 and 1938, crewmen aboard the USS *Langley* (AV-3), en route to Coco Solo, Panama, sighted what they believed was the phantom ship just as the sun rose one calm and clear morning. When the sun was not yet bright enough to hurt your eyes, a full-rigged sailing ship was spotted with all sails full and headed right at the carrier. Word spread as the ship was studied with binoculars by the officers and sailors, who quickly lined the rails to get a glimpse of the beautiful sight. When the sun finally ascended above the horizon, the sailing ship suddenly disappeared as sounds of disbelief reverberated through those watching the spectacle. Because the incident lasted nearly ten minutes and was seen by so many there was little doubt that a phantom ship had been sighted.[12]

Atholl Murray, a former crewman on the passenger steamer *Cayuga,* related an incident that occurred aboard that vessel while sailing on Lake Ontario in 1942. Several of the crew were on the fantail swapping yarns, when one man saw what looked like two full-rigged ships cross the ship's wake amid the clouds as the sun was setting. An old steward grimly told the group about the ghost fleet of Lake Ontario. If the phantoms were seen sinking after crossing your wake, it meant that one of your mates would surely die. Several men then believed they saw what the old man described, and later that night the old steward died.

Grooming

Clippings of cut hair were considered unlucky aboard a ship. In Scotland if a sailor's hair clippings would not burn when thrown in his fireplace, it was a warning not to go to sea. In the same regard, women would not burn their hair clippings when any blood relation was at sea for fear that they would be doomed to drown. It was considered unlucky for a sailor to have his hair cut during a calm, the common belief being that it was lucky for hair to be trimmed during a storm.

Paring fingernails during a calm was thought to bring good winds, but was also an unlucky thing to do during a storm. It was important as well to take proper care of fingernail clippings under the belief that if the clippings fell into the hands of witches they might be used in wicked spells against those who dropped them.

Most sailors of old wore a full beard, except when it was necessary to shave to stop lice infestations. Wigs were believed to have become popular when it was discovered that lice flourished in natural hair.

Daily bathing was looked down upon and was not common until it was realized that it reduced lice and fleas and made for a healthier environment for all. For hundreds of years these vermin were an accepted part of sea life, and the elimination of the pests was not achieved until better hygiene and bathing facilities became a part of daily routine.

Clean clothes not only reduced filth and pests, but also safeguarded one from the risks of infection if wounded. It was said that naval officers preparing for battle dressed with fresh clothes for two reasons. It reduced chances for infection if wounded and if you were killed in battle you would be properly attired to meet your maker.

Notes

1. Van Dervoort, *The Water World*, 322.
2. Garrett, *Voyage into Mystery*, 149-53.
3. Canning, *Fifty True Mysteries of the Sea*, 246-47.
4. Beck, *Folklore and the Sea*, 288.
5. Malcolm, *Navies of the Night*, 9-11.
6. Ibid., 11.
7. Ibid., 11-12.
8. Ibid., 12.
9. Brock, *Floating Phantom of the Icy North*, 29-33.
10. Brown, *Phantoms of the Sea*, 65-68.
11. Ibid., 24.
12. "Langley's Flying Dutchman," in *Tailhook*, Fall 1989, p. 6.

9. Heavenly Signs

Hexes

Heavenly signs of wind and rain,
Long the seafarer's weathervane.
The witch's spell in memory burned,
When the hexed ship never returned.

Heavenly Signs

Since ancient times seafarers have associated celestial phenomena with good and evil. The sun with its halos, the moon in its strange phases, the intensity of the stars, the streaking meteor, the auroras, solar eclipses, and even the rainbow were perceived as signs of good or ill fortune.

Although explicitly forbidden in the Ten Commandments, the worship of stars as gods was common in the ancient Middle East. The widespread practice of reading the constellations and other signs of heaven as portents of the future most likely originated in this worship.

One of the first recorded good-omen signs of heaven was the rainbow, created by God as a promise to Noah: "This is the sign that I am giving for all ages to come, of the covenant between me and you and every living creature with you: I set my bow in the clouds to serve as a sign of the covenant between me and the earth. When I bring clouds over the earth, and the bow appears in the clouds, I will recall the covenant I have made between me and you and all living beings, so that the waters shall never again become a flood to destroy all mortal beings."[1] Thus the rainbow has become a sign of clearing weather and a symbol of good things to come. The rainbow, it was thought, even had the power to command the rain to cease.

Many other beliefs and proverbs relating to the rainbow followed. If the green of the bow was large and bright, it was a sign of further rain. If the bow's red was the brightest, rain and wind would come together. If there had been a drought, the rainbow indicated rain. After much rain it foretold fair weather. If a bow suddenly broke up or disappeared severe weather would follow. When a bow appeared in the morning, rain would follow; a bow at noon would bring slight and heavy rain; a bow at night meant fair weather was coming. When two or three rainbows were sighted, it indicated fair weather for the time being and unsettled weather or heavy rains in the next few days. A rainbow in the eastern sky foretold that the next day would be clear. A bow in the west would usually be followed by more rain that day. When a rainbow did not touch the water, clear weather was in the offing. The rainbow as a sign of fair weather is alluded to in this proverb:

> The boding shepherd heaves a sigh,
> For see, a rainbow spans the sky.

A popular ancient belief was that the moon could cause harm and affect fertility. It was also thought to influence seed germination, childbirth, rain, shellfish growth, and the human brain. The belief that the moon affected the feebleminded or caused insanity is reflected in the terms "lunatic," "lunacy," and "moonstruck." Plagues, war, and disaster were believed tied to eclipses of the moon. Weather change was thought associated with the moon's phases.

Marking the beginning of the month, a new moon, in biblical times, was a holiday of rejoicing. Silver was associated with the moon, as gold was with the sun; hence the term "silvery moon," and the superstition that it was lucky to turn over silver coins at the sight of a new moon. An old Icelandic legend advised that if the points of a crescent moon were pointed toward the earth, a shipwreck would occur during that moon. When the points of the moon were sharp it indicated dry weather. A new moon in the far south meant dry weather for a month. If the points of the new moon were turned up, the month would be a dry one; if the points were down, it would be wet. If the new moon was on its back it meant wind. If the moon was standing on its point, expect rain in the summer or snow in the winter. If the shadow of the old moon was seen in the new moon's arms, it was a sign of fair weather.

Irish seafarers believed that a "star-dogged moon" (one star ahead of and towing the moon) portended storms. Seafarers of old believed that the moon could eat up the clouds when it rose in a storm.

Fishermen in England believed that fish spawned during a full moon and that fish would spoil after being caught or would soon turn bad in the full moon's light. If the moon rose clear, fine weather could be expected. A halo around the moon indicated rain, and the number of stars visible within the halo indicated the number of rainy days. The larger the halo, the closer the rain clouds, and the sooner the rain would come. A large ring with low clouds suggested rain within twenty-four hours; a small ring with high clouds indicated rain in a few days. A red, dim, or pale moon indicated rain; a red moon meant wind. A large red moon with clouds was a sign of rain within twelve hours.

Some mariners believed that the sighting of the aurora borealis in the Northern Hemisphere or the aurora australis in the Southern Hemisphere was a sign of upcoming violent tempests or cold weather.

A Viking legend tells of Odin (the supreme god in Norse mythology), who sent the Valkyrie, or warlike virgins, to every battle to gather heroes to join his forces to oppose the giants in the great final battle. The Valkyrie, whose name meant "choosers of the slain," decided who would be slain in each battle. When they went forth in their pursuit, their brilliant armor reflected a strange, glimmering light, which spread over the northern skies, producing what we know as the aurora borealis, or northern lights.[2]

Indian legend regarded the aurora as the spirit of their forefathers roaming through the land of souls.

Before they were understood, eclipses of the sun and moon caused great fear and apprehension. The first recorded solar eclipse happened October 22, 2136 B.C. Because the unknowing believed that the eclipse would destroy the sun, rites were held to stop the attack. Along with the racket of drumbeats, gongs, and other clamor, spears and arrows were shot into the air at the spectacle to drive the threat away.

As recent as 1878, there was still widespread fear of eclipses among primitive people, as this account in the *Philadelphia Inquirer* on July 29 of that year relates: "It was the grandest sight I ever beheld but it frightened the Indians badly. Some of them threw themselves upon their knees and invoked the Divine blessing; others flung themselves flat on the ground, face downwards; others cried and yelled in frantic excitement and terror. Finally one old fellow stepped from the door of his lodge, pistol in hand, and fixing his eyes on the darkened sun, mumbled a few unintelligible words and raising his arm took direct aim at the luminary, fired off his pistol, and after throwing his arms about his head in a series of extraordinary gesticulations, retreated to his own quarters."[3]

Columbus was said to have used the lunar eclipse of April 2, 1493, to his advantage. When Jamaican natives refused to supply him provisions, the explorer declared that divine vengeance would follow, "for that very night the light of the moon would fail." When the eclipse occurred the frightened islanders came to him for help, and when the moon again was bright he was guaranteed his provisions.[4]

Present superstitious belief tells us that if you see a shooting star streak across the sky, it is an omen of good luck. If you make a wish for money, your wish will come true. If an ill person sees the star, their health will be regained within a month. To see a shooting star while on a voyage is a good omen. The old mariners, however, saw them as a sign predicting tempests.

If a shooting star streaked toward the north, a north wind was expected the following day. Many shooting stars in the summer indicated upcoming hot weather and thunder. By determining which edge of the Milky Way was the brightest, mariners believed they could predict from which direction an approaching storm would come. When many stars were sighted, rain was expected. Many stars in winter was a sign of frost. When many stars twinkled in the summer, clear weather was indicated. If the stars appeared large and clear, rain or wind was coming. When comets were sighted it was thought they would bring cold weather.

Hexes

Witches were thought capable of affixing hexes, raising storms, and wrecking ships as early as A.D. 45. According to writings by Pomponius Mela, the Ile de Sein off the coast of France was inhabited by certain women druids who controlled the winds: "It contained some of these venerable virgins, who pretended that they could raise storms and tempests by their incantations." Called gallicenae at the time, they were believed to be of great genius endowed with the rare ability to foretell the future and to transpose themselves into whatever animal they pleased.

The Anglo-Saxons, Scandinavians, Laplanders, Scots, English, and colonial Americans all had early dire regard for witches and their storm-raising evil ways. King James VI, while on a voyage from Denmark in 1590, was caught in a tempest believed to have been caused by witches. The Scottish witch Isobel Gowdie confessed to raising a storm in 1662 by imploring the help of Satan, wetting a cloth, and beating it upon a stone. Another Scottish witch, Margaret Barclay, was believed to have sunk her husband's brother's ship by crafting a wax model of that ship and throwing it into the sea. Marian Peebles, reputed witch of the Shetland and Orkney islands in 1642, reportedly took the shape of a porpoise and sank a boat along with five lives. Mrs. Hicks and her daughters, tried as witches in England in 1716, were accused of raising storms and wrecking ships by making a sudsy potion from their shoes. Upon searching the cabin of another suspected witch from Devonshire, England, witchcraft paraphernalia was discovered in the form of a mop handle fashioned into a miniature sail and a dried fish.

Some witches, especially those native to Europe, worked at their craft commercially, selling good or bad weather and calm or fierce winds to mariners for cash. They also read fortunes and sold charms and cauls. Squak, an old Negro woman from Liverpool, was a popular attraction for American sailors. The seer would foretell one's future by reading the person's pulse. Her two green-eyed black cats with nightcaps on their heads added flavor to her mystique. The renowned witch Molly Pitcher was said to have been the only American witch who sold her powers in this manner. It was said that many vessels were idled because of her ominous predictions to skippers and ordinary seamen.

Goody Cole of Hampton, New Hampshire, was finally imprisoned in 1680, after nearly a quarter century of witchcraft suspicion. Widely feared by the citizens of Hampton, she was said to have made a pact with the devil and was accused of causing the wreck at Rivermouth, one of the most renowned sea disasters of the time.

A large group of townsfolk, out for a fishing excursion, saw the witch at her spinning wheel when they passed her hut near the mouth of the river. Upon seeing her, someone on the boat cried out, "Fie on the witch!" and the captain grimly advised:

> "She's cursed," said the skipper; "speak her fair:
> I'm scary always to see her shake
> Her wicked head, with its wild gray hair,
> And nose like a hawk, and eyes like a snake."

At this the witch spoke her veiled threat:

> "Oho!" she muttered, "ye're brave today!
> But I hear the little waves laugh and say.
> 'The broth will be cold that waits at home,
> For it's one to go, but another to come!'"

> They dropped their lines in the lazy tide,
> Drawing up haddock and mottled cod;
> They saw not the Shadow that walked beside,
> They heard not the feet with silence shod.
> But thicker and thicker a hot mist grew,
> Shot by lightnings through and through;
> And muffled growls, like the growl of a beast,
> Ran along the sky from west to east.

> The skipper hauled at the heavy sail:
> "God be our help!" he only cried,
> As the roaring gale, like the stroke of a flail,
> Smote the boat on its starboard side.

> Suddenly seaward swept the squall;

> But far and wide as the eye could reach,
> No life was seen upon wave or beach;
> The boat that went out at morning never
> Sailed back again into Hampton River.

Male witches, or wizards, who also "sold wind and weather," were likewise thought to have control over tempests. Legend tells of the wizard Aeolus, who gave the departing Ulysses a leather bag full of fair and other winds. According to a Great Lakes legend, there once was an Indian wizard who stored his winds in a bag. Another Cree Indian wizard offered three different winds for a pound of tobacco.

A Canadian weather wizard by the name of Wiggins caused major disruption of fishing and shipping vessels when he predicted "the great Wiggins storm" in 1882. The tempest did not occur but still kept scores of vessels idle until the day of doom had passed.

Notes

1. Gen. 9:12-15.
2. *Bulfinch's Mythology*, 331.
3. *Encyclopedia of Magic and Superstition*, 168.
4. Ibid.

10. Icebergs

Insects, Islands

Glistening palaces, the ocean's wonder,
Docile giants that sent ships under.
Bad luck spiders and the pesky roach,
Devil's isles only fools approach.

Icebergs

Said to have assumed every style of architecture imaginable, icebergs, the great palaces of nature, rank as the most monumental and majestic wonders of the oceans. Their varied magnificent shapes and colossal configurations designed by their breakaway birth, re-formation, or erosion appear as massive contemporary artworks rendered by the giant hands of God.

Sometimes shaped into abandoned edifices afloat in the vast loneliness of the sea, they have played with the imaginations of awestruck mariners who have viewed their grandeur. Enormous cathedrals with steeples, arches, and pillars; castles with towers in the sky; ruins of lost cities; pyramids, obelisks, bridges, trees, animals, human figures, and even gigantic collapsed balloons have been seen in icebergs by unbelieving Arctic navigators. Marble cities of ice, rising cliffs, mountains, and other giant forms, cloaked in the reflected hues of the sky and sea, or mystically appearing through fog, icebergs have deceived and astonished even the most experienced mariner.

Tabular icebergs are those launched from the circular barrier of Antarctica, whose dimensions are measured in miles. Similar formations, substantially smaller but by no means tiny, originate from the shelf ice breakup in northern Canada and Greenland, and are called ice islands. The vast quantity of icebergs in the Antarctic is astounding. In just the American sector of the Antarctic continent, an area known as the devil's graveyard, during Admiral Byrd's last expedition, eight thousand separate bergs were sighted in one day![1]

The dimensions of some of the monster bergs defy one's imagination. One crescent-shaped giant was sighted by several ships in the South Atlantic in 1854 and 1855. This iceberg was formed like an enormous floating harbor with one arm forty miles long, the other sixty miles long, and a bay forty miles long between the arms.[2] It was believed that many ships were lost to this berg when they sailed parallel to one of the arms, and then discovered too late that they were embayed and unable to come about. Navigating in iceberg seas at night was treacherous enough. By adding fog to the menace, one might imagine the gripping fears encountered by mariners in these regions.

A giant L-shaped berg was reported by Capt. C. C. Dixon in Cape Horn waters in 1860. A threat to the area for months, the berg measured fifty miles long on one leg and thirty miles long on the other. The disappearance of several ships in that area at the time was thought due to this menace. Many other horseshoe-shaped Cape Horn bergs, some of which reached twelve hundred feet in height, were reported by Cape Horn sailors in 1892 and 1893.[3]

What is believed to be the record height of an iceberg was that of one sighted by Captain Pattmann on the *Loch Torridon* near Cape Horn on January 20, 1893. It was only three miles long but its peak reached fifteen hundred feet above the sea.[4]

Another monster berg, 100 miles long, 100 miles wide, and 130 feet high, was sighted in 1927. The granddaddy of all icebergs, however, was sighted about 150 miles west of Scott Island by the U.S. Navy icebreaker USS *Glacier* in 1956. Sixty miles wide and 208 miles long, this berg was more than twice the size of Connecticut![5]

By comparison, the largest ice island sighted in the Northern Hemisphere was one 7 miles long and 3-1/2 miles wide reported off Baffin Island in 1882. Another measuring 4 miles long was sighted in the North Atlantic in 1928.[6]

The perils encountered by mariners in Arctic seas include fog, collision, and entrapment in ice fields or ice islands. An unusually fearful experience and narrow escape was described when one ship was caught in an ice floe with icebergs:

> It was awful to behold the immense icebergs, working their way to the northeast from us, and not one drop of water to be seen; they were working themselves right through the middle of the ice. The dreadful apprehensions that assailed us by the near approach of the iceberg, were this day awfully realized. About three P.M. the iceberg came in contact with our floe, and in less than one minute it broke the ice we were frozen in quite close to the shore; the floe was shivered to pieces for several miles, causing an explosion like an earthquake, or one hundred pieces of cannon fired at the same moment. The iceberg, with awful but majestic grandeur, came almost to our stern, and every one expected it would have run over the ship. The intermediate space between the berg and the vessel was filled with heavy masses of ice, which, though they had been previously broken by the immense weight of the iceberg, were again formed into a solid body by its pressure. The iceberg was drifting at the rate of about four knots an hour,— and by its force on the mass of ice, was pushing the ship before it, and, as it seemed, to inevitable destruction. A gracious Providence ruled this otherwise: the iceberg, that so lately threatened destruction, was driven completely out of sight to the northeast.[7]

The steamer *President* was crushed between icebergs in 1841. The brig *Anne,* bound for England from Newfoundland, met with a similar experience but was borne along with its massive ice field menace for twenty-nine successive days.[8]

The explorer ship *Resolute* was not so lucky. Abandoned in Melville Straits, this vessel became encased in a field of ice estimated three hundred thousand square miles in extent, to wind up in Baffin Bay, after being carried over a thousand miles from its original position.[9]

Sometimes the placid beauty of an iceberg lures the unwary to its dangers. A vessel that might venture too close to a berg could encounter the strong current that usually runs along its sides and be violently dashed against its mass. Another danger was for the unknowing to moor a vessel to a berg for shelter against strong winds. An iceberg's mass and beauty almost makes them seem docile and harmless. But, as often happens, if a large enough piece of the berg breaks off, in seconds the entire mass can suddenly turn over, causing a rush of massive waves by the sudden change of configuration. Even vessels lying a great distance away could be upset or destroyed.

The precarious instability of icebergs is related in an incident that occurred when two sailors were trying to attach an anchor to a berg. They had scarcely begun to hack away at the ice when suddenly the entire mass split in two from top to bottom, the two halves plunging into the sea with a thunderous crash. Luckily the men escaped with their lives.[10]

Another foolhardy incident took place near Temple Bay, Labrador, when two young officers from a French man-of-war, ignoring all warnings, boarded a nearby iceberg for a picnic. The bright and calm summer morning evaporated any fear of danger, and by noon the two had scaled the glistening palace walls to reach the very top of the berg. There they shouted and drank toasts to their fellow officers and the lady passengers watching aboard the ship. They hacked at the ice and made fun of the dread supposedly attached to the beautiful wonder of the sea. Finished with their horseplay, the men clambered back down to the ship. No sooner had they boarded when the giant iceberg broke up like an eggshell into infinite fragments which filled and tormented the surrounding sea. Knowing they had barely escaped certain death, they never forgot their first and last picnic on an iceberg.[11]

Perhaps the strangest of all iceberg yarns is that of an abandoned square-rigger discovered sitting on an iceberg clearly out of the water as if in dry dock. The unbelievable sight was reported in 1904 by the French bark *Emilie Calline*, which could not maneuver in close enough for identification. The ultimate fate of the mystery ship and its crew was never known.[12]

Before venturing out on the *Titanic* search in 1983, I procured daily iceberg reports from the Defense Mapping Agency; the idea was scoffed at by several members of the crew. After all, I thought, the reason we were going on the search mission in the first place was because the *Titanic* hit an iceberg. Regardless, I just wanted the data out of curiosity. I was surprised, though, when the first report showed no fewer than thirteen major bergs and many growlers in the area of the North Atlantic that we were going to. Growlers, or small bergs, which could be the size of a house, were not even plotted. Although many of us were anxious to see an iceberg, by the time we departed Halifax we spotted nothing but a bit of ice floe. However, being familiar with the number of vessels lost to bergs, I couldn't help wondering what role complacency played in all their losses. It also evoked the sickening dread that *Titanic* lookout Frederick Fleet must have felt when he realized that a huge quadrant of the starry sky he was gazing at that ill-fated night suddenly blacked out. Too late he sighted the enormous black iceberg that his ship was racing into.

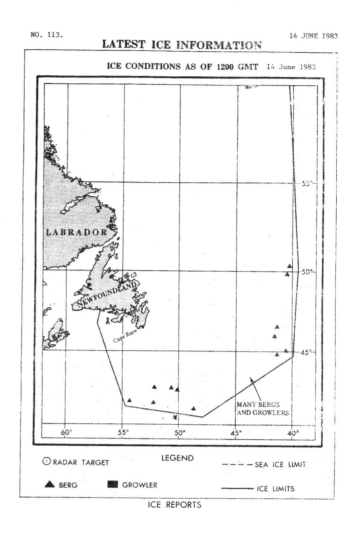

NO. 113.

LATEST ICE INFORMATION

14 JUNE 1983

ICE CONDITIONS AS OF 1200 GMT 14 June 1983

LABRADOR

NEWFOUNDLAND

Cape Race

MANY BERGS
AND GROWLERS

LEGEND

⊙ RADAR TARGET   — — — SEA ICE LIMIT

▲ BERG   ■ GROWLER   ———— ICE LIMITS

ICE REPORTS

The magnificent liner *Normandie* launched October 29, 1932, was fitted with an instrument that detected other ships and icebergs within a four-mile range through radio beams sweeping the horizon. This vessel was the first to carry a radar system.[13]

Insects

Bees were welcome and considered good luck to have aboard a ship. Spiders were usually thought a sign of bad luck. Icelanders believed that a spider should not be bothered when hanging by its web. Whoever found one had to put their hand beneath it and say, "Up, up, fishing-carl! Your wife lies ill in her child-bed"; or "Row up from below, fishing-carl, if you betoken fair weather; row down, if you betoken foul."

Fishermen of Greenock, Scotland, used to say that it is a sign of good luck if a fly drops into a glass of water.[14]

Cockroaches, instead of being a sign of good or bad luck, were just plain pesky. They were known to eat boot leather, oilskins, and the labels of food tins. It was near impossible to rest because they crawled over those trying to sleep and gnawed at their toenails. China clippers often hired the Chinese to rid their vessels of the pests. Using rattan bushel baskets and a special bait, they often carried off more than thirty bushels of the dead pests from a single ship.[15]

A highly unusual and primitive surgical procedure used on early seventeenth century sailing vessels involved a species of leaf-cutting ant. With no material or small needles available for suturing severed gut in abdominal wounds, the mandibles of the ants were situated to join the gut; when the body of the ant was cut off, its mandibles closed to act as sutures. Because human gut can be manipulated and even cut with little pain, the patients suffered only minor discomfort.[16]

Islands

Islands encountered or imagined by searfarers through maritime history can be divided into two major categories: mythical islands, or those storied islands never visited, whose existence is doubtful; and islands that appear and disappear, such as volcanic formations, icebergs, and weather-related mirages.

Books could be filled about the vast number of enchanted or bewitched islands said to have existed since ancient times. It was a common practice of early explorers, including Marco Polo, to label all lands islands if something unusual or marvelous was heard about them, whether they were visited or not. Here are some of the renowned ones.

According to Hawaiian legend, when the earth was covered with water, a giant bird laid an egg that hatched in the sun and formed Hawaii. Polynesian legend states that islands were created by being thrown from the heavens by the will of their gods. In Tahitian legend there was once a moon brighter than the one we know, which was broken into many pieces and thrown into the oceans.

Tahitian islanders told Captain Cook of an island where giants dwelt who were taller than his ships. They were known to be friendly unless upset and could carry a ship on their back. If they became enraged they had the strength to snatch a man and fling him like a pebble into the sea. A Greek and Scandinavian myth told of islands being formed when clods of earth were thrown into the sea by semigods.[17]

There was said to exist somewhere in the sea of darkness (western Atlantic) a phantom isle called the Island of Satan's Hand. Sighted only at night, in fog, or in foul weather, it was a place no mariner ever looked for. Always enshrouded in mist and continually changing its position, the island was believed to be the hand of a giant demon that snatched men and entire ships in its grasp. Once in the clutches of this monster the victims were lost forever.[18]

Sailors dreamed of islands inhabited by beautiful women who catered to seafarers, refused no advances, and showered them with delights. The Island of the Amazons was thought to be a Fiddler's Green on earth. The legend, said to have orginated with Marco Polo, told of two islands, Feminea and Masculea, the first inhabited only by women and the other only by men. Masculea as might well be expected was soon forgotten. All the women dwelling on Feminea were young, passionate, and beautiful; for three months of each year, they sought intimate relationships with sailors. The visitors were not required to work and their entire stay was devoted to amorous indulgences. No male children past adolescence were on the island because the visitors had to agree to take them along when they departed. Columbus planned to bring back several of the women from the island during his homeward voyage in 1493. He set his course for the island known today as Martinique, but the unseaworthy condition of the *Nina* and *Pinta* made him change his mind.[19]

The Isles of Demons, first identified as the *Insulae Demonium* on a 1507 map, were north of Labrador near the mouth of what is now called the Hudson Strait. A later map depicted two islands and another showed a single island, but both maps placed them north of Newfoundland. As late as 1620, mapmakers still positioned them somewhere off Labrador. Belle Isle, at the mouth of the Belle Isle Strait between Newfoundland and Labrador, was regarded by sixteenth-century French fishermen as the Isle of Demons because of the chilling screams emanating from its shores. The screams were later figured to be Indian ceremonial cries. The island was believed named Belle Isle, "Beautiful Island," in an effort to exorcise, or drive away, the demons.[20]

Navigators in 1610 referred to Bermuda as the Isle of the Devils because of the storm fiends thought to inhabit that place. Seafarers during the time of Columbus believed demons rose from the waters off St. Brendan's Isle. This supposedly devil-infested island may well have been Bermuda. The legend of St. Brendan's tells of miraculous events occurring during the life of St. Brendan, born in Ireland and christened on a day when a white mist called "broen finn" surrounded the village. Brendan's Isle was said to have been discovered during the Voyage of Brendan, when he and a group of other monks made their remarkable Atlantic voyage to the promised land of the saints. His legend does live on, for St. Brendan's, the name of the Bermuda psychiatric hospital, was chosen to reflect how the hospital cares for those whose lives might be enshrouded in a white mist or "broen finn."

The ancients believed that Ireland was a floating island during the time of the great Deluge. Seafarers in the Middle Ages, and in more recent times, believed in floating isles, the belief no doubt nourished by the sighting of immense icebergs in the Arctic seas. Demons, whose purpose was to deceive and mislead mariners, were said to dwell on floating islands. Great areas of floating seaweed also gave the appearance of floating islands.[21]

French fishermen believed in islands where the souls of the dead were carried to on summer nights. When the sea was quiet the oars of white spirits could be heard cutting the water as they rowed to the isle in their black boats.[22]

There have been countless sightings of islands the positions of which were concurrently verified that later proved nonexistent. Low-lying cloud formations, particularly those in tropical regions, could easily be mistaken as islands. Mirages, volcano eruptions, and sandbars that appear, move, and dissappear have all no doubt been perceived as islands.

The strange mechanics of volcano eruptions have certainly caused the demise and birth of islands. When Krakatoa exploded in 1883, it was the most violent eruption the modern world had seen. However, experts believe that at one time an enormous volcano sat where the waters of Sunda Strait are now. Sometime in the ancient past, a massive explosion, far greater than Krakatoa, blew the giant volcano away. All that remained was its base appearing as a severed ring of islands, the largest of which was Krakatoa. Although the explosion of Krakatoa obliterated what was left of the original crater's ring, a new island, Anak Krakatoa, or Child of Krakatoa, arose in its place in 1929.[23]

What happened to the Aurora Islands? Named after the Spanish ship *Aurora* that sighted them in 1762 and in 1774, they lay southeast of the Falkland Islands. Another Spanish vessel, the *San Miguel,* verified and fixed their location, they were sighted by several other vessels, and in 1794 the Spanish corvette *Atrevida* found them again. The features of the islands were described, their latitude and longitude were confirmed, and they were thereafter placed on maps. They were forgotten until Antarctic explorer Capt. James Weddell searched for but could not find them in 1820. Another unsuccessful search was conducted by the American sealer *Benjamin Morrell* in 1822. Although they remained on many maps until the 1870s, they were never sighted again.[24]

Captain Swain, in a Nantucket whaler, sighted and named Swain Island in 1800. He charted its position as latitude 59° south latitude, 90° to 100° longitude slightly southwest of Cape Horn. Captain Dougherty, in the whaler *James Stewart* reported sighting an island in 1841 at latitude 59° 20' south latitude, longitude 120° 20' west. Believing he had discovered a new island, he named it Dougherty Island. Other mariners also reported sighting an island in the same area. Then in 1860, Captain Keates of the *Louise* sighted the island and described its features in detail, relating that he even saw a grounded iceberg on its shore. After these sightings Dougherty was on all the maps and the British Admiralty charts. It was sighted in 1886 and again a few years later by Captain Stannard of the *Cingalese*, who told of seeing many seals nearby. However, after 1889 many explorers and other navigators searched for the island but it was never again to be found, although it was carried on the Rand McNally map until 1938. The mystery of this disappearing island has never been solved.[25]

Since the first sighting of Bogoslof Island in the Aleutians in 1796, the small black rock isle changed its appearance and position several times. First named Castle Rock after its shape, it originally appeared as a towering black rock castle. In the 1950s only one or two rock towers and a long spit of rocks remained.[26]

Sable Island, a ship graveyard in the Atlantic, 150 miles off Nova Scotia, was long thought to be an island where the ghosts of the wicked often appeared.

The banana-shaped, narrow spit of sand often changes its appearance, sometimes reduced in size by the tides, other times expanded to cover the countless wrecks of ships that have run a foul of it in dirty weather. It is estimated that over five hundred shipwrecks lie on or around the tiny island, ninety percent of which occurred after 1825.

Goodwin sands, six miles east of the little town of Deal, England, is by far the biggest ship graveyard of the world. Only ten miles long and four miles wide, this area became known as the "shippe swallower" in medieval times. Fifty-one vessels foundered on the sands, with a loss of 290 lives, between 1850 and 1860 alone. Detailed statistics are vague, but it is believed that over fifty thousand vessels lie wrecked around the British coast, many of which were lost to the Goodwins.[27]

Eynhallow, an island in the Orkneys (north of Scotland) between Rousay and Pomona, is said to this day to be enchanted. As the location of one of the earliest monasteries of the area, its name is Norse for "Holy Island." The isle is said to be the domain of sea folk, and is believed to now and then appear and disappear. A popular legend contends that if a man held steel in his hand as he approached its shore, the island would lose its enchantment. As the story goes, one courageous man was said to have accomplished this feat and therefore snatched the island from the sea folk. Because of this, the enraged sea people still torment the surrounding island waters. It is further believed that iron or steel will not remain on the island overnight and that rats cannot survive there.[28]

Notes

1. Riesenberg, *Cape Horn*, 344-45.
2. Bowditch, *Waves, Wind, and Weather*, 66-67.
3. Riesenberg, *Cape Horn*, 342-43.
4. Ibid., 343.
5. Bowditch, *Waves, Wind, and Weather*, 67.
6. Ibid.
7. Van Dervoort, *The Water World*, 57-58.
8. Ibid., 58-59.
9. Ibid., 59.
10. Ibid., 60.
11. Ibid., 60-61.
12. Allen, *The Windjammers*, 107.
13. Maddocks, *The Great Liners*, 108.
14. Bassett, *Legends and Superstitions of the Sea and of Sailors*, 430.
15. Low, *Cabin Boy on a China Clipper*, 23.
16. Thrower, *Life at Sea in the Age of Sail*, 149.
17. Rappoport, *Superstitions of Sailors*, 127-28.
18. Shay, *An American Sailor's Treasury*, 238.
19. Ibid., 239.
20. Ramsay, *No Longer on the Map*, 116-20.
21. Rappoport, *Superstitions of Sailors*, 128-29.
22. Ibid., 131-32.
23. Carson, *The Sea around Us*, 86-87.
24. Ramsay, *No Longer on the Map*, 97-98.
25. Ibid., 103-6.
26. Carson, *The Sea around Us*, 87.
27. Clemans, *Ye Olde Shippe Swallower*, 15-18.
28. Beck, *Folklore of the Sea*, 272-73.

11. Jewelry

Jinxes, Jonahs

His ship was safe, no drownin' fears,
He wore gold earrings on his ears.
"Jinxed ship she was, God rest her dead,
There was a Jonah aboard, they said."

Jewelry

Earrings engraved with spiritual or magical symbols were worn by the ancients to ward off evil spirits and to prevent satanic influences from entering one's body through the ears. Because the ear was believed to be the center of intelligence, it was common to touch one's ears at the mention of death in an effort to make lingering evil spirits deaf. Amber jewelry as an amulet was an old and common protection against witchcraft and disease. Coral stones offered protection from lightning, hail, and the evil eye. Sailors believed in the therapeutic value of having their ears pierced. It was thought that piercing one ear would improve the sight of the opposite eye. Some seafarers pierced the ear opposite to the eye used for looking through a telescope for this reason. Piercing both ears offered better sight in both eyes. The wearing of a plain gold earring assured protection against going down with a ship or drowning.

161

Jinxes

A dignified gentleman dressed in a trim black suit carrying a black valise stepped aboard a docked vessel seeking the whereabouts of a person unknown to the ship's crew. Many of the men who saw the stranger thereafter considered their ship jinxed because of the simple and innocent inquiry. Hundreds of other voluntary or involuntary actions, events, deeds, expressions, and circumstances that occurred aboard a ship caused the superstitious mariner to believe his vessel was jinxed.

The infamous jinxed Finnish ship *Grace Harwar* was said to have killed a man on every voyage. All the deaths were blamed on her first captain's preserving his wife's body in the ballast.

Scottish fishermen sternly believed that if a boat capsized with the loss of lives, it was permanently jinxed and should never be used again. Destruction by fire was the only way to end the jinx.

Many seafarers died or were gravely injured from avoidable accidents because they believed they were "jinxed." Living with the constant fear of being unlucky, that something dreadful was going to happen to them, they often carried a fatalistic attitude that made them more accident prone.

Jonahs

After the sailors cast lots to determine on whose account they met the misfortune of a violent tempest during their voyage to Tarshish, they singled out Jonah. "Tell us," they said, "what is your business? Where do you come from? What is your country, and to what people do you belong?" Knowing that Jonah was fleeing from the Lord, the men asked him, "What shall we do with you that the sea may quiet down for us?" Jonah said to them, "Pick me up and throw me into the sea, that it may quiet down for you; since I know it is because of me that this violent storm has come upon you." Then they took Jonah and threw him into the sea, and the sea's raging abated.[1]

Thus ended the first seafaring witch-hunt, so to speak. It was the first record of an action, in this case a drastic action, taken by mariners against a person thought dangerous to their ship. Thereafter "Jonah" became the catchall name for anyone or any vessel thought to bring about ill fortune. The belief was widespread, profound, and serious: When everything ran smoothly on a voyage, usually everyone got along with one another, friendships developed, and sea life was good. However, just as soon as misfortune occurred—bad weather, doldrums, sickness, injury, or death, especially for unknown reasons, a Jonah was thought to be the cause, and the witch-hunt began. Anyone ill-favored, deformed, lame, or viewed as unlucky in any way was suspected. So far-reaching were these suspicions that even those sailors reluctant to pay for their pleasures on liberty were viewed as Jonahs. As often was the case, many vessels were manned by those of one nationality or from one city. Any outsider was generally

Out There

considered unlucky. Once discovered, the Jonah was singled out and abused either openly or indirectly until the actions forced him off the ship. Skippers faced with extremely low crew morale and unrest found no other alternative than to put the Jonah ashore at the first opportunity.

Lawyers and dressmakers were near the top of the list of Jonahs. So taboo were these professions that these words were not even to be uttered in the presence of those going to sea. Stowaways, barefoot women, flat-footed people, virgins, whores, brides, tailors, insane people, black men, red-bearded men, brown-eyed people, narrow-headed folks, hunchbacks, chinless men, lame people, albinos, nuns, priests, spinsters, and those with speech impediments were all considered Jonahs. Cross-eyed people were considered Jonahs and because these unfortunates were thought unable to hold a ship on its course, cross-eyed sailors were seldom signed on a ship.

The greatest number of people to ever embark on one vessel sailed on the *Queen Mary* from New York to the Clyde on July 25, 1943, as the converted Cunard liner sped troops across the Atlantic. Making the passage of 3,353 miles in four days, twenty hours, and forty-two minutes, 16,683 people made the trip at speeds up to 28.73 knots. One wonders how many of these passengers were viewed as Jonahs by the superstitious.[2]

An example of how deep the belief in Jonahs ran is related in an old story about the coastal packet ship *President* that encountered a violent storm off Cape Hatteras during a voyage to New York. A crewman, admitting his wickedness, declared himself a Jonah and jumped overboard. After this the storm abated awhile but soon engulfed the ship again. Believing that the Jonah's presence was still with them, the crew quickly threw his sea chest overboard, and the storm stopped again. When the gale attacked them with renewed fury, a desperate search was made for any remaining effects of the Jonah. When the dead man's shoes were at last found and thrown to the sea, the storm finally stopped for good.[3]

The "bad luck boat," Great Lakes schooner *Erie Wave,* was renowned as a Jonah ship. On her maiden voyage she went over on her beam ends when taken by surprise in a gale on Lake Erie. Two crewmen were lost when the vessel sank. On her first voyage after she was salvaged and sent back in service, she met with another violent squall and went over again with the loss of two passengers. Repaired again, on her last trip the *Erie Wave* was blown ashore near Long Point. That same night, after freeing herself from shore, she got caught in a gale that pushed her over on a bar where the seas opened her up. Two survivors made it to the beach, but the other crewmen and passengers were lost, their bodies washing ashore near the Old Cut. She was long remembered as "the schooner with a Jonah."

Probably because of their association with the clergy, even Bibles were considered Jonahs. Few sailors kept a Bible among their possessions, believing the Good Book should stay in the captain's quarters except when used for prayer service or burials.

One lady passenger read passages aloud from the Bible to her children on deck each morning. Dressed against the weather, her black hooded wraps caused serious uneasiness among the crew, who blamed the plaguing head winds on the matron and her book. Some of the crew were certain the lady purposely tried to procure bad weather by her actions. Finally, a bold Dutchman approached her and pleaded that she stop or he would throw the book to the deep six.

Ignoring the threat, the lady, with her children beside her, continued reading, now nearly leaning over the rail at the bows of the ship. The unheeded warning and her renewed actions being too much for the Dutchman to stand, he grabbed the Bible from her grasp and threw it overboard.[4]

While crewmen fought a dangerous fire aboard the tanker *Standard* in the Gulf of Mexico in 1915, they remembered that the ship's Bible, which was on the vessel when in German hands, was still aboard. Believing the Bible to be the cause of their misfortune, several of the crew left the fire raging, found the book, and threw it to the sea.[5]

An old Gloucester Jonah story tells of a man who gained a berth on one of the best haddock boats with one of the keenest skippers in the business. Despite using every trick in the book, the hauls were so poor that after several months each fisherman's share was exceptionally meager. Discouraged and nearly broke, the stranger, who was said to be unlucky, left the crew for another boat. On the very next trip the fishing boat he had left began to take better hauls and by the end of the winter realized a good profit. However, the second boat the stranger went to, again worked by an expert captain, likewise took few fish, resulting in skimpy shares. In transferring to a third boat, equally poor hauls of fish were caught as well. While each boat the stranger worked caught an unusually low number of fish when he was aboard, they took better than average catches the rest of the season—after the Jonah left.[6]

Notes

1. Jon. 1:1-15.
2. Maddocks, *The Great Liners*, 154.
3. Shay, *An American Sailor's Treasury*, 283-84.
4. Ibid., 284-85.
5. Ibid., 285.
6. Ibid.

12. Knives

Knots

Knives made the winds come and go,
Blunt knives only could a sailor throw.
To know the ropes, he was part of the crew,
But his smarts showed by the knots he knew.

Knives

Greek seamen believed that by sticking a knife into the mast of a ship, gale winds could be made to die down. English sailors used the same practice to bring on a wind when in the doldrums. To stick a knife into the deck, however, was generally believed to bring bad luck. Scottish sailors carried knives for protection against the devil and other water spirits who were afraid of cold iron. It was a rarity to see a sailor carry a white-handled knife, which was considered unlucky. In the old days of sail, as a guard against sabotage or stabbings, only blunt knives were permitted aboard ship. A sharp blade was necessary for cutting rope or carving, and its blunt end greatly reduced the possibility of slashed sails or wounds inflicted during fights.

Some knife superstitions observed on shore were also practiced aboard ships. If you gave a knife to a mate, it was common to receive in return a small amount of money, so as not to *cut* the friendship. To cross the knife and fork at the table invited misfortune. If you spun your table knife and it pointed at you when it stopped spinning, it was a sign that death was pointing at you.

Knots

What is believed to be the first portrayal of rope making is a depiction from the tomb at Thebes in Egypt of the Pharaoh of the Exodus. Although the drawing is thought to represent the making of leather strips for sandal lacing, the process is considered the same as that required for making rope. A workman is shown cutting and revolving a strip of leather from a hide. Another worker is seen arranging and paying out the strips to a third man, who is twisting the cord as he steps backward.[1]

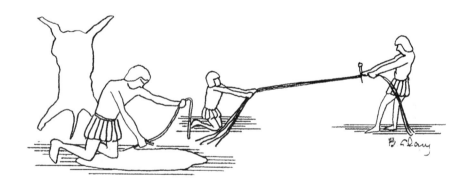

Ancient shipbuilders used ropes and cordage made from materials available in their respective countries. The very design of his vessel made the seafarer depend on rope. From this necessity came many different knots whose origins were born out of the requirements of a ship's rigging. The sailor's skill of working with rope came more from the necessity of his work than by idle-time study. To be adept in his work, a sailor would come to know by heart every inch of line, knotting, and splicing in the many miles of required rigging on his ship.

The general Properties belonging to the common Mariner is to hand, reef, steer, Knot and Splice, with which Qualifications he may safely value himself upon the Calling of a good seaman.

—*A Naval Repository,* 1762

Originating from the skill of the sailor's labor, fancy knot work was one of the oldest forms of folk art, and the most prolific shipboard handicraft. An abundance of condemned rope always on hand, sailors could often be found fashioning knot work to wile away their idle time.

According to *The Ashley Book of Knots*, a veritable encyclopedia on the subject, there are over thirty-eight hundred different knots, splices, hitches, and stitches known, many of which date to the early seafaring days. The more knots a sailor knew, the more respect he commanded and the higher he stood in the "pecking order" among his shipmates. There was widespread interest in knot tying, competition was keen, and the tricks to master many of the more difficult knots were often divulged only under the pledge of secrecy, or bartered for the knack of tying some other complicated knot. A seaman showed off his skill, and his integrity was often judged by the beckets (decorative rope handles) on his sea chest.[2]

Naive greenhorns, aspiring to climb the salty ladder of success, were often the target for "knotty" pranks. Sent off to find Matthew Walker, a novice would eventually discover that Matthew Walker was a stopper knot. Some apprentices were given the job of "feeding the camel" to embarrassingly find that the camel was a fender. A shellback might have asked a newly assigned sailor if he knew the most important knot of all, the dragon bowline. The tenderfoot, of course, stated that he had not even heard of the knot, so the veteran would tie a common bowline for the lad. "That's just a bowline," the neophyte exclaimed in confidence. "Aye, and if you drag it along the deck, it's a dragon bowline."[3]

Close in similarity are the reef and thief knots. Seamen tied up their seabags with the thief knot to ward off pilfering. It was figured that the unknowing thief, often a greenhorn, would most likely retie the bag with a reef knot and give himself away.[4]

The double overhand knot often tied in the strands of a cat-o'-nine-tails was called a blood knot because it quickly drew blood from those who received the lash. The strands on the "thieves cat," the cat used for the most severe offenses, were heavier and tied with harder knots.

Though few sailors were hanged at sea, the hangman's knot has always carried some interesting superstitious connections. The knot was fashioned with either nine or thirteen turns to the noose and adjusted so that the knot was placed immediately behind and below the left ear. The bulky design of the knot helped to better snap the victim's neck. A noose with nine turns reflected the thinking that even if a man had nine lives there would be a turn for each of them. Thirteen turns in the noose, it was said, represented the symbol of bad luck. The turns in the noose were wound counterclockwise so that the devil could, after death, take his victim easier.

One of the most familiar knots is the Turks-head, believed to have been in use since the time of Leonardo da Vinci (1452-1519). The knot was often tied around the top spoke of a ship's steering wheel. A helmsman could thereby see at a glance or feel in the dark that the helm was centered. The knot was also made as bracelets, anklets, gathering hoops, and a wide assortment of handgrips.

Almost like the Turks-head knot is the monkey's fist knot. Used on the end of a heaving line, the knot is tied around a small ball of stone or iron for the weight required to heave a light line from a ship to the dock. A dock attendant could then take in the heaving line, which was attached to a messenger line, which in turn was fastened to the heavy hawser. We can imagine that many an unwary longshoreman was surprised with a nasty blow from a weighted fist thrown with the practiced aim and perfection of a big league pitching ace. The bos'n was in charge of the heaving lines, his stature measured by how far and accurately he could throw the line.

For the right price, witches supplied sailors with a cord having three knots. When becalmed, untying the first knot was thought to produce a light breeze, undoing the second produced a moderate wind, and the third a strong breeze. Scottish fishermen were known to buy knotted handkerchiefs of wind from sorcerers. The desired strength of wind could be obtained by slowly undoing the knot. Once loosened, the knot was useless and for additional winds another purchase was required.

If a sailor found a knot in a painter, he could expect a long voyage. When a sailor referred to "tying a knot in the devil's tail," he was relating to the "well done" completion of a difficult task.

Notes

1. Bodmer, *The Book of Wonders*, 353-54.
2. Ashley, *The Ashley Book of Knots*, 1-3.
3. Beck, *Folklore and the Sea*, 193.
4. Ibid.

13. Launching

Luck

Christened with blood, sent down the ways,
Rituals still followed since ancient days.
A marred launch, no ceremony or name,
Marked ships sailed with unlucky fame.

Launching

What is thought to be the first record of a sacrifice commemorating the completion of a ship was found on an Assyrian tablet of 2100 B.C. that bears the king's inscription: "To the gods I caused oxen to be sacrificed."[1]

When a Turkish ship slid down the ways, a sheep was sacrificed and its flesh was given to the poor. The spilling of human blood solemnized the launch of Tahitian war canoes, and in a ceremony fittingly termed "roller reddening," Viking ships entered their element after first sliding over slaves tied to the launch rollers.

The ancient practice of spilling blood at boat launchings is still taking place on the island of Carriacou in the West Indies. Ken Legler of Carriacou Boat Builders relates that as recently as 1992 the deck of a fishing boat was sprinkled with the blood of a he-goat as part of the launching ceremony.

The christening of French vessels in Brittany involved crumbling biscuits on the deck and the smashing of a bottle of wine against the prow, while the owner of the new vessel recited:

"Biscuit and bottle of wine insures that my
boat will never lack bread."

An assigned wood-godfather and wood-godmother afterward bent down to pick up the biscuit crumbs and lick up the wine. Because they were christening a wooden vessel and not a human being, they were addressed as wood-godparents.[2]

After vessels were completed in PasdeCalais, France, a tent made out of the mainsail was erected on board under which a priest would bless the new ship. Wine and cakes were served to the crew and wine was also offered to passing spectators. If a drink was refused, it was a sign of bad luck.[3]

After boats were launched to a flowing tide in Scotland, ample quantities of whiskey, bread, and cheese were offered to guests. The vessel then received its name and the following was recited:

"Fae rocks an saands
An barren lands
Anill men's hands
Keep's free
Aeel oot, weel in
Wi a gueede shot."

A bottle of whiskey was then broken over the prow or the stern depending on which way the boat was sent down the ways.[4]

Boats were also christened in Scotland by a woman who sprinkled corn or barley over it. The launching of ships in the Middle Ages included bedecking the vessel with flowers, a blessing by a priest, anointing the ship with eggs and sulphur, a consecration ceremony, and the naming of the craft after some saint. A Fijian belief involved the throwing of stones in the house where a new canoe was built to charm the carpenter gods.[5]

Ship launching and christening rituals, reverently adhered to since ancient times, were more important than the construction of the vessel itself. These ceremonies were strictly followed and conformed to lest the newly built craft be marked a failure. No matter how well the shipwrights performed their tasks or how well built the vessel was, mariners relied most on the launch of a ship to determine if the vessel would be a lucky or unlucky one. Just after the vessel went down the ways, it was carefully scrutinized to determine if her momentum was halted properly by her arresting gear or yard boats, how she sat in the water, if she floated on an even keel, and whether or not she had a list.[6] Care was also taken immediately after launch so that the attendant yard tugs could guide the new vessel's first turn in a clockwise, or "with the sun," direction for good luck.

It was always considered a sign of ill fortune if at a launching any mishap occurred. If the vessel did not move, if wine or champagne was not spilled, or if any accident happened, especially one that resulted in injury or death, it was thought to be a bad omen and the vessel was believed to be unlucky.

To assure that a vessel would not "stick" on the ways, launching skids were coated with soap, tallow, or some other slick substance. Over twenty-two tons of tallow and soap were used to launch the *Titanic*. As a substitute for tallow, bananas, and even clams, were used as a lubricant. Lard or any substance containing lard was strictly forbidden because lard comes from pigs, which signified bad luck.

Launching when the moon was full, during high tide, or in the morning was thought to be lucky. To assure a perfect launch beyond that which nature could provide—a sunny day and fair winds—it was reported that in Nova Scotia and in Maine, shipbuilders often threw bits of fish in the surrounding waters so that sea gulls would be cheerfully on the wing and dolphins would be lured into playing about.[7]

It was firmly believed that if a vessel was not christened, it was more susceptible to hazard. An old-time fishermen's belief was that the owner of a boat would drown if his vessel was not christened. Moreover, in many early shipping communities, if a vessel was launched without a christening or ceremony, it was near impossible to find a crew for that marked vessel.

There are many recorded instances of vessels that met with mysterious misfortune or were lost, whose launch was accomplished without proper ceremony, or marred by some unfortunate accident.

Moments before the great White Star liner *Titanic* was launched, a worker, James Dobbins, was pinned beneath the great ship after support beams he was cutting collapsed. His leg was crushed and fellowworkers freed him just in time, but he died the next day. It is hard to believe that although over a hundred thousand spectators viewed the launch, there was no ceremony for the famous ship and no customary breakage of a bottle of spirits across her bow.[8] The ill-fated *Titanic* was never christened!

The launch of the *Great Eastern* was finally accomplished on the Thames, January 30, 1858, after four months and many unsuccessful attempts. Guests repeatedly invited to witness the would-be event became so disinterested that the vessel was labeled "Leave-her-high-and-dry-a-than." Although she did successfully lay the Atlantic cable in 1866, the rest of her troubled career was believed by many a result of her marred launch.

After the loss of the *Edmund Fitzgerald* with all hands on Lake Superior, November 10, 1975, the superstitious would recall the launch of the ore carrier during which the sponsor, Mrs. Edmund Fitzgerald, had to strike the champagne bottle three times across the bow before it broke. It was also revealed that a spectator, Jennings Frazier of Toledo, Ohio, died suddenly at the scene of a heart attack.

The Great Lakes' worst storm of November 1913 sank twelve vessels and claimed some 235 lives. Even though the bulk carrier *John McGean* was lost because of the severe storm, there were those who remembered her marred launch at Lorain, Ohio, on February 22, 1908. The great push of water created as the vessel entered the water washed into a platform of spectators, thirty of whom were catapulted into the icy water. Two of the victims were seriously hurt.

Some American vessels were launched with ginger ale in lieu of spirits during Prohibition, and milk was used to launch missionary ships. The Japanese originated the use of birds at launchings. At the launch of the *Chicago* in 1885, three doves were released from red, white, and blue ribbons.[9]

The use of red ribbons or banners at launchings is handed down from the belief that red was a witch deterrent and the color of blood and life, which supposedly protected a vessel from the evil eye.

Deviating from custom by launching a ship with water or flowers, during Prohibition or not, might have been proper according to temperance advocates, but to the superstitious sailors on the vessel it meant that an indelible stain of bad luck was put on their ship.

Said to have been the grandest clipper built by the renowned shipbuilder Donald McKay, the *Great Republic* was christened at McKay's Boston yard, October 4, 1853, with a bottle of cochituate water, as a last-minute substitution for champagne. The beverage, called "Boston's drinking water," had just been put on the market and was reportedly used to soothe those who advocated temperance. Another version of the story related that the water was used at the last minute because someone had found and consumed the champagne intended for the launch. Nevertheless, many viewed the water christening as the cause of the tragic fire that destroyed the *Great Republic* in New York on December 26, 1853.

It is believed that water was used to launch the *Constitution* whereupon she moved only twenty-seven feet. The use of jacks and other mechanical devices proved useless in attempts to budge her. She was stuck because of a slight dip in the ways caused by the previous and premature launch of the frigate *United States*. After a second launch attempt moved her only thirty feet farther, it was found that the ways near her stern had settled. Because of the time required to rebuild that portion of the ways, excessive pressure on her keel caused a permanent hog (sag) of fourteen inches amidships, which she has to this day. Most probably her obstinacy was due to the aforementioned problems; however, it was said that not until a bottle of choice old Madeira wine was broken across her bow on October 21, 1797, did she finally slide into the sea.

Selecting the right day and time for a launch was more often than not seriously considered. A few shipbuilders, ignoring superstitions, carelessly looked the other way and launched on a day best suited to their schedule. Friday was the unluckiest day of all for launching, Wednesday was perfect, and the thirteenth of any month was profoundly taboo. The launch of the *Carroll A. Deering* with flowers on Friday, April 4, 1919, was, according to some, the reason for her mysterious loss in 1921. (See chapter 5, Disaster.)

Cunard Lines poked fun at the superstition when the *Countess* was launched at San Juan on Friday, August 13, 1976.[10] Without having any apparent ill fortune, the *Countess* still sails a seven-day schedule in the Caribbean.

Officials at the Bath Iron Works in Bath, Maine, and at Bay Shipbuilding in Sturgeon Bay, Wisconsin, still avoid Fridays for the laying of keels or the launching of vessels.

There have been some unusual ship launchings and incidents that occurred during launchings that deserve mention. Perhaps the most unusual launch of all is that of the first iron ship of the U. S. Navy, the USS *Michigan*. Because she was made of heavy iron, as launch time approached, in December 1843, her critics watched with mixed feelings of amusement and wonder, certain that the ship would never float. As tension mounted, the *Michigan* slid down the ways, but abruptly stopped short of entering the waiting waters of Lake Erie. When many attempts to move her failed, the scoffers and well-wishers finally dispersed. Determined to launch the vessel, shipyard workers returned the next morning to discover that the new ship, proudly flaunting her seaworthiness, had launched herself![11]

USS *Michigan*

The 730-foot self-unloader *Tadoussac* accidentally launched herself on May 29, 1969, at the Collingwood Shipyards, Collingwood, Ontario. With a 350-man launch crew beneath her, several wooden trigger levers broke near the stern causing the uncontrolled and premature release of the ship. Two men lost their lives and over forty others were injured, some seriously.[12] The vessel as of this writing is still sailing.

Working beneath a vessel at launching was exceptionally hazardous especially in the early days of shipbuilding. During the Middle Ages, criminals were assigned the life-threatening job of removing the last blocks to free a vessel before launch. In later years shipwrights in New England received bonus hazardous duty pay as extra grog for "under bottom" work.[13]

Side launching a vessel is a most spectacular event. Many complex calculations are required to safely slide a vessel evenly off the ways and into a usually narrow adjacent slip. Apparently far too many calculations were figured into the side launch of the steamer *Lake Fernando* by the Buffalo Dry Dock Company in 1919, for the vessel was more than side-launched—she was launched on her side.

Tense moments and unexpected situations can occur when a side-launched vessel "hangs up" on the ways. Such was the case when the 730-foot self-unloader *Algowood* stuck on the ways at the Collingwood shipyard during an October 7, 1980, launch. She was stuck on the ways for fourteen minutes; jackmen worked hydraulic jacks to free the vessel. When the *Algowood* started moving again, fears of an uneven launch were realized as the forward end of the vessel moved down the ways some thirty feet ahead of the stern. The vessel's uneven entry into the water caused an unexpected rush of water that "baptized" spectators edging out on the launch basin for the best view. One spectator related that it was the first time he had ever heard a thousand people say "oooooooooooh" all at once when the cold October slip water washed up thigh high on trousers and skirts.[14]

A small miracle some believe occurred at the launch of the nuclear submarine *Nautilus* resulted in a phrase that will be forever associated with its launch. A pea soup fog enshrouded the shipyard at Groton, Connecticut, right up until the time that Mrs. Dwight Eisenhower was about to christen the boat with champagne. Moments before her swing, the fog burnt away and the sun shined through on the event. From this very dramatic moment on, it was said that "the sun always shines on *Nautilus*."[15]

The first woman to sponsor an American Navy ship was Miss Watson of Philadelphia, who used a combination of water and wine to launch the ship of war *Germantown* on October 22, 1846.[16] Since that occasion, thousands of prominent women have experienced the spine-tingling honor of launching ships. Once a lady breaks a champagne bottle across a navy ship's bow, she becomes a member of the exclusive Society of Navy Ship Sponsors. The club's nearly six hundred members include such notables as first ladies Mrs. George Bush, Mrs. Ronald Reagan, and Jacqueline Kennedy. Three nuns who participated in the launch of the destroyer *Laboon* are also members.

Launching ceremonies are still considered a very serious and important event at the General Dynamics Electric Boat Division at Groton, Connecticut. Although over a hundred submarines have been built and launched, careful plans are still religiously followed to assure a safe and lucky launch. So articulate is the planning for a launch that standby bottles of champagne are always on hand should the lady sponsor accidentally drop the ceremonial instrument. Two standby bottles are near at hand on the launch platform, as well as one aboard the new vessel. If by chance the vessel moves away from the platform without the smack of one of these bottles, an immediate signal is sent to the "second" lady aboard the vessel to quickly smash that bottle over the bow before the vessel touches the water. It may appear that the ceremony is unrehearsed; however, a practice session is held before the event, the sponsor using a weighted wooden bottle so that nothing will be left to chance. The bottles are even scored to produce a sure break, and encased in pewter and mesh to prevent injury from flying glass.

Perhaps the most humorous incident in connection with a launch happened just before the ferry *Delaware* was sent down the ways. Clarence B. McCormick, chairman of the Delaware River and Bay Authority, was advising the ship's sponsor on last-minute details. When he pointed to the spot on the prow where the ferry was to be christened, the sponsor quickly smashed McCormick's hand with the champagne bottle. There is no record of any ill fortune caused by the incident.

Luck

There are three reasons why a horseshoe is believed to be lucky. It is shaped like a cresent, which from ancient times is considered lucky; it is from a horse, which in English mythology was a lucky animal; and it is made of iron, which from the time of its discovery was thought to offer protection and luck. Together the three reasons lead the superstitious to conclude that the horseshoe is a truly lucky sign.[17]

If you believe in a horseshoe for good luck, you should know that unless the shoe is nailed with the ends up, the good luck it might bring will certainly drain out.

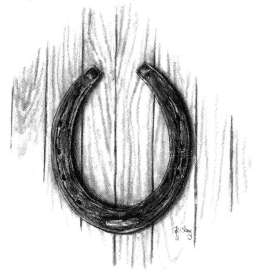

Fishermen often carried the Hammer of Thor, a tiny hammer shaped like a bone from a sheep's head. The tiny bones (there are two in each head) were believed to bring good-luck results.[18] Sailors carried, believed in, and relied on many charms to afford them good luck. There were sailors, however, that were just outright lucky, whether they carried charms or not. Just as some seamen were consided Jonahs, or unlucky, there were those who could always avoid bad luck. We all know people who seem "to have all the luck." They are characterized by the Russian proverb: "If a person is born lucky, even their roosters will lay eggs." Sailors who were seemingly always at the end of a rainbow were classified as white Anglo-Americans with blond hair and blue eyes. Seafarers born with a caul were also thought to be perpetually lucky. It seems too, that the bell-bottomed lads, whether handsome or downright homely, were always the lucky ones who had to beat the pretty ladies off with a belaying pin.

The fear some sailors had of being unlucky seemed to place them in a behavior pattern of believing that misfortune would come their way. There also were those who made their own luck through forethought or the knack of taking advantage of what life offers. Psychologists, who study human behavior, have all but proven that things accepted as chance are due to one's response to events, which reflects the thinking that a pattern of worry exists before an accident, or confident behavior is linked with success.

To believe that there are phases of good or bad luck and that some people are almost always luckier that others was termed *synchronicity* by psychologist Carl Jung. There may be a connection between a person's psychological state and the circumstances or events that are somehow drawn to that person. Luck is a weapon against pandemonium, and, like fate, it infers belief in a posture unrelated to probability, cause and effect, human endeavor, or morality. Luck, unlike fate, is generally thought of as favorable, while fate is generally considered ominous. An associated belief is that luck is fleeting, thereby affecting situations for only a short time. Fate, on the other hand, is thought of more as longevity—that distress, old age, death, or all of these will eventually come our way. Luck, coming to us on a day-to-day basis, may be good or bad.[19]

Notes

1. Kennedy, *Ship Names,* 10.
2. Rappoport, *Superstitions of Sailors,* 268-69.
3. Bassett, *Legends and Superstitions of the Sea and Sailors,* 401.
4. Rapporport, *Superstitions of Sailors,* 269.
5. Bassett, *Legends and Superstitions of the Sea and Sailors,* 399-402.
6. Beck, *Folklore and the Sea,* 27.
7. Ibid., 26.
8. Eaton and Haas, *Titanic Triumph and Tragedy,* 21-22.
9. Lovette, *Naval Customs, Traditions, and Usage,* 36.
10. Baker, *The Folklore of the Sea,* 29.
11. Clary, *Ladies of the Lakes,* 105-6
12. Woodcock, *Side Launch,* 72.

13. Baker, *The Folklore of the Sea*, 32.
14. Woodcock, *Side Launch,* 91.
15. Baker, *The Folklore of the Sea*, 29.
16. Lovette, *Naval Customs, Traditions, and Usage*, 36.
17. Bodmer, *The Book of Wonders,* 311.
18. Opie and Tatem, eds., *A Dictionary of Superstitions*, 234.
19. *Encyclopedia of Magic and Superstition*, 24-25.

14. Marriage

Mermaids and Mermen

Hard to splice for the hearts they got,
They seldom tied the marriage knot.
Though hearing not their lover's plea,
They longed for the mermaids of the sea.

Marriage

Out of fear of desertion, vessel commanders from many nations in the days of the man-of-war refused to grant seamen shore leave even in their own home ports. Instead, hundreds of prostitutes and other abandoned women were ferried out to the ships for the crew's entertainment. Because officers were allowed liberty ashore they were not permitted to indulge in this frivolity in accordance with admiralty regulations.

When a vessel or a fleet came into port, a flotilla of small boats was filled with the best looking and most provocatively dressed women carefully selected by watermen who conveyed them out to the waiting sailors. The men were then permitted on the ferries to choose a woman by paying a shilling or two for her passage. Because the women most often tried to smuggle spirits aboard, they were thoroughly searched at the gangway. Sometimes they would be hoisted aboard in a cut-down cask fashioned into a chair, which was raised and lowered in a ceremony called "whipping the ladies." The women would then be free to go below with their "husbands." Jammed together without the slightest privacy, in an area barely

large enough to accommodate the men, as many as five hundred seamen and nearly that many women would spend the night. The stench, vile conversation, obscene conduct, lurid indecency, fighting, rioting, and every other debauchery imaginable were all part of what was described as "hell afloat."

The only way a sailor could obtain shore leave in those days was to get married, and about the only way to obtain an audience with a vessel's commander was to seek permission to get married. One lowly British seaman aboard a man-of-war at anchor off Spithead[1] approached his captain for this permission after hearing it was the only way to go ashore. The lad was elated to find that he indeed had the blessing of his commander, but was soundly taken aback when he was escorted ashore by marines under the order of his superior, who questioned the truth of his request.

As he was being rowed ashore, his mind raced for a way out of the predicament. To be caught in an outright lie meant certain severe punishment. Although having enough money for a license, he did not know how he would find the right girl—any girl. As soon as he arrived on shore, he asked for the hand of the first girl he encountered. After the lady accepted his proposal, he immediately bought a ring, obtained a license, and was hastily joined in matrimony at Kingston Church, near Portsmouth.

Right after kissing his new bride, without so much as an exchange of conversation, let alone any honeymoon, the marines ushered the groom back to his ship, which immediately departed. No longer an outcast loose single woman of the city, the new navy wife soon received half the lad's pay, and it was doubtful that the two newlyweds ever laid eyes on each other again.[2]

It has been said that for every woman who disdainfully decried that sailors had a wife in every port, there were ten others who married the sailors for a share of his pay, to promiscuously serve as the "wife" for other itinerant seamen while her other half was away. Sweethearts or wives of a sailor who had taken up with another lover and did not want the absent seaman to come home were defined as those who "had not got hold of the tow rope."

Perhaps it was the romantic itinerant life of the sailor that made him a difficult catch. His worldly travels, at any rate were his resolute grounds and convenient alibi for remaining aloof from serious involvement and marriage. Despite their shortcomings, it seemed that sailors always got the girls, as related in this eighteenth century song:

> Don't you see the ships a-coming?
> Don't you see them in full sail?
> Don't you see the ships a-coming
>   With the prizes at their tail?
>   Oh! my little rolling sailor,
>   Oh! my little rolling he;
>   I do love a jolly sailor,
> Blithe and merry might he be.
>
> Sailors, they get all the money,
> Soldiers they get none but brass;
>   I do love a jolly sailor,
> Soldiers they may kiss my arse.
>   Oh! my little rolling sailor,
>   Oh! my little rolling he;
>   I do love a jolly sailor,
> Soldiers may be damned for me.[3]

An old farewell superstition was that when it came time for that last good-bye, if a sailor tasted the salt of his loved one's tears, he would come home safely and his wife or sweetheart would remain true. Those heart-broken sweethearts left tearfully waving at the wharf are epitomized in this anonymous verse:

> Goodbye! Goodbye!
>
> When his ship is trimmed and ready

191

And the last good-byes are done,
When the tugboat's lying waiting,
And Jack aboard is gone,
Then the lasses fall a-weeping,
As they watch his vessel's track,
For all their landsman lovers
Are nothing after Jack.[4]

Some women, smuggled aboard a husband's or lover's ship, became an asset by performing various duties during battle. Living together in cramped quarters between the guns meant, it was said, that many new lives were born below at the same time men were dying on the decks above. The phrase "son of a gun" originated from the time when women gave birth between the guns. On the HMS *Goliath* during the battle of the Nile in August 1798, a woman whose labor was believed induced by the roar of battle gave birth to a boy.

An entry in a captain's journal of a brig in 1835 gives an example of a true "son of a gun" birth: "This day the surgeon informed me that a woman on board had been labouring in child for 12 hours and asked if I could fire a broadside to leeward. I did so and she was delivered a fine male child."[5]

Although women were officially prohibited from going to sea aboard British ships in 1817, some sailed with their husbands as late as 1837. The seventy-four-gun, man-of-war HMS *Genoa* carried the wives of nine petty officers during the last battle under sail in 1827. A baby born aboard the HMS

Tremendous during the Glorious First of June was baptized Daniel Tremendous Mackenzie. The marriage of seaman David Jones and surgeon's attendant Anne Robinson resulted from the care Robinson rendered to Jones aboard the frigate *Le Seine* in May 1802.[6]

Although it was generally considered unlucky to have women aboard ships, despite the superstition many wives went to sea with their husbands. Many sailors, too accessible to the bickerings and criticism of the first ladies, referred to as "kittle cargo," shied away from ships, or "henfrigates" as they were called, that sailed with the captain's wife. Beyond being unlucky to have aboard, often when an accident or shipwreck occurred, strangely the woman was the only casualty.

When two ships collided and were beam to beam in a gale off Cape Horn, one captain, sensing his vessel would sink, tried to throw his wife aboard the other ship. The lady, the only casualty on either vessel, was crushed to death when she fell between the ships.[7]

Rather than spend lonely years pacing a widow's walk, many wives of whaling captains who withstood the rigors of seasickness accompanied their mates on voyages that lasted as long as five years. Forty wives hailing from Martha's Vineyard sailed with their husbands; countless others sailed from the more than twenty other American whaling ports. Aside from the companionship, whaling ladies were "at home" to sew, bake, wash clothes, read, keep journals, and bear and tutor their children aboard ship.[8]

Scottish fisherfolk believed that marriages among their kind would bring stormy weather. The best time for a marriage was thought to be right after the herring season was over.[9]

Huron Indians were said to have "married" their fishing nets to young maidens for good fishing luck.[10]

Present policy does not permit a husband and wife serving in the U.S. Navy to go to sea together. The married couple will further not be ordered to sea duty at the same time, unless permission is granted through waiver.

Perhaps the most difficult hardship suffered by a navy marriage today is the separation common between a submariner and his wife. Away and submerged for as long as a three-to six-month deployment, crew members on submarines such as the USS *Michigan* have only the bare minimum contact with their wives. Each man is allowed two 100-word "family-grams" a month as a means to stay in touch. The small paragraphs of exotic phrases, love, and family news are hardly private. Once received by the sub's communication section and given to the recipient, by mutual agreement the love notes are posted with names omitted, for the benefit of all the crew.

Mermaids and Mermen

Eons ago when creatures of the sea ventured to land and adapted limbs for that new environment, could they not have left behind unimaginable and strange relatives? How does one pass off as total myth the mermaid's existence when we know so little of the mysteries of the deep? Astonishing and baffling ocean finds in our time have proven man's ineptness to fully comprehend what strange creatures still exist in the dark reaches of the sea. A coelacanth, the fish thought extinct 70 million years ago, was found near Madagascar in 1938. A previously unknown species of shark, weighing nearly a ton, was found entangled in a U.S. Navy vessel's sea anchor in Hawaiian waters in 1976. The fourteen foot plankton-feeding creature and four others taken since that time have been called, for lack of a better name, megamouths after their enormous bathtub-shaped jaws containing over 450 teeth.[11]

Only within the last twenty years have scientists discovered thermo vent communities of fish and other invertebrate that exist without sunlight in primitive fashion around thermo vents, or hot spots produced by volcanic action on the ocean floor.

In the light of these discoveries it is a wonder how one can disregard the possibility that mermaids and mermen exist or have existed, especially when reports of their sightings by persons of unquestionable veracity and integrity have been documented throughout the centuries. The age-old legend is worldwide. An ocean, lake, or river bordering practically every country is steeped in its mermaid lore.

The fishtailed Babylonian god Ea, or Oannes, Lord of the Waters, was first worshiped in Accad in 5000 B.C. and is considered the first merman in recorded history. Portrayed with a human body to the waist, and a fish's tail, he was believed to appear on land during the day, returning to the sea at night. He was also known as the great fish of the ocean.[12]

Derceto, also known as Atargatis, a Semite moon goddess, was believed to be the first mermaid worshiped as a goddess by the Philistines, Syrians, and Israelites. According to a fifth century B.C. Greek account, Derceto, who resided in the territory known as Ascalon in Syria, had a head of a woman and a body of a fish. She has, according to a Phoencia drawing, the distinction of being the first of her kind undisputably portrayed as a mermaid.[13]

Oannes and his mermen successors faded into the dusty pages of history, but the mermaid, the principal figure of all the half-human, half-fish legends, has survived for over two thousand years.

The perpetual youth, striking beauty, and allure of the mermaid has fascinated people of every land, but her seduction power is renowned as her most famous characteristic. As if epitomizing a goddess of vanity, she typically appeared combing her long hair with a mirror in hand while the rapture of her voice was heard sweetly in calm or storm luring unresisting man to his doom. The customary theme of her desire is constant: her quest for a soul; her magical power to grant wishes; the wrath she exacts when injured or defeated; and her intervals of stay on land as a spouse of mortals who have acquired her magic hat, which prevents her return to the sea.[14]

A mermaid superstition relates that the creature often dove and rose to the surface of the water with her hands full of fish. If the mermaid threw the fish at their ship, the sailors believed several of the crew would be lost. On the other hand, if she threw the fish away from them, with her back to the ship, it was a good omen.[15]

Norwegian seafarers believed the sight of a mermaid told of a coming storm. Many sailors were in fear when mermaids and mermen rose from the deep abyss. To injure them was foolishly dangerous. A story tells of a seaman who lured a mermaid to his boat. Hanging on the side of the gunwale, the sailor struck the mermaid causing her hand to be severed from her body. Because of this cruel act, his boat was engulfed in a storm during which he was nearly lost.[16]

There was also an association with Friday and the mermaid. If a mermaid spoke to a vessel in a storm on Friday, that vessel would be sure to reach port safely. The superstition is related in this verse:

> On a Friday morning we set sail,
> And our ship was not far from land,
> When there we saw a pretty fair maid,
> With a comb and a glass in her hand, brave boys.[17]

The sightings of mermaids have long been attributed to manatees or dugongs, even though the appearance of these blubbery creatures in no way resembles the lissome beauty of the mermaid, nor, in most cases, do they inhabit the same locale. Much closer in resemblance to the mermaid and her mannerisms is the seal. The seal's svelte shape, the way a seal sits on rocks, its utterance of melodious sounds, its rounded, humanlike head, eyes, expressions, and flipper movements seem more apt to be mistaken as a mermaid. However, the vastness of the mermaids legend and countless worldwide sightings far outnumber the handful of these mistaken identities.

In the third century before Christ, Megasthenes, the Greek ambassador to the court of the Hindu Chandragupta, stated that around the shores of Taprobane (former name of Ceylon) were half-fish creatures that looked like women. Later off the coast of Mandar, Ceylon, in 1560, seven mermen and mermaids were reported caught in a net and verified by several Jesuit priests and the physician to the Viceroy of Goa. The physician, Bosquez, after dissecting and examining the creatures, related that they were exactly like humans both externally and internally. His report was published in the *Histoire de la Compagnie de Jesus*, No. 276.[18]

The seventeenth-century explorer Henry Hudson, while on expedition to find a passage to the East Indies, recorded in his log on June 15, 1608:

> This morning, one of our companie looking over boord saw a Mermaid, and calling up some of the companie to see her, one more came up, and by that time shee was come close to the ship's side, looking earnestly on the men: a little after, the Sea came and overturned her: From the Navill upward, her backe and breasts were like a womans (as they say that saw her) her body as big as one of us; her skin very white; and long haire hanging down behinde, of colour blacke; in her going downe they saw her tayle, which was like the tayle of a Porposse, and speckled like a Macrell. Their names that saw her were Thomas Hilles and Robert Raynar.[19]

Perhaps the most detailed report of a mermaid sighting was that given by Captain Whitbourne in Newfoundland Harbor in 1610:

> Now also I will not omit to relate something of a strange Creature that I first saw there in the year 1610 in a morning early as I was standing by the waterside, in the Harbour of St. Johns, which I espied verie swiftly to come swimming towards me, looking cheerfully, as it had beene a woman, by the Face, Eyes, Nose, Mouth, Chin, Eares, Necke and Forehead: It seemed to be so beautiful and in those parts so well proportioned, haveing round about the head, all blew

strakes, resembling haire, downe to the Necke (but certainly it was haire) for I beheld it long, and another of my companie also, yet living, that was not then farre from me; and seeing the same coming so swiftly towards me, I stepped backe, for it was come with the length of a Pike. Which when this strange Creature saw that I went from it, it presently thereupon dived a little under water, and did swim to the place where before I landed; whereby I beheld the shoulders and backe downe to the middle to be as square, white and smooth as the backe of a man, and from the middle to the hinder part, pointing in proportion like a broad hooked Arrow; how it was proportioned in the forepart from the Necke and shoulders I know not; but the same came shortly after unto a Boat, wherein one William Hawkridge then my servant, was, that hath bin since a Captaine in a ship to the East Indies and is later there imploied againe by Sir Thomas Smith, in the like voyage, and the same Creature did put both his hands upon the side of the Boate, and did strive to come in to him and others then in the said Boate: whereat they were afraid and one of them strooke it a full blow on the head: whereat it fell off from them: and afterwards it came to two other Boates in the Harbour: the men in them, for feare fled to land: this (I suppose) was a Mermaide.[20]

One of the most incredible stories of a mermaid is that of the miniature Benbecula, mermaid of the Outer Hebrides. About 1830, a woman near the end of a reef was shocked to see a creature "in the form of a woman in miniature" a few feet from her. The little maiden, oblivious to those watching, cavorted in the water, turning somersaults. When several men waded out to try to catch her, she quickly swam from their midst. An impish little boy then began throwing rocks at the creature, one of which hit her in the back.

Several days later, townspeople flocked to the shore to see the dead little sea creature, who had washed ashore two miles from where she was first sighted. After a thorough examination it was stated the "the upper part of the creature was about the size of a well-fed child of three or fours years of age, with an abnormally developed breast. The hair was long, dark and glossy, while the skin was white, soft, and tender. The lower part of the body was like a salmon, but without scales." All who saw her believed that she was a mermaid. So filled with compassion were those people of the district that, directed by the sheriff, Mr. Duncan Shaw, a coffin and shroud was made for the little mermaid, and she was buried a short distance from where she was found, the simple service attended by many people.[21]

A mermaid encounter was described by Dr. Robert Hamilton in the *History of Whales and Seals*, published in 1839. Six Shetand fishermen reported that a mermaid was caught entangled in their nets off the island of Yell. They removed a fishhook imbedded in her body and she remained in their boat for three hours. Nearly three feet long, her upper body was like a woman's except that her face and neck were like a monkey's. Her hands were not webbed and she kept her small arms folded over her breast. "A few stiff bristles were on the top of the head, extending down to the shoulders, and these it could erect and depress at pleasure, something like a crest." The creature's body was without gills, fins, hair, or scales. Its lower part was like a fish, the tail of which looked like a dogfish's. Offering no resistance but uttering continual moans, the little creature, soon playing on the superstitions of the fishermen, was released into the water to quickly dive out of sight.[22]

A more recent mermaid encounter occurred on January 3, 1957, and was reported by Eric de Bisschop while on the raft *Tahiti-Nui* during a voyage that matched the ancient Polynesian trek from Tahiti to Chile.

A short while after midnight, Bisschop discovered the sailor on watch nearly incoherent with fear. He had heard the sound of what he believed was a large fish or dolphin flop onto the deck. To his shock he found the creature erect and standing on its tail, with what looked like fine seaweed on its head. Although frightened, he approached and touched the creature, which bolted, knocked him off his feet, and dove into the water. Positively sure he had seen a mermaid, the sailor found many silvery fish scales on his arms.[23]

Notes

1. The waters between Portsmouth, England, and the Isle of Wight.
2. Robinson, *Jack Nastyface,* 93-95.
3. Spectre, *The Mariner's Book of Days.*
4. Ibid.
5. Beavis and McCloskey, *Salty Dog Talk,* 79.
6. Lovette, *Naval Customs, Traditions, and Usage,* 275.
7. Lubbock, *The Last of the Windjammers,* 111.
8. Laing, *Seafaring America,* 168.
9. Opie and Tatem, *A Dictionary of Superstitions,* 240.
10. Bassett, *Legends and Superstitions of the Sea and Sailors,* 411.
11. *The Best of Smithsonian,* 16.
12. Benwell and Waugh, *Sea Enchantress,* 23.
13. Ibid., 28.
14. Ibid., 13.
15. Van Dervoort, *The Water World,* 335-36.
16. Rappoport, *Superstitions of Sailors,* 72-73.
17. Bassett, *Legends and Superstitions of the Sea and Sailors,* 445.
18. Benwell and Waugh, *Sea Enchantress,* 87.
19. Ibid., 95.
20. Ibid., 96.
21. Ibid., 117.
22. Ibid., 118.
23. Ibid., 262.

15. Names

Navigation, Numbers

Those unlucky names of ships and men
Were thought to be a curse back then.
Into the Sea of Darkness they sailed,
And with the devil's compass, prevailed.

Names

Certain surnames were considered unlucky by some Scottish fishermen. In one village alone, those with the names Rosse, Cullie, and White were said to have been banned from going out to sea. If men with such an unlucky name worked for the fishermen ashore, they were often denied wages when the catch was meager. If they were even caught looking at the fishing nets or boats, or were met early in the morning, it was a sure bad omen. An old story relates how two such unlucky men happened to come across each other early one morning; because they were so steadfast in their belief of the omen, no one fished that day.[1]

The 167-foot Egyptian cedarwood vessel *Praise of the Two Lands*, built about 2680 B.C., had what is believed to be the earliest known ship name. Thought to be named for a symbol of unity between the north and south Nile, the name was also believed to be the first one with a political connection.[2]

Ship names that began with the letter *S* or *O* or those ending with *A* were thought by some to be unlucky. Others felt that any name beginning with *A* was unlucky. Names with seven letters were thought to be the most lucky particularly if the name contained three *a*'s. Too many *a*'s in a name perhaps spelled ill luck for the Great Lakes bulk freighter *Mataafa*. Although having a lucky seven-letter name, she was lost near Duluth in 1905 with nine lives. Salvaged and rebuilt in 1906, she rammed and sank the steamer *Sacramento* in October 1908, and collided with the steamer *G. Watson French* in 1912.

Bulk Freighter *MATAAFA*   Courtesy Great Lakes Historical Society

Thirteen-letter ship names are still thought to be unlucky by some shipping companies. When in recent years the Erie Sand and Steamship Company of Erie, Pennsylvania, acquired the self-unloader *Richard J. Reiss,* the new owners painted out the initial *J* on the ship as a precaution against any unlucky fate.

Ninety-five Great Lakes vessels and oceangoing merchant ships operating on the inland seas with thirteen-letter names are listed in the 1993 *Know Your Ships*. One of these, a

Taiwan bulk carrier of the First Steamship Company, is named *Ever Advantage*.

Spanish ships were considered unlucky if given a nonreligious name. Seemingly in deference to Athene, goddess of the sea, ancient Greek vessels most often bore a feminine name.[3] Some sailors were reluctant to sail on vessels with masculine names because ships were thought to be feminine.

After the snake-named British ships *Cobra*, *Viper*, and *Serpent* were lost, there was great public dissatisfaction in naming a new submarine *Python*. Giving in to the outcry, the name was changed to *Pandora* even though over fifty other Royal Navy vessels with snake names sustained no losses.

A ship launched without a name is thought seriously unlucky. When a frigate was built in 1966 for a Ghana regime that was overthrown before the ship's completion, there was doubt that the new regime would take the ship, so she was launched without a name, and the yard workers would not even watch her slide down the ways.[4]

If a vessel met with disaster or defeat, most often her name was not used again (there was only one *Titanic*). Good luck ships, those famous in battle, or those known for achieving records gallantly passed their names on to many successors. There have been no less that eight U.S. Navy ships named *Enterprise*, the present namesake being the nuclear aircraft carrier USS *Enterprise*, CVN-65.

The ancients believed a ship's name was integral to the ship and if it was changed a deadly curse would follow the unlucky vessel. Because many vessels were named after gods, kings, or countries, it was further thought that a name change would at least be offensive. Although according to Lloyd's records the names of thousands of ships have been renamed in apparent unconcern for the belief of ill luck following such a practice, the superstition in some shipping circles lingers. Name changing, unless a ship's name is changed with new ownership of a vessel, is still considered by some as unlucky. If the change is absolutely necessary, it is usually accomplished by simple announcement void of fanfare or ceremony.

Seemingly daring fate, some ships were renamed after the reefs they struck. The ship *Gainsborough* was salvaged and renamed *Diamond Head* after being wrecked on Diamond Head in 1898. Intentionally run aground on Manga Reva Reef, near Pitcairn Island during a cargo fire in 1900, the bark *Pyrenees* was later salvaged and renamed *Manga Reva* but was lost at sea in 1917.[5]

One would think that the unluckiest ship name of all was that given to the schooner *Devil* in 1868. Among other ominous or unsavory ship names were those given the vessels *Casket, Hard Luck, Rotten Apple, Black Cat, Black Bird, Black Crow, Black Spread Eagle, Black Watch, Bittersweet, Bruiser, Endless Summer, Great Storm, Hard Luck, Hard Times, Horse Turd, Irreproachable, Isn't, Lucifer, Melanope, Pickle, Precious Ridicule, Snake of the Sea, Wandering Jew, and Sheitan.*[6]

A most unusual combination of names was gathered on a ship during a sea battle between the English and the French in 1757. Captain Death in command of the English man-of-war *Terrible,* which had been fitted out at Execution Dock, also carried among her crew a ship's surgeon named Ghost and an officer named Devil.[7]

Navigation

Other than the winds and stars, the most ancient mariners of the Mediterranean had only the sounding-lead and line with which to gage the depth of water to guide their vessels.[8]

The first primitive compass, known as a wind rose, is traced to Amalfi, Italy, in the twelfth century after Christ. The device had a magnetized needle affixed to a circular card and balanced on a sharp point. Instead of showing the north, south, east, and west points, the card indicated the direction of the four winds known by Greek seamen as Boreas, the north wind; Euros, the east wind; Notos, the south wind; and Ephinos, the west wind. An eight-wind card was soon established by the Romans, who named them Tramontana, Greco, Levante, Sirocco, Mezzodi, Garbino, Ponente, and Maestro.[9]

Although Arabian merchants were thought to have acquired the method of navigating with a needle from the Chinese, who were known to have used the method much earlier, the first mention of this instrument with an Italian name (Amalfi) was by the Arabs in the mid-thirteenth century.[10] Even though scholars of the time thought mariners would not trust their vessels and lives to this first compass believed invented by the devil, the instrument was used in the Mediterranean near the end of the twelfth century and also in northern Europe within the next hundred years.[11]

The oldest known marine chart, the *Carta Pisana,* is believed to have been made in Pisa, about 1275.[12] With these first charts, which depicted compass bearings and scaled distances, and the invention of the sandglass, which aided the seafarer in estimating speed, extended voyages gradually enlightened and guided him through the dark uncertainty and fear of distant seas.

The Polynesians, those genius navigators of the Pacific, known to have populated nearly every island in the tropical sector of that ocean, began their incredible voyages several thousand years ago. They saw the stars as moving areas of light over the inverted heavens, and sailed in the direction of the stars that passed over their islands of destination.[13] They were believed to have also used a peculiar system of navigation unknown in other parts of the world, which was accomplished by an elite group of priests. Peering through a small hole in the rim of a bowl of water, they studied and noted reflections of the stars on the water in the bowl. Using this procedure, though not having the means to measure distance traveled, they were thought able to determine both latitude and longitude.[14]

Other methods of navigating included: watching flocks of birds and following their migration, noting the color of the sea and the mist from surf breaking on distant rocks, looking for floating vegetation and cloud formations hanging over islands.

They were also thought to be able to determine the position of islands by lying low in the hull of their craft to feel how the waves affected the motion of their boats. It was said that this method was so accurate that the Polynesian navigator could determine the position of landfall a hundred miles away.[15]

History records the use of birds by ancient navigators, which were released and followed to land. The frigate, or man-of-war, bird was known to have been used for sighting land by the Polynesians, and in recent years carried messages from island to island. Norsemen were also known to carry ravens for finding land. Interestingly, this ancient method of navigation is still recommended for making landfall in dirty weather in the *United States Pilot* for Antarctica: "Navigators should observe the bird life, for deductions may often be drawn from the presence of certain species. Shags are a sure sign of the close proximity of land. The snow petrel is invariably associated with ice and is of great interest to mariners as an augury of ice conditions in their course."[16]

Numbers

Widespread superstition has surrounded the number thirteen since the time of Christ. In company with the chosen twelve apostles, thirteen sat at the last supper. Jesus answered them, "Did I not choose you twelve? Yet is not one of you a devil?" He was referring to Judas, son of Simon the Iscariot; he would betray him, one of the twelve.[17]

The superstition of being the thirteenth person to sit at table is still thought by many as unlucky. Overly superstitious sailors would not ship out on a vessel that had thirteen persons aboard. Death is represented on the number thirteen tarot card, and according to legend a coven is composed of thirteen witches.

Viewed more as a symbol of evil than ill luck, the dangerous digits 666 are known as the frightful sign of the devil.

Folklore relates that the numbers three, seven, nine, and their multiples were thought lucky.

Lucky numbers, however, sometimes did little to help an unfortunate ship. The supposedly lucky seven-masted schooner *Thomas Lawson*, the only seven-masted vessel ever built, capsized in a severe storm off the Scilly Islands on Friday, December 13, 1907.

The origin of firing three volleys at funerals to drive away evil spirits is believed to be from the mystical significance of the number three as utilized in ancient Roman funeral ceremonies. Dirt was thrown three times in the sepulcher, mourners called the dead by name three times, and when leaving the tomb they spoke the word *vale,* meaning "farewell," three times.

The numbers three, five, and seven, though, bore mystical significance long before Roman times. The symbolism continues today in "the Holy Trinity," Macbeth's "three witches," the frequent use of three in Masonic ceremonies, three cheers, and even in the familiar auction phrase, "going once, going twice, sold."

Wives of some sailors believed that if their husband was washed overboard three times and was saved, they need not worry because the sea did not want him.[18]

The mystical significance of seven as a sacred number is derived from the seven planets in the solar system, the seven-day moon change, and the creation of Earth in seven days. In the very early days, a seven-gun salute was the official British national salute. Because gunpowder was easier to store ashore than aboard ship, early regulations decreed that although a ship could fire only seven guns, shore batteries could fire three shots for every shot fired from a ship. Thus the twenty-one-gun salute. When improved gunpowder came into use, the ship and shore salutes were made the same—twenty-one guns, the highest national honor. The United States offically adopted the twenty-one-gun salute August 18, 1875. Before this time, our national salute was with thirteen guns, one for each state.[19]

Notes

1. Bassett, *Legends and Superstitions of the Sea and Sailors*, 428.
2. Kennedy, *Ship Names*, 14.
3. Bassett, *Legends and Superstitions of the Sea and Sailors*, 431.
4. Kennedy, *Ship Names*, 12.
5. Ibid., 112-13.
6. Ibid., 161-75.
7. Lorie, *Superstitions*, 182.
8. Scandurra, *The Maritime Republics*, 214.
9. Kemp, *The History of Ships*, 36.
10. Scandurra, *The Maritime Republics,* 214.
11. Carson, *The Sea around Us*, 212-13.
12. Scandurra, *The Maritime Republics*, 214.
13. Carson, *The Sea around Us*, 211.
14. Thrower, *Life at Sea in the Age of Sail,* 162.
15. Pacific Voyages, *The Enclyclopedia of Discovery and Exploration,* 363.
16. Carson, *The Sea around Us*, 212-16.
17. John 6: 70-71.
18. Opie and Tatem, *A Dictionary of Superstitions*, 403.
19. Lovette, *Naval Customs, Traditions, and Usage*, 51-54.

16. Offerings

Omens

Offerings to still the angry wave,
Solemn promises the ancients gave.
Guided by omens of evil or good,
Through all ages the symbols stood.

Offerings

Through sacrificial offerings ancient sailors beseeched the help of their gods to protect them from the tempest. Solemn vows made to God, the Holy Virgin, patron saints, or other sea deities by sailors were common during times of peril. Other offerings were made by seamen or their loved ones at home for their protection and safe return from sea.

Legend states that the king of Crete, Idomeneus, promised Neptune that if he survived a tempest he would sacrifice the first being he encountered after making landfall.

The first person he met was his son, but unfailing he held true to his solemn vow.

It is said that Saint Anthony's church in Cornwall, England, was constructed by people who had vowed to build the church after being saved from shipwreck.

Like the animal sacrifices for the launch of a new vessel, rituals involving human sacrifice were also performed for protection on long voyages or to calm an angry sea. When Norsemen's ships could not make way, it was common to throw a man overboard. Ancient Scottish mariners drew lots to select and then condemn the poor soul they were sure was responsible for a calamity at sea. Chinese seafarers likewise were known to have cast humans into a stormy sea as a sacrifice to appease their gods.

213

Human lives were selected by the king and sacrificed to the sea by many African tribes of old. Wrapped in a hammock and cloaked in ceremonial dress, the human offering was taken out to sea and thrown to the sharks. Human sacrifices were also offered to the shark gods of the Fijians and Samoans. Polynesian fishermen offered their deceased to the sharks. They were clothed in red wrappings and thrown into the sea in the hope that the sharks would be pacified by the spirit of the deceased and thereby not harm the fishermen.

Although many early seafarers offered a human sacrifice to the sea in times of grave peril, animal sacrifices were usually offered before and after voyages and upon going into or returning victorious from battle.

Barbary pirates would offer sacrificed sheep or fowl to the storm gods, Arab mariners offered a cock to the demons, Norsemen dedicated a black lamb, horses were offered to the river spirits by Russian tribes, and the Chinese in recent years still offered sacrificed fowl to the river goddess Loong Moo. Animal sacrifices were thrown to river alligators by Philippine Islanders, dogs were thrown to the sea to eliminate bad luck on Fijian canoes, and offerings were also made to whales in those islands.

According to a German custom of the fifteenth and sixteenth centuries, fishermen offered carp and pike to their patron saint, St. Ulrich.

Norwegian and Danish sailors offered cake to the sea. Vessels of straw along with fruits and meat were offered to the sea by women in the East Indies during the seventeenth century in an attempt to lure disease and sickness into the sea. Greek mariners threw bread to the sea as an offering to St. Nicholas to ward off storms. Sumatra islanders offered cakes and sweetmeats to the sea as a precaution against injury, and Chinese boatmen offered food to crows perched in their rigging in the hope of securing a favorable passage. In a plea for good weather, Japanese junk sailors threw saki and coins into the sea as an offering to Kompira, the god of the elements.

Native American Chippewas offered a Manitou stone to the wind spirits for faster canoe speed. The Algonquins were known to have thrown tobacco in the water as an offering and other tribes smoked their pipes to solicit fair winds. Indians arriving on the banks of the Mississippi or other large rivers were known to make offerings to the spirits there.

In the islands north of Scotland an old remedy to calm storm waves was the sprinkling of holy water on the sea. Spilling oil on an angry sea to calm the waves is believed to have originated from the time when oil was used in this manner as an offering.

In 1397, the master of the *Trinity*, after being saved from shipwreck, offered to the Holy Virgin a silver replica of his ship. The Romans frequently made marble models of the ships that survived peril and placed them in the temple of Jupiter Redax.

During a severe gale on one of Columbus's voyages, peas were drawn from a cup to determine who would make a pilgrimage to the shrine of Our Lady of Guadeloupe with a five-pound taper. Columbus himself drew the lot and fulfilled the promise in gratitude for being saved from the storm.

The captain and crew of a Portuguese bark that barely escaped a violent tempest during the eighteenth century was said to have immediately gone in procession to offer thanksgiving at a nearby shrine after coming ashore. They decorated their ship's mainsail with flowers and carried it to the church for the mass.[1]

Sailors throwing their hats into the sea for a good luck offering was a tradition followed for many years after the days of the man-of-war. Homeward bound, homesick sailors were known to dangle a line overboard as a symbolic offering for wives and sweethearts to "pull the ship home."

In the early 1800s, as an offering for her son's safe return from sea, the lady owner of The Widow's Son Inn in Bow, London, set aside a hot cross bun every Good Friday if the lad was still at sea. Faithfully continuing the gesture after her son was lost, each Good Friday she added a hot cross to the moldy collection in a basket at the inn. Years after the old lady died, the tradition lived on; each Good Friday a sailor was invited to hang a fresh hot cross bun by the hearth to replace the one hung there the year before. Just as the owner had done, the stale hot cross bun was then placed in a basket and the sailor was given a free beer.

In a touching prayer for their father's safety at sea, English children would blow a kiss out to him at sea and chant the "kiss blessing": "I see the moon and the moon sees me, God bless our father on the sea." Children of Somerset, England, would throw an apple into the Bristol Channel and recite: "Come high tide or low tide whatever it be. Oh, God, bring my father home safely to me."

During the biggest Chinese festival of the year, the annual day of worship and thanksgiving to Tin Hau, Goddess of the Sea, thousands of boat people renew their heritage and pay tribute to their Queen of Heaven, Holy Mother, and protector of the Boat People. Junks, trawlers, freighters, tugs, workboats, and crane barges, all decorated in a blaze of bunting, banners, and flags, sail in procession down Hong Kong Harbor to two sacred shrines where homage is paid to their guardian angel of seafarers.[2]

Omens

This section will cover unusual omens and their related stories not already discussed.

Ted Richardson, former wheelsman on the Great Lakes freighter *Henry Phipps,* related that when sailing in the Straits of Mackinac in the late 1950s his vessel approached a U.S. Steel freighter that had gone aground. The captain of the *Phipps* warned his entire crew not to look at the beached vessel. To do so, he believed, represented an omen of ill luck, and the same fate was sure to fall upon those who looked at the grounded ship.

A veteran sailor serving aboard a U.S. Navy nuclear submarine informed me of a strange incident aboard his boat that was perceived as a bad omen. Each time the movie *Gray Lady Down* was shown, a life-threatening tragedy occurred aboard the sub. The movie, shown three different times, was about a submarine that sank and trapped its crew inside. After three serious misfortunes believed triggered by the showing of the movie, it was barred from being shown again.

Some of the most common bad omens include a black cat crossing one's path, which is a sign of bad luck for a day; the sight of a new moon through glass, which presages bad luck for twenty-eight days; a bird flying into a house or a picture falling from a wall, both frightening signs of death; and the breaking of a mirror, the familiar omen of bad luck for seven years. Because the seafarer was so susceptible to supernatural influences, the number of omens associated with maritime superstition is endless. Countless omens, signs of future good or evil, most often perceived by the mariner as evil, filled his life and everyday routine. Even if an omen was thought by

some as a good one, many others interpreted the sign as a forecast of bad luck.

The loss of an anchor, the sight of an umbrella aboard ship, a hatch cover upside down or dropped into a hold, the loss of a water bucket or mop at sea, an earthenware basin upside down, a deck of playing cards, and sneezing on the port side of a vessel were all believed omens of bad luck.

Fishermen believed that if you rowed a dory with the left hand, turning it against the sun, it was a sure bad omen. A suitcase carried on a ship, a violin aboard, or a partly filled bucket were particularly bad omens. It was a further bad sign if the first fish of a day was sold to someone with broad thumbs.

A strict superstition among submariners was that flowers should not be taken aboard their boat, as it was an omen portending the flowers would become a funeral wreath for a shipmate or the entire sub.

Chinese sailors considered shoes on deck a bad omen, West Indians saw the calabash gourd as a bad sign, and Scottish mariners saw bad luck coming upon seeing an upturned washbowl.

Fearful of enraging the devil by mocking the winds, most sailors will not whistle aboard a vessel. If a greenhorn whistled a happy tune while going about his work, he may have appeared to some as a happy sailor at work. To the superstitious, however, to hear someone whistling was an omen of bad luck.

While birds often aided the mariner to navigate or to predict storms, they were often considered either good or bad omens.

A bird on the liner *Queen Elizabeth* was believed to be the cause of delays, storms, and fog.[3]

Was it pure circumstance or was the strange bird that attacked the captain of the barque *Ellen* on September 12, 1857, a messenger of mercy? Seemingly out of nowhere an unknown bird with dark gray feathers, a wingspan of three and a half feet, and an eight-inch beak with teeth like a saw flew around and grazed the shoulder of Captain Johnson as he stood beside the helm on the quarterdeck. The bird then began to circle the vessel but soon flew back to and directly into the face of the captain. The bird violently flapping its wings, Johnson was able to grab the attacker but only after receiving a stinging bite on his thumb.

Two crewmen who joined in the fight managed to tie the bird's legs but were also bitten. Not giving up, the bird still tried to bite all within reach until its head was cut off and its body thrown into the sea. The barque was on a north northeast course when the bird was encountered. Believing the bird was an omen and a sign for him to change course, the captain did so by steering due east. Had the bird not come to the ship in this manner, Johnson would not have altered his course and he would not have found and saved from certain death forty-nine desperate survivors of the sunken vessel, *Central America*.[4]

Other strange and unexplained bad seafaring omens include women in white aprons, swans, tolling bells, pins or spinning wheels aboard a ship (because of their connection with witches), spitting into the sea, and counting fishing boats at sea.

The sound of a ringing glass (such as a wine glass) after it was accidentally struck was thought to be an omen of death for a sailor if the ringing was not stopped. When the ringing was stopped, a sailor was thought to be saved from drowning.[5]

Although sailors generally saw most omens as evil, there were a few sincerely believed good ones.

Whalers believed that if the carcass of a whale drifted away with the tide instead of sinking, it was an omen of good luck. Children aboard a vessel was always a good omen. Having bird droppings fall on a hat or cloak was an omen of good fortune. Sneezing on the right side of a vessel as well as sneezing three times was a good sign. A mouse seen swimming in a pail of water was taken as an omen for a prosperous voyage. Scottish fishermen believed that the first shedding of blood at the beginning of the new year was a good omen.

One of the most renowned omens is that of Saint Elmo's fire, or corposant, the fiery light that often appears at the tips of mastheads, yardarms, stays, etc. The glowing discharge, often accompanied by a crackling sound, takes place when the air in a storm is charged with electricity.

The belief in the supernatural character of the light is traced to ancient times when Roman sailors believed the lights were Castor and Pollux, patrons of mariners, and twin sons of Zeus, the king of gods in Greek mythology.

Erasmus, a Christian martyr (A.D. 303), was believed to have been a Sicilian bishop who died at sea during a tempest after vowing to appear to the imperiled crew if they were meant to be saved. The light, which appeared at the masthead after his death, was named after him. Elmo is thought to be a variant of Erasmus.[6]

Chinese sailors believed that their sea goddess, the Mother of Heaven, appeared in the lights, German mariners believed the lights were spirits of their dead comrades, French sailors saw the lights as a sign of death and referred to it as the wandering candle, Roman Catholic sailors saw the lights as the Holy ghost, corpus sancti, and in more recent years Greek sailors called it Telonia after a demon tax gatherer believed to extract toll from souls on the way to heaven.[7]

The Venetian Antonio Pigafetta, who wrote an articulate journal during Magellan's journey in 1519, said that during a violent storm, when the flotilla of five ships was under great fear of being lost, Saint Elmo "appeared in the form of a lighted torch at the height of the maintop, and remained there more than two hours and a half, to the comfort of us all. For we were in tears, expecting only the hour of our death." Whenever Saint Elmo's fire appears, Pigafetta wrote, "the ship never perishes."[8]

An excerpt from the second voyage of Columbus reads: "On Saturday, at night, the body of St. Elmo was seen, with seven lighted candles in the round top, and there followed mighty rain and frightful thunder. I mean the lights were seen which the seamen affirm to be the body of St. Elmo, and they sang litanies and prayers to him, looking upon it as most certain that in these storms, when he appears, there can be no danger. Whatever this is, I leave to others, for, if we may believe Pliny, when such lights appeared in those times to Roman sailors in a storm, they said they were Castor and Pollux."[9]

Generally considered a sign that the worst of a gale was over, if the fire was seen to rise it was a good omen; if it descended the omen was bad. Chinese sailors' belief was the opposite.

If the fire descended to the deck, it was an even more ominous sign, and should the light fall upon a sailor's head it meant that his death was near at hand. If the fire was seen in double form, it was thought to be an especially good omen.

Notes

1. Bassett, *Legends and Superstitions of the Sea and Sailors*, 379-98.
2. Maitland, *Setting Sails,* 125-27.
3. Opie and Tatem, *A Dictionary of Superstitions*, 26.
4. Beck, *Folklore and the Sea*, 292-93.
5. Opie and Tatem, *A Dictionary of Superstitions*, 173.
6. Bassett, *Legends and Superstitions of the Sea and Sailors*, 319-20.
7. Ibid., 314.
8. Humble, *The Explorers*, 124-25.
9. Bassett, *Legends and Superstitions of the Sea and Sailors*, 304.

17. Patron Saints

Piracy, Punishment

Sailors heard in their desperate plea,
By trusted patrons of the sea.
Ruthless pirates the world knew well,
Endless floggings, the sailor's hell.

Patron Saints

Although mariners viewed the black-robed clergy as the representatives of the Almighty on earth, a sign of the devil, or of death, many God-fearing Catholic sailors believed that Christ, the Holy Virgin, and the saints could still the wind and calm the angry sea.

The Virgin's aid to mariners is recorded as far back as A.D. 200 when, during a Varangian attack on Constantinople with Russian ships, Bishop Photius was said to have raised a tempest that destroyed the fleet by spreading the mantle of Our Lady of Blachernes on the waves. Many sea-side shrines and temples were built in her honor. Great miracles were attributed to an ancient statue of her at Venice, which was saluted by passing ships. The shrine of Notre Dame de la Garde at Marseilles was dedicated in honor of the Virgin's appearance to seafarers in peril. In 1700, Norman mariners who believed in her powers paid homage to Notre Dame de Deliverance, and the Norman legend of Notre Dame des Neiges at Havre relates how the Virgin caused a snowstorm to hide blockading ships and save them from the enemy.[1]

Saint Anne, whose apparition was also connected with Saint Elmo's fire, was especially honored as the patron saint of Canadian mariners. Depictions of her hovering over vessels in peril are hung at a church in Beaupre, Canada.[2]

Saint Anthony, thought to be one of the most powerful saints, was known to have preached to the fishes and was the patron saint of fishermen. When there was lack of wind, old French sailors believed that Saint Anthony, their patron of the wind, was angry or in slumber. In the doldrums, sailors sometimes swore or loudly whistled to wake him. Disrespect in this regard is related in an old story of becalmed Portuguese seamen who prayed to Saint Anthony but received no help. Against the wishes of the ship's pilot, the statue of the saint was lashed to the mast but still no favored winds came. Finally, after the sailors harshly insulted the saint, fair winds arose, and the statue was reverently returned to its niche.[3]

The prayers of Flemish fishermen were believed heard by Saint Arnould, who, it was said, assisted in bringing a whale to shore that was too large for the bay into which it was towed.[4]

A legend tells of Saint Asclas, who by his prayers prevented the movement of a boat on the Nile.[5]

Gun and powder sections on Mediterranean ships were long referred to as the *La Sainte Barbe* rooms in honor of Saint

Barbara, the patron saint of gunners. Mariners on the Koenig sea in Bavaria often invoked Saint Bartholomew before venturing out in their boats: "Holy Bartholomew! Shall I return? Say yes." An echo reportedly responded yes in fair weather and no in bad.[6]

It was believed that Saint Benedict could make iron float and would embark on a mat to help drowning sailors.[7] French sailors believed that Saint Beuzec merely had to lift his finger to calm a violent storm.[8]

Saint Christopher, said to have carried Christ across a river, has long been the patron saint of travelers. The theft of a statue of Saint Columba, a patron saint of northern nations, was said to have raised a tempest.[9] Saint Clement, whose emblem was an anchor, was another patron saint of mariners. He was believed to have suffered martyrdom when cast into the sea with an anchor around his neck.[10]

Saint Cyric was the favored patron of Welsh mariners.[11]

Saint Erasmus, or Saint Elmo, discussed in an earlier section, was connected with St. Elmo's fire, and St. Elias was a patron of Slavonic mariners[12]

Saint Francis Xavier was figured as a most powerful patron saint of sailors.[13]

The power of Saint Genevieve, the patron saint of harbors, was believed to have obliterated a tree in a Spanish harbor that contained two demons that wrecked many ships. Saint George, honored by Sardinian fishermen, was said to have driven away enemies of the tunnyfish. Saint Germanus was known to quiet a stormy sea with a few drops of oil in 429. Saint Gonzales de Tuy was also connected with Saint Elmo's fire legends.[14]

Saint Hermes was a famed patron of sailors in old England, Saint Helena calmed a storm by throwing pieces of the holy cross overboard, Saint Hilariion, when attacked by pirates, stopped their ship while under full sail, and French sailors honored Saint Houarden, who could calm the seas with a slight movement of his hand.[15]

Saint James the Greater, patron saint of Spanish seafarers, was believed to have sailed to Spain on a strange marble ship without sail or steering. Saint Kea was said to have sailed to shore on the rock he was praying on when surprised by the incoming tide. Saint Leonore was known to have rescued a sinking ship by waving a bishop's letter at it. Saint Loman was believed to have sailed against the wind and tide.[16]

Saint Marculf, by raising a storm with prayer, was believed to have destroyed an advancing pirate fleet. Saint Mark, the patron saint of Venetian fishermen, was believed to have calmed a tempest that raged when his body was being brought from Egypt. Saint Michael, god of the wind, renowned for winning a diving contest with the devil, was another patron of Sardinian fishermen. Legend tells that when the devil took his turn to dive, Saint Michael, by making the sign of the cross over the sea, caused it to freeze over the demon.[17]

Saint Nicholas is perhaps far more renowned as a maritime patron than even Saint Peter the chosen leader of the twelve apostles and the rock upon which the Catholic church was built. He was a bishop of Myra, an ancient seaport on the River Andracus in the province of Lycia on the southwest coast of Asia Minor. Once a great grain center, the site is now know as Dembre.

His connection to the sea came during his endeavors in piloting grain ships to the city of Myra beset by famine. These efforts were accomplished despite the fact that the man was not known as a sailor, nor was he familiar with the sea. After this undertaking, an incident took place that would permanently affix his name in a high place of honor among all seamen.

A ship heading for Myra was caught in a vicious storm that gravely threatened all those aboard. Given to prayers, some of the sailors who recalled hearing of the famous Bishop Nicholas called on him to save them from the great peril. Out of nowhere there suddenly appeared a total stranger working among the crew as if he had been aboard for the entire voyage. Whether or not this was taken as a sign is not known, but sails were trimmed, and the ship, set on a sure course, came through the storm. The stranger had vanished before their eyes as quickly as he had appeared. When the storm-tossed vessel finally reached port, the sailors went to the nearby church to give thanks for their survival. There, to their astonishment, they found Bishop Nicholas, the very stranger who had mysteriously appeared on their stricken vessel and rescued them from the tempest. It was through this lifesaving deed that word of the miraculous works of Saint Nicholas spread throughout the Mediterranean, to Europe, and to America.

His good works were known to landsmen as well. The legend relates how he tucked money beneath the pillows of young ladies in trouble, or under the doors of the poor and elderly. While spending the night at an inn, he also brought back to life innocent victims of a heinous murder. In the inn's pantry, perhaps to satisfy mid-night hunger, he discovered that the innkeeper had murdered and dismembered three boys, stuffing them in a pickle barrel in a plan to sell the fresh meat from their limbs at the market. Saint Nicholas, it is said, brought the lads back to life and saw them home to their beds. From this legend statues of the saint sometimes depict him with three boys and a barrel.

He was also known as the patron saint of rivermen. Statues of his likeness were commonly seen near bridges or hazardous rapids where from his vantage he would guide the unwary tug or barge skipper past the danger. Many are the stories of those captains who, not saluting Saint Nicholas out of indifference or irreverence, would wind up wrecked on the rocks. Once a barge was caught in violent flood waters on the River Saone in France. The captain pleaded to a nearby statue of Saint Nicholas before entering the raging rapids: "If you will but save me, I promise to place before you a candle as tall and thick as the mast of my ship." When the rapids went calm, the barge captain turned back to St. Nicholas and cried out, "Ha! You will get no candle from me, Bishop!" His insult, it was said, was the reason his vessel was lost on an uncharted reef at the very next bend of the raging river.

Saint Nicholas, the Good Samaritan and mystical figure known throughout most of the world, still performs his legendary and wondrous deeds for those who believe. If you disbelieve his works, look closely at the magic in children's eyes at Christmas time and ask them about St. Nick, whom they know as Santa Claus.[18]

Saint Ninian was a Scottish maritime patron. Saint Phocas was a patron maritime saint of Greek seamen. In the legend of Saint Patrick, who was believed mighty against the sea, it is related that when a leper was refused passage on a ship, the saint cast a stone altar into the sea, which the leper sailed on in company with the ship. Saint Peter, the apostle fisherman, often invoked during storms, is the chief patron saint of fishermen.[19]

Saint Ringar and Saint Ronald were also favored patrons of Scottish sailors, and Saint Rosalia was venerated by Sicilian mariners.[20] Saint Sauveur is the fishermen's patron saint in Normandy. Saint Telme and Saint Thomas were also favored patron saints of the sea. Saint Peter, Saint Hyacinth, Saint Marinus, Saint Columba, Saint Blaise, Saint Telme, Saint Francis de Paul, and Saint Scothinus were all known to have walked on the sea.[21]

Piracy

Piracy is thought to be the world's third oldest profession behind prostitution and medicine. Bold, organized depredation of ships at sea was widespread among the earliest seafarers in the Middle East. In the Mediterranean, treacherous thieves of the sea, during the last hundred years of Roman rule, plundered four hundred towns, captured and held hostage Julius Caesar, and threatened the very core of Roman expansion. Arabs of the Red Sea, the Barbary corsairs of Algiers and Tunis, the highly feared pirates of the Persian Gulf, and the active Chinese and Malays all plagued and seized ships with ruthless abandon.[22]

Sea raiders fell under two distinct classifications. Pirates were those who attacked ships of every nation; buccaneers, or *boucaniers* from the French for "smoker of meat," defined the early herdsmen of the Caribbean island of Hispaniola, who smoked their meat in *boucans*. When these islanders took to sea roving, even though their depredations were piratical, their acts were considered lawful because they were directed only against the Spanish.

By the beginning of the nineteenth century, piracy had died away leaving behind a romantic heritage of legends and adventures of some of the most feared men ever to sail the seas. Word of their treachery, hideous torture, and wanton killing spread far and wide, striking mortal terror in those who espied the "jolly roger," the feared skull and crossbones flag of the pirate. Some of these fears were much exaggerated. The widely rumored and horrible fate of blindfolded victims, prodded by a pirate's sword, walking a plank to their death in the sea, it appears, was mostly rumor, for there is only one known case of this ever taking place. This single incident was believed to have been accomplished by Major Stede Bonnet, who, it was said, took to pirating after retiring from the army with the rank of major to escape his nagging wife.[23]

After outfitting a ten-gun sloop at his own expense, in 1717, he and a crew of seventy men launched a career that brought him a high degree of success among those of his kind. It was estimated that at the time fifteen hundred pirates were working the waters off the coast of North America. Even though Bonnet was pardoned when he surrendered and vowed to end his pirating to help curtail the marauders, he changed his name to Captain Thomas and went back to piracy. His adventures ended with his capture and hanging at Charleston, South Carolina, in November 1718.[24]

It is ironic that no other pirate captured worldwide attention, and admiration as did Capt. William Kidd. As far as being successful at his work, he ranked only second or third compared with his ruthless peers, having captured only two or three ships. In 1695, Kidd signed articles that gave him a commission from King William III to apprehend and suppress pirates off the coast of America. He set out on this mission in the ship *Adventure*, financed by a privateer enterprise, and was not heard from again until 1698, when ugly word spread of his piracy in the Indian Ocean. He next appeared in New York in 1699 in a small vessel flaunting valuable booty, and was arrested in an embarrassing and awkward situation by the royalty who appointed him. Returned to England in chains and charged with piracy and murder, Kidd could not produce documents to prove that the ships taken by him were lawful prizes. He became the scapegoat of the scandal, and a charge of murder was apparently drummed up to assure his conviction. Kidd was innocent and within his right, because the man he killed was a mutinous gunner aboard his ship *Adventure*. Captain Kidd was found guilty and executed on May 23, 1701. His body afterwards hung in chains on public display at Execution Dock, Wapping, England. A sad and much belated postscript to this story is that the documents that would have proven Captain Kidd's innocence were found in a Public Records Office two hundred years later.[25]

No pirate struck more terror in the lives of those that ventured on the sea than Capt. Edward Teach, better known as Blackbeard. He threatened and often paralyzed shipping in Atlantic waters from Trinidad to Newfoundland.

Sporting a long black beard plaited into many tails that grew from below his eyes, the tall, fierce-looking man presented a grim and fearful appearance. In combat, he wore slings that holstered three pairs of pistols. To further promote his hellish looks, he would stick lighted matches under the brim of his hat.

Originally from Bristol, England, Teach began his pirate career in 1716. Taking at first smaller vessels, he soon seized a large forty-gun French ship, which he named *Queen Ann's Revenge*. With this vessel he was capable of taking larger prizes. Ship after ship fell into his hands. Laying off Charleston, South Carolina, he took every vessel that came into or left that port, "striking great Terror to the whole Province of Carolina." Soon commanding three ships, he turned his treachery against his own by wrecking two of his vessels, sailing off with the booty and his closest comrades, while deserting the remainder of the lot on a small island. He next surrendered to, received a pardon from, and entered into a close friendship with North Carolina Gov. Charles Eden, with whom, it was rumored, he shared a good portion of his treasure.

The good governor officiated at the marriage of the pirate and a sixteen-year-old girl, Teach's thirteenth wife. Bidding farewell to his new bride in June 1718, he continued his work taking many ships while sailing to the Bermudas, the booty of which was shared with his governor friend.

Lt. Robert Maynard, dispatched by Governor Spotswood of Virginia colony in the sloop HMS *Ranger*, found and attacked Teach's ship, which was aground near the mouth of the James River. Furious hand-to-hand fighting ensued between Maynard and the pirate, who died after receiving twenty-five wounds. Maynard returned with Blackbeard's head to Bath Town, Virginia, where he received a triumphant and relieved ovation. Teach being dead, for a time piracy fears subsided; his career lasted only about two years.[26]

The Welsh Capt. Bartholomew Roberts, considered the most successful pirate, was said to have taken over four hundred vessels from Brazil to Newfoundland. A strict disciplinarian, this tall black man drank only tea, ordered lights out by 8:00 p.m., disallowed gambling, and threatened death to any man who brought a woman aboard his vessels disguised as a man. He even tried to persuade a parson taken as prisoner to sign on his ship to care for the spiritual needs of his crew.

He flew a flag of his own design depicting a figure of himself with sword in hand standing atop two skulls that signified Barbadian and Martinican heads. His pirate career began about 1720 and ended when he was hit in the throat with grapeshot on February 10, 1722, and was thrown overboard in his full ornate dress. He was only about forty years old at the time.[27]

Another renowned pirate was Capt. John Avery, nicknamed Long Ben, who was the subject of several popular plays and novels of his time. Like the famous Captain Kidd, at the height of his career in 1695, his supposed romantic adventures generated much public attention. He died a pauper in his thirties.[28]

Capt. Thomas Goldsmith, said to have amassed a great fortune as a pirate during the reign of Queen Anne, was believed to have been the only pirate to have died in bed. The epitaph on his tombstone read:

Men that are virtuous serve the Lord;
And the Devil's by his friends ador'd;
And as they merit get a place
Amidst the bless'd or hellish race;
Pray then, ye learned clergy show
Where can this brute, Tom Goldsmith, go?
Whose life was one continual evil,
Striving to cheat God, Man, and Devil.[29]

The careers of two female pirates, Anne Bonny and Mary Read, crossed paths when, disguised as men, they signed on with Capt. John "Calico Jack" Rackam. When still living at home, the hot-tempered Bonny was said to have killed her maidservant with a knife. The equally hostile Mary Read forced an argument with a pirate who was to engage in a duel with her lover and killed him on the spot.

Seizing many Jamaican ships, the band she ran with was captured after a short period. Mary Read died of fever in prison in 1720. Anne Bonny's execution was postponed for health reasons, and her ultimate fate is unknown.

Known to have butchered his prisoners without the slightest provocation, the pirate John Phillips became a most successful marauder after his career began in 1723. Through nine months of command, Phillips seized more than thirty ships from Barbados to Newfoundland.[30] Insight into a pirate's life can be gained through the articles drawn up by Capt. John Phillips's crew aboard the *Revenge*:

1.

Every man shall obey civil Command; the Captain shall have one full Share and a half in all Prizes; the Master, Carpenter, Boatswain and Gunner shall have one Share and quarter.

2.

If any Man shall offer to run away, or keep any Secret from the Company, he shall be maroon'd with one Bottle of Powder, one Bottle of Water, one small Arm, and Shot.

3.

If any Man shall steal any Thing in the Company, or game to the Value of a Piece of Eight, he shall be Marroon'd or shot.

4.

If at any Time we should meet another Marrooner (that is, Pyrate,) that Man that shall sign his Articles without the Consent of our Company, shall suffer such Punishment as the Captain and Company shall think fit.

5.

That Man that shall strike another whilst these Articles are in force, shall receive Moses's Law (that is 40 Stripes lacking one) on the bare Back.

6.

That Man that shall snap his Arms, or smoak Tobacco in the Hold, without a cap to his Pipe, or carry a Candle lighted without a Lanthorn, shall suffer the same Punishment as in the former Article.

7.

That Man that shall not keep his Arms clean, fit for an Engagement, or neglect his Business, shall be cut off from his Share, and suffer such other Punishment as the Captain and the Company shall think fit.

8.

If any Man shall lose a Joint in time of an Engagement, shall have 400 Pieces of Eight; if a limb, 800.

9.

If at any time you meet with a prudent Woman, that Man that offers to meddle with her, without her Consent, shall suffer present Death.[31]

Surprisingly, the famous explorer Sir Francis Drake and the father of the U.S. Navy, John Paul Jones, were considered pirates.

For his buccaneer molestation of Spanish shipping, Drake was called "the Pirate" by the Spaniards. He took and then burnt Portobelo and sacked Vera Cruz in 1572. In 1578 he plundered Valparaiso and seized a great treasure ship from Acapulco. After he was knighted by Queen Elizabeth for being the first Englishman to circle the globe, his exploits, under commission, were thereby not considered piratical.

As a rebel, John Paul Jones, in command of a privateer in 1777, was feared as the terror to British shipping off the British Isles.

At one time in South Carolina forty-nine pirates were hanged in a single month. Life expectancy of pirates was woefully short. It was said that there was only one pirate to have died in bed and only one pirate grave marked with a tombstone.

Piracy has been blamed for many mysterious ship losses, especially those in the Bermuda Triangle. According to the International Maritime Bureau records, there have been 450 pirate attacks since 1984 and over 90 attacks in 1993. Capt. Edward Agbakoba, the bureau's expert on piracy, estimates that his agency receives only half of the reports that occur.

Most of the attacks took place in the South China Sea and north Asia, where piracy is seen to be on the rise. While the South-east Asia region is currently experiencing the most attacks, West Africa and the northeast coast of South America are also considered highly dangerous areas. The marauders dash out from shore in speedboats to capture larger vessels. Extra watches are posted and fire hoses are kept handy to repel attackers. As an added precaution, some vessels are even wrapped in barbed wire.

Most of the pirates go after the ship's safe, which could contain tens of thousands of dollars for payrolls and port fees. Although entire cargoes are taken too, sometimes a specific container is targeted, suggesting that the attackers have received inside information.

Aside from the danger to the crew who become the victims of a pirate attack, the sobering navigational and environmental threat is also of great concern. In some instances the crews of ships have been tied up with the vessel left to steam ahead on its own at full power with no one in control.

Led by the stench of rotting flesh, when workers began cutting up the Australian freighter *Erria Inge*, they found the remains of ten men who had been doused with gasoline, burned to death, and stuffed in the ship's long vacant refrigerator. The 17,000-ton vessel was attacked in 1991.

Pirates killed the British captain and his Filipino first officer when they boarded the Danish-owned freighter *Baltimar Zephir* off Indonesia in December 1992. These increasingly vicious and fatal attacks indicate that the same ruthlessness and audacity practiced by pirates of old is still taking place today.[32]

Punishment

In the early navy days cruel and severely harsh punishment for the slightest infraction permeated a sailor's life with fear. For the seaman to exist in a world governed by the strict articles he signed was harsh enough. However, those unfortunates who served under unscrupulous authorities that ruled with an absurd interpretation of those articles, or who supplemented the articles with their own regulations, made life even more miserable for the lowly sailor. An old article of war in the Royal Navy stated that "all crimes not capital shall be punished according to the customs and manners used at sea," thereby allowing captains to resort to any mode of punishment they considered proper. Countless and repetitive acts of inhumane cruelty were issued under the guise of discipline.

The most widely issued punishment was flogging. Out of a red bag would come the cat-o'-nine-tails, thus the expression, "Letting the cat out of the bag." The bag was red to hide bloodstains. Tails of knotted cord about two feet long were attached to a short wooden stick. For more serious offenses, such as theft, the thieves' cat was used, having longer and heavier tails knotted along the full length of each tail. Lest those who administered the flogging be flogged themselves, the punishment had to be applied with fervor and was carefully scrutinized to assure compliance. A "fresh hand" often took over after six or a dozen lashes. "All hands to witness punishment" was a cry that sent chills up the spines of those who would receive or even watch the flogging. The only humane aspect about the punishment was that a fresh cat was used instead of a bloodstained one to guard against infection. Typical sentences on U.S. man-of-wars before 1850 when flogging was abolished were: "Pilfering rum, unpaid shore debt, spitting on another man, or dropping a bucket from aloft, 12 lashes; disrespectful language to master-at-arms or being slow to enter a boat, 6 lashes; appearing naked on deck, 9 lashes; mutinous disrespect to officer, 40 lashes; drunkenness or mutinous conduct, 50 lashes." Because blood was usually drawn after only the fourth lash, the ship's doctor was nearby to tend to the victims, whose back received a bucket of saltwater after the scourging. In hope of lessening the intensity or the number of lashes, some sailors had a cross tattooed on their backs.

In the Royal Navy, flogging punishment was the most severe of all with regard to the number of lashes issued per offense. As many as five dozen lashes could be dealt without trial or court-martial for any offense the captain or his officers considered a crime.

In the early 1800s, on a vessel lying off Spithead, the escape of four impressed seamen was foiled when word of their plans leaked out. Tried by court-martial, they were sentenced to three hundred lashes each through the fleet. A launch containing the offenders, the master-at-arms, and a doctor was prepared so that the unfortunates could be rowed from ship to ship enabling the entire fleet to witness the spectacle. Stockings were placed over the men's wrists before they were lashed to a pole rigged fore and aft of the launch to prevent the tearing of flesh, common when a man writhed in agony from the high number of lashes. After an officer read the sentence, the punishment began. Receiving about two dozen lashes, the prisoners were then conveyed to the next ship escorted by a flotilla composed of boats from each vessel and accompanied by the strains of "the rogues' march." Because the victim often lapsed into unconsciousness during the ordeal, every effort was made to bring him around, including the pouring of wine down his throat. When the doctor declared that the man could take no more, he was placed in sick bay until such time that he recovered enough to withstand the remainder of his punishment. If there were many ships in the fleet and a man could withstand the lashes, the ceremony might have taken half a day.[33]

Some offenders, knowing they could not withstand so many lashes, humbly asked to be hanged instead, but the request was coldly denied and carried out whether the prisoner was dead or alive.

Punishment in the U.S. Navy was left up to the commander's discretion as well. Officers did not receive physical punishment, but enlisted men did; flogging was most often prescribed. More serious crimes, such as treason or desertion, resulted in hanging. Under regulation, captains were forbidden from issuing more than twelve lashes, a court-martial being required if the offense necessitated more. Some commanders, however, by dividing the offense into several smaller charges, could sidestep the ruling by administering twelve lashes for each of the lesser offenses. When seaman Thomas Ayscough was found drunk aboard the USS *Constitution,* he was, on November 23, 1804, given forty-eight lashes, in four increments of twelve for four separate offenses. By not charging the man with drunkenness, which would have called for a court-martial, he was found guilty of four lesser counts and flogged accordingly.[34]

The punishment called "starting" was more spontaneous and common, but no less brutal. The boatswain's mate, directed by the officers, would *start* a man by beating him with a rope's end. Often stripped to the waist, the offender was beat without being tied up and was therefore often injured trying to escape the blows. So severe was this punishment that many men could not wear their jackets for several days.[35]

Cobbing was a punishment issued by striking the offender's backside twelve times with a barrel stave. When beginning the punishment, the man striking the offender would cry, "Watch!" and all those nearby would remove their hats or receive the same treatment. The last stroke, called the "purse," was the hardest one given.[36]

Gagging was prescribed for those daring enough to make an ill comment to superiors. His hands bound behind him and his legs in irons, the offender's mouth was forced open to take an iron bolt that was bound and tied behind his head. An offender was also often hoisted aloft regardless of the weather or left guarded on deck until the captain in his good time decided to release him. Tongue scraping was another remedy for those with sharp words. Voiced discontent was seldom heard, for to do so bordered on mutiny.

Being made to run the gauntlet was a punishment inflicted without courtmartial, most often issued for petty theft. The offender was tied in a tub with his bare backside in a highly vulnerable position. After first receiving four dozen lashes by the boatswain and his mates, the offender was then pulled around the deck by boys passing through two rows of men who were each provided with a three-rope knotted scourge. Depending on the number of men aboard, the victim might receive as many as six hundred lashes.[37]

Hardly imagined as a more drastic punishment than flogging, keelhauling was considered even more cruel. The offender was hoisted by tackle to the fore yardarm and dropped into the sea. Weights were attached to the victim so that he would sink deep enough to be hauled beneath the keel and hoisted up from the opposite yardarm. The punishment was sometimes made more dreadful by the firing of cannon directly above the man after he plunged into the water.

Boys were punished by holding or confining them in the dark and foul reaches of the ship's hold for an hour or longer. If the offender was not penitent enough, the practice of "letting in the light" followed: lowering a lantern near the youngster, which illuminated the rats and filth in the area. The left hands of boys were sometimes tied together while their right hands whipped one another as they danced around in a spirited jig. Mastheading, or confinement aloft in all kinds of weather, was also a favorite punishment for boys, especially in the early navy.

Specially devised corporal punishments were dealt to cooks or stewards for uncleanliness, hoarding, wasting, or burning food. In 1852, a cook on the ship *Columbus* was made to gulp down the scorched pudding he had prepared for the crew. For those who avoided work by feigning illness, called "sogering" or "playing possum," offenders might have received an extra heavy dose of salts or a mixture of Spanish flies and pepper sauce.

Ducking, a punishment phased out near the end of the seventeenth century, consisted of fastening a rope around the offender's body, hauling him high to a yardarm, then dropping him repeatedly into the sea.

A punishment for lying was to be hoisted to the mainstay for an hour, after which the offender was made to clean the seats in the head, where he received the honor of being "the liar of the head." For undue profanity, officers gave up a day's pay; seamen were made to wear a wooden collar, which could be made more burdensome by adding weights according to the degree of the offense.

Minor offenses brought restrictions of pay, liberty, food, sleep, and water. It was punishment enough when water was scarce to place the drinking cup at the masthead. If a man was thirsty enough, he was made to climb to get the cup, bring it down to drink, and then return it. Not being allowed to pass the cup to another, each man had to make the climb himself or go thirsty.

In 1842, the highly controversial and shameful hanging of three men wrongfully suspected of mutiny took place aboard the U.S. brig *Somers*. Ambiguous evidence—a dime novel, a dirk, and a list of crewmen's names—was discovered in a midshipman's seabag. After the mid was observed whispering to a boatswains mate and another seaman, the three were placed under arrest. When others in the crew appeared to be "muttering mutinously," four others were put in irons. The three "ringleaders" pleaded their innocence during a drumhead trial, and thereafter were held in irons with canvas bags over their heads. The next morning, on the captain's recommendation and junior officer's concurrence, the three supposed leaders were hanged from the yardarm. Word of the incident leaked to the press and enraged the public after the vessel reached the Brooklyn Naval Yard. The three men had been hanged at sea on scant and flimsy evidence when the vessel was near St. Thomas, where they could have been tried in port. Although a court of inquiry concurred with the captain's actions, Secretary of the Navy Upshur charged him with murder, but he was later acquitted. The last hanging at sea took place in 1855, and the last reported mutiny aboard a U.S. Navy vessel was in 1890.[38]

Pirates dealt victims their own special brand of sadistic cruelty, which was more torture than punishment. A game was played by lashing captives while the pirates rode atop their shoulders. Some victims were tied to the mast and pelted with broken bottles before being killed. Other prisoners were made to run around a mast while being jabbed with sharp weapons in a game called "sweating." Intoxicated pirates sometimes made teetotaling prisoners drink large quantities of rum without stopping. Perhaps the most sadistic of all tortures was the stuffing of pitch in a victim's mouth and setting it afire.

In an effort to obtain information a mild taste of their own medicine was given some captured pirates when heavy weights were placed on their chests as they lay on their backs.

Notes

1. Bassett, *Legends and Superstitions of the Sea and Sailors*, 76.
2. Ibid., 81.
3. Rappoport, *Superstitions of Sailors*, 88-90.
4. Bassett, *Legends and Superstitions of the Sea and Sailors*, 85.
5. Ibid., 83.
6. Ibid., 81.
7. Ibid., 83.
8. Rappoport, *Superstitions of Sailors*, 87.
9. Bassett, *Legends and Superstitions of the Sea and Sailors*, 84.
10. Ibid., 83.
11. Ibid., 82.
12. Ibid., 84.
13. Ibid.
14. Ibid., 81-83.
15. Ibid.
16. Ibid., 83.
17. Ibid., 82-83.
18. Lindquist, *The Legend of Saint Nicholas*, 24-27.
19. Bassett, *Legends and Superstitions of the Sea and Sailors*, 84.
20. Ibid., 82-83.
21. Ibid., 85.
22. Gosse, *The Pirates' Who's Who*, 11.
23. Ibid., 51-55.
24. Ibid.
25. Ibid., 180-82.
26. Ibid., 291-95.
27. Ibid., 261-65.
28. Ibid., 40-43.
29. Ibid., 137.
30. Ibid., 244-45.
31. Ibid. 16-17.
32. *Detroit Free Press*, Nov. 30, 1993.
33. Robinson, *Jack Nastyface*, 139-41.
34. Fowler, *Jack Tars and Commodores*, 137-38.
35. Robinson, *Jack Nastyface*, 147-48.
36. Thrower, *Life at Sea in the Age of Sail*, 96.
37. Robinson, *Jack Nastyface*, 143.
38. Roscoe and Freeman, *Picture History of the U.S. Navy*, 491.

18. Regions Feared

Rescue

Ageless feared regions on the main,
Where seamen test the Triangle's fame.
Where brave ships sail 'n the strange sea takes.
The Horn, the Forties, the November lakes.

Regions Feared

The first region feared by the ancient mariners was the waters of the central Mediterranean. There, in what they thought was the great ocean that flowed around the world, lurked all the unknown terrors of the deep. After extended and unmolested sailing in these waters, it was thought that all sea perils must lie west of the Isle of Sicily, then beyond the Straits of Gibraltar (thought by some to be the end of the world), and soon to the so-called sea of darkness in the western Atlantic.

Although many of these unfounded fears subsided, through later voyages of discovery, other sinister and life-threatening regions of the oceans came to be known. Some of the ancient fears linger as mariners today still fearfully respect the legendary waters of the western Atlantic, in the area now known as the Bermuda Triangle, the Dragon's Triangle in the Pacific, and other dreaded regions of the seas.

Of all the oceans, two renowned regions have similar unexplained phenomena, aberrations, and anomalies of communication blackouts, pronounced compass deviations, navigational instrument failures, and freak weather and sea conditions. These regions are the famed Bermuda Triangle in the western Atlantic and the Dragon's Triangle in the western Pacific.

The Bermuda Triangle is known to lie within the area bounded by Bermuda, Puerto Rico, and Miami. It is not indicated on any map or chart except the air and sea charts of the British Admiralty that delineate the area as a zone of magnetic aberration.

The Dragon's Triangle, or as called by the Japanese the Ma-no Umi, Sea of the Devil, falls roughly within the triangular boundaries of Tokyo, the Mariana Islands, and Guam.

The unique characteristics the two triangles share and how they are related is most fascinating.

Both triangles are situated southeast of a continental land mass in areas where warm and cold ocean currents clash. The deepest part of the Atlantic Ocean, the 27,510-foot deep Puerto Rico Trench, lies in the Bermuda Triangle, and the deepest part of the Pacific Ocean, the 35,800-foot deep Mariana Trench, lies within the boundaries of the Dragon's Triangle. Both triangles are situated almost exactly on opposite sides of the earth from each other. They both lie between longitude 20° and 35° east and west and both are close to the same latitude north and south.

Also intriguing is the fact that both triangles are either crossed or bounded by the earth's agonic lines (invisible magnetic paths between the North and South magnetic poles) along which, because of irregularities in the earth's magnetic field, compass needles indicate magnetic north and true north at the same time.[1]

Both triangles are associated with the strange disappearance of ships and aircraft that vanish without a trace of survivors, wreckage, or flotsam. The mysterious losses sustained in these two regions far outweigh those in any other waters of the world.

Some historians believe that the Dragon's Triangle has claimed ships for more than a thousand years, pointing to records of vessels lost from the time of the Chinese dynasties of Sung and Yuan and the Japanese medieval shogunates.[2]

Ancient sailors in this region blamed the mysterious losses of fishing boats on dragons, which are said to snatch the boats and their occupants from the surface of the sea and drag them down to their abode. According to a Chinese legend of

900 B.C., waters near of a small island within six days sail from Suzhou, in Kiangsu province, were unapproachable even in calm weather because of a dragon's underwater palace beneath the island. It was said that those who ventured near the area heard strange noises and saw strange lights over the sea at night visible from a hundred miles away.[3]

About 1945, Japanese maritime communities and scientific authorities noted the disappearance of several patrol ships and fishing boats off the coast of Japan. As early as 1950, the growing number of missing seamen together with the continuing disappearance of larger vessels and their crews led the Japanese Shipping Administration to declare the Ogasawara Island chain and environs an official danger area for shipping.[4]

The simultaneous disappearance of five Japanese warships in early 1942 is still a mystery. Because the three destroyers and two small aircraft carriers were operating in home waters near Japan, it is unlikely that they were sunk by enemy forces, who, had they been involved, would surely have taken credit for the losses. Moreover, in those early days of the war, it was unlikely that the United States and Great Britain had warships in that area.[5]

In connection with the believed magnetic disturbances in this triangle, the operation of our navy submarines was greatly impaired because of the malfunction of magnetic detonators on their torpedoes. Sometimes the hunters became the hunted when torpedoes turned and streaked toward the subs that launched them. Even though the magnetic detonators were state of the art, torpedoes had to be refitted with the older contact detonators.[6]

Like the strange messages heard from those who vanished in Atlantic's triangle was the one made by a Japanese pilot on a night patrol in a Kawanishi Flying Boat before the invasion of Iwo Jima. Before the plane disappeared he radioed: "Something is happening in the sky . . . . The sky is opening up. . . ."[7]

Ten vessels along with their crews and passengers disappeared or mysteriously sank in the triangle from 1949 to 1954. One of these, the *Kaio Maru No. 5*, sent out on a research expedition to determine the cause of the many losses, also disappeared in calm seas and good weather. No oil slick was found even though the vessel carried 150 tons of oil, and all seemed normal at the time of its last radio contact. Five empty oil drums from the vessel were the only items ever found. Ancient legends were recalled when a Japanese magazine suggested that the *Kaio Maru* might have been swallowed by dragons.[8]

Within a two-week period in March 1957, three U.S. military aircraft disappeared.

It is known that many more bigger ships and larger aircraft have mysteriously disappeared in the Dragon's Triangle than in the Bermuda Triangle. The estimate of losses may be exceptionally low even though a pattern of losses has been established. Many more early losses could be hidden under the veil of myth or legend, or in later years, when unexplained, were attributed to adverse weather or war casualties.

According to the Japanese Maritime Safety Agency, 1,427 vessels disappeared with no trace in the area of the Dragon's Triangle between 1968 and 1972.[9]

The area also claimed the largest vessel ever lost. The 227,912-ton *Berge Istra* sank a few moments after a massive explosion 170 miles southwest of Mindanao in the Philippines on December 29, 1975. She was bound from Brazil to Kimitsu in Tokyo Bay with a thirty-two-man crew and a cargo of iron ore. Although two of her crew miraculously were saved after being blown off the ship, they were at a loss in trying to determine the cause of the explosion.[10]

The only reference by ancient mariners of a danger zone in the Atlantic with plausible relation to the Bermuda Triangle is that alluded to in their description of the "sea of darkness" in the western ocean and in the Islands of the Bermudas thought to have been inhabited by devils.[11]

No "official" danger area exists in the Bermuda Triangle according to the United States Coast Guard. Upon requesting information in this regard from the Seventh USCG District, which handles search and rescue in that region, one will receive a form letter stating:

> The "Bermuda Triangle," or "Devil's Triangle," is a mythical geographic area located off the southeastern coast of the United States which is noted for an apparent high incidence of unexplained losses of ships, small boats, and aircraft.

> Countless theories attempting to explain the many disappearances have been offered throughout the history of the area. The most reasonable seem to be citing human errors and environmental factors.

> The U.S. Coast Guard is not impressed with supernatural explanations of disasters at sea. It has been our experience that the combined forces of nature and the unpredictability of mankind outdo science fiction stories many times each year.

It is believed that Columbus was the first to encounter the same sinister phenomena that have given the Atlantic Triangle its famed reputation. The first record of a mysterious experience in the area now known as the Bermuda Triangle comes from the explorer's first voyage. Before sighting land, he witnessed "glowing waters" off the Bahamas, a fireball that plunged into the sea after it circled his flagship, and irregular spinning of his ship's compass. During a later voyage he experienced an unusual "whirlwind" that claimed three of his vessels by "turning them three or four times about . . . without any storm or roughness of the sea."[12]

Charles Berlitz, in his book, Without a Trace, has composed a list of 143 sailing vessels, steamers, freighters (including colliers, cargo, and tankers), pleasure boats, aircraft, and other craft that have disappeared in the general area of or believed heading into the Bermuda Triangle since 1800. Resulting from these 148 losses, over 2,000 people vanished. In 46 of the cases, the number of lives lost is unknown.[13] The largest loss of lives were those missing from the USS Cyclops, a navy collier that vanished in March 1918 with 309 officers and crew, and whose disappearance is considered, according to a Department of the Navy, Office of Information, fact sheet, "one of the most baffling mysteries in the annals of the Navy."

Charles Lindbergh may have been the first pilot to encounter and record erratic aircraft instrument behavior in the area. During a flight from Havana to the mainland in the *Spirit of St. Louis* on February 13, 1928, he made the following log entry:

> Both compasses malfunctioned over Florida Straight [sic], at night. The earth indicator needle wobbled back and forth. The liquid compass card rotated without stopping. Could recognize no stars through heavy haze. Located position, at daybreak, over Bahama Islands, nearly 300 miles off course. Liquid compass card kept rotating until the Spirit of St. Louis reached the Florida Coast.[14]

Also in 1928, a Fokker trimotor on a similar flight from Havana to Miami "lost" Florida because of a serious compass deviation. Ditching in the sea resulted in the loss of the aircraft, passengers, and cargo. The pilots and a radio operator lived to relate the strange compass malfunction.[15]

Through the thirties and forties, continued malfunction of compasses and the strange disappearances of aircraft, including the loss of ten planes from two military flights from Bermuda to Europe in World War II, were not mysteriously related to the Triangle until December 5, 1945, when public attention was aroused with the famed disappearance of five TBM *Avengers* and a PBM *Martin Mariner* rescue plane dispatched to find the five lost aircraft.[16]

Flight 19, an over-water training flight under the command of instructor and lead pilot Lt. Charles C. Taylor, departed NAS Fort Lauderdale intending to accomplish a triangular route navigation problem.

Lieutenant Taylor, a combat veteran with over twenty-five hundred hours flying time in TBMs, was accompanied by four naval pilots in an advanced training program and nine aircrewmen, who, except for one man, were undergoing advanced aircrew training. The four student pilots had about three hundred hours flying time each with about sixty of those hours in TBMs or TBFs.

During preflight of the aircraft, instruments were checked, survival gear was examined, and fuel tanks were checked full, having enough fuel for 5-1/2 hours of flight. It was noted without concern, that none of the aircraft had a clock. Aircraft clocks were a much sought-after souvenir and each airman was issued a watch anyway.

A takeoff time of 1345 was delayed because of the late arrival of Lieutenant Taylor, who requested to be replaced by another pilot. Stating he did not want to take this flight out, his request was denied; no replacement pilot was available. Having recently transferred from NAS Miami, where he had been assigned similar duty, it would be his first exercise with this training hop.

The weather in the area of the flight was checked as favorable with a moderate to rough sea as confirmed by another flight that had conducted the same training exercise an hour earlier.

The flight departed at 1408; a student was in the lead and the instructor, Fox Tare two eight (FT-28), tracked the four trainees at the rear. Cruising at 150 miles per hour, the flight would arrive at a bombing target, accomplish their runs, and continue for 67 miles on the first leg. The flight would then turn to course 346 degrees for 73 miles on its second leg, and then turn to course 241 degrees for a distance of 120 miles on the return to Fort Lauderdale. At about 1500 the captain of a fishing boat near the target area recalled seeing three or four planes heading east.

About 1540, FT-74, the senior flight instructor at Fort Lauderdale, while flying around the field, heard what he believed was a radio transmission from a boat or an aircraft in distress. Someone was transmitting a message to Powers, one of the student pilots of Flight 19. The voice asked Powers several times what his compass read. Powers finally replied, "I don't know where we are. We must have got lost after that last turn."

The senior instructor radioed Fort Lauderdale that a boat or a plane was lost, and then sent the message, "This is FT-74 . . . plane or boat calling Powers please identify yourself so someone can help you." This message received no response but the voice radioed again asking the others (student pilots) if there were any "suggestions." After FT-74 sent the message again, the voice seeking help was identified as Lieutenant Taylor, FT-28. "FT-28 this is FT-74, what is your trouble?" Sounding rattled and confused Taylor replied, "Both my compasses are out and I am trying to find Fort Lauderdale, Florida. I am over land but it's broken. I am sure I'm in the Keys but I don't know how far down and I don't know how to get to Fort Lauderdale." Startled at what he heard, FT-74 told FT-28 to "put the sun on your port wing if you are in the Keys and fly up the coast until you get to Miami. Fort Lauderdale is twenty miles further, your first port after Miami. The air station is directly on your left from the port." FT-74 thought that FT-

28 should certainly know if he was over the Keys because he had flown the area for six months while stationed at Miami. FT-74 radioed, "What is your present altitude? I will fly south and meet you." "I know where I am now. I'm at twenty-three hundred feet. Don't come after me," was FT-28's strange reply. One could surmise that the newly assigned Lieutenant Taylor would have suffered much embarrassment had he been "rescued" by the senior instructor pilot.

Not convinced, FT-74 radioed, "Roger, you're at twenty-three hundred. I'm coming to meet you anyhow." A few moments later FT-28 radioed, "We have just passed over a small island. We have no other land in sight." FT-74 thought in disbelief that if FT-28 was in the Keys, how could he run out of islands? How could he not see the Florida peninsula?

FT-28 came on the air and requested that Miami or someone try to track them on radar, adding, "We don't seem to be getting far. We were out on a navigation hop and on the second leg I thought they [his students] were going wrong, so I took over and was flying them back to the right position. But I'm sure now that neither one of my compasses is working." What did Lieutenant Taylor mean by the strange statement, "We don't seem to be getting far"?

Apparently flying in opposite directions, FT-74 soon lost radio contact with the Flight 19 but believed it was somewhere over Bimini or the Bahamas. Disoriented, with the weather deteriorating, the lost FT-28 kept changing course. Confusion is apparent in his radio transmissions: (At 1631) "One of the planes in the flight thinks if we went 270 degrees we could hit land." (At 1645) "We are heading 030 degrees for 45 minutes then we will fly north to make sure we are not over the Gulf of Mexico." About 1700 Taylor called to his flight: "Change course to 090 degrees for ten minutes." About that same time a transmission from one of the students was heard: "Damn it, if we would just fly west we would get home: head west, damn it."

Obviously heeding the student's suggestion, at 1716 FT-28 called out that they would fly 270 degrees (west), "until we hit the beach or run out of gas."

Not sure whether he was over the Gulf of Mexico or the Atlantic, at 1804, he called to his flight again: "Holding course 270 degrees . . . . We didn't go far enough east . . . . Turn around again . . . . We may just as well turn around and go east again."

At about 1820 this grim transmission from FT-28 was heard: "All planes close up tight . . . . Will have to ditch unless landfall . . . . When the first plane drops to ten gallons we all go down together."

Meanwhile, a PBM, *Martin Mariner* at Banana River was being made ready for a search mission to find the lost planes. With twelve hours of fuel, the plane was said to be in A-1 condition, all equipment checked, and engines operating normal. As this type of aircraft was labeled "the flying gas tank," mechanics carefully checked and found no indication of gas fumes.

The British tanker *Viscount Empire* in waters north of the Bahamas reported tremendous seas and high velocity winds.

At 1927 the PBM *Mariner* lifted off with three aviators and a crew of ten aboard. After sending an "out" report to its home base, the aircraft was never heard from again. At 1950 the tanker S S *Gaines Mills,* off the coast of Florida, reported a burst of flames and apparent explosion, flames leaping a hundred feet high and burning for ten minutes. The captain of the vessel later recounted seeing a plane catch fire and crash, exploding on the sea.

A massive five-day air and sea search produced not a single scrap of wreckage from any of the planes. Many logical reasons for the loss of Flight 19 have been considered: compass failure; the lack of a necessary radio frequency on which the senior flight instructor and Lieutenant Taylor could have continued to communicate; poor radio reception; the sudden change to foul weather complicated by nightfall; delays in locating the flight with radio bearings and the failure to transmit that data after it had been determined.[17]

Flight 19 was the cornerstone of the Bermuda Triangle fame, generating many mythical and erroneous accounts, but there still remains a veil of mystery surrounding the incident. Why did Lieutenant Taylor not want to go on the flight? A sick, intoxicated, or hungover pilot would have added a grave dimension to the already serious situation. Did he have a watch? His repeated radio transmissions asking other aviators how long they had been flying on various headings suggest he did not. Why did both compasses fail? Was there not one compass in all the planes that could be relied upon? Radio transmissions suggest the flight eventually ran out of fuel and ditched in heavy seas. If this in fact occurred, it raises the most worn of all questions: Why was no wreckage or flotsam ever found?

Aside from compass, gyro, radar, sonar, and navigational instrument malfunction and failure associated with the Bermuda Triangle, other strange experiences of those sailing or flying through the area, defy logical explanation. Even satellites orbiting above the area are affected. Unusual localized luminous fog, green haze, or clouds, the phenomenon of "white water" produced by bright lights in the sky or under the sea, time-warp anomalies, violent or freak sea activity, uncanny sightings, and errie messages before and after disappearances have weaved the unbelievable fabric of the sinister triangle.

On a clear night during a flight from Andros Island to Miami in November 1964, pilot Chuck Wakeley suddenly observed a fuzzy glow on the right wing of his plane. The glow traveled to the fuselage, to the left wing, then inside to his instrument panel, and finally to his body, which also began to glow. He also witnessed the failure of his indicators and electromagnetic equipment during this time.[18]

The sixty-five-foot shark fishing boat *Wild Goose* was said to have disappeared with all aboard after being engulfed in a sudden localized fog in the Tongue of the Ocean, a 1-1/2-mile stretch of deep water between Andros and Exuma islands.[19]

Unexplained gain or loss variations in aircraft clock time, not indicated on aircraft clocks but monitored by ground personnel, have provided some of the most bizarre aberrations of the Triangle.

Pilot Bruce Gernon tried to climb above rather than fly through an elliptic cloud in the triangle on a routine flight from Andros Island to Palm Beach, Florida on December 4, 1970. The cloud turned into a tunnel that touched the wingtips of his aircraft, causing what he termed "zero gravity."

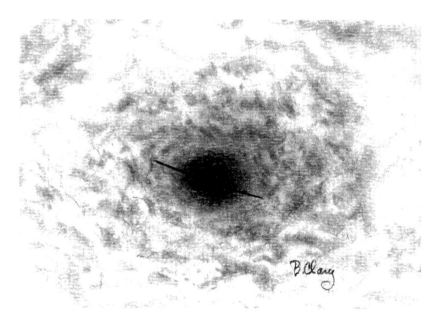

He then flew into a green haze of zero visibility and witnessed the complete failure of all instruments. After clearing the haze, he made radio contact with Palm Beach ground control and landed safely. However, the routine flight of seventy-five minutes had instead only taken forty-five minutes, and his aircraft flew only two hundred fifty miles instead of the usual 200. The top cruising speed of his plane was 195 mile per hour.

When Gernon checked the fuel records of his previous flights, he determined that his plane used about forty gallons of fuel for that trip whereas during this strange flight the aircraft had used only twenty-eight gallons. His final calculations were mind-boggling, for it appeared that either his aircraft had flown at 1,182 mile per hour or the cloud that he had entered had been moving at that speed to allow for the reduced consumption of fuel.

It was said that about that same time during the late afternoon of that December day, many other aircraft had become lost in cloud formations in the same area.[20]

The pilot of a U.S. Navy P2 radioed a mayday call, which was not acknowledged. An engine cylinder had failed during a rapid climb out of heavy turbulence encountered during a training flight near Bahama. After accomplishing a safe landing at Jacksonville despite the difficulty, the pilot was asked to participate in finding an aircraft that had sent a mayday call. He was asked to look for himself, for that mayday call, somehow detained in time for a quarter of an hour, was his own! [21]

An unusual increased time extreme occurred when Air Force pilot Tim Lockley flew a NATO mission along with several other aircraft from Pope, North Carolina, to Mildenhall, England, in November 1970. The planes had taken off in half-hour intervals, but Lockley reported a gain of 3-1/2 hours of flight time over the other aircraft in his group. With no adverse weather conditions, no electrical disturbance, and no strong tail winds, his airspeed was as indicated but his ground speed was several hundred knots faster that it should have been. The unexplained time anomaly was confirmed by ground control. Lockley later related, "You hear a lot of rumors about things like this—when planes fly into white-outs—where the sky and water look exactly alike. You get disorientated about everything, even about time."[22]

A National Airlines 727 experienced a ten-minute radar failure while flying in a light haze. After landing, the plane's clock and all watches aboard showed a corresponding ten-minute lag even though a time check was accomplished a halfhour before landing.[23]

The loss of two U.S. Air Force KC-135s during normal flying conditions in an area three hundred miles southwest of Bermuda on September 22, 1963, coincided with a radio blackout on the Coast Guard cutter *Chiola* at about the same time the two aircraft were lost.[24]

Not only aircraft are affected by the Triangle's mysterious forces. Prof. Wayne Meshejian, a physicist at Longwood College, Virginia, has confirmed the malfunction of weather satellites but only when passing over the Bermuda Triangle while orbiting eight hundred miles above the earth. The temporary malfunctions are attributed to an unknown and powerful energy source beneath the sea. The force can erase videotapes while not altering the satellite's orbit.[25]

After the pilot of a Cessna 172 lost radio contact with Grand Turk Island, Bahama, ground control, the tower overheard the pilot tell a passenger they must be over the wrong area because "there's nothing down there." The aircraft was never heard from again.[26]

A seaman on the *Queen Elizabeth II* observed a plane flying directly at the ship, then abruptly and silently plunge in the sea about a hundred yards from the liner. No wreckage or oil slick was found.[27]

Crew members aboard the US *Josephus Daniels* reported a large "hill" of water rising from the ocean resulting in a logged course change. After the log was examined by port authorities it was never seen again.[28]

The pilot of a Boeing 707 observed a similar phenomenon on April 11, 1963, when he reported a massive raised level of the sea, estimated to be a half mile high. A sailor on the *Queen Mary* observed the color in a section of the sea in the Triangle change from dark to pale green. The sea then erupted with a twenty-five-foot wide column of water rising in the air to about fifty feet. Shortly thereafter a second column was seen about a half mile from the first one. When the columns settled the ocean returned to its normal dark green color.[29]

Off Key West, Florida, in May 1965, fisherman Irwin Brown and his wife reported seeing a "trench" in the water, which appeared perpendicular to his boat's path. The twenty-foot wide, four-foot deep gully looked as if it were created by a giant aquatic bulldozer.[30]

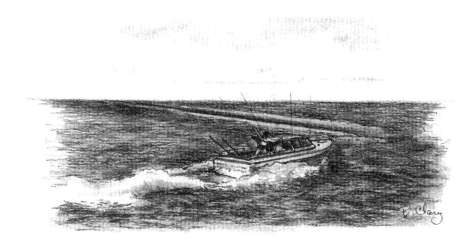

Restauranteur Chuck Muer, his wife, and three of his children, while sailing his boat, *Charlie's Crab*, in the Abaco Island group, near Turtle Key, was engulfed by a enormous rogue wave on November 27, 1981. In clear weather and approaching undetected, the wave, called a "rage" by the islanders, was at least forty feet high as it covered their boat. The Muers were fortunate to survive this calamity, but the incident shook them to the core. Chuck was a big collector of my work, but thereafter would have nothing to do with storm scenes.

Chuck, his wife, and another couple, while sailing *Charlie's Crab* from the Berry Islands to Jupiter, Florida, in the early morning hours of March 13, 1993, were lost in what has been called the worst storm of the century. Approaching near-hurricane strength, the storm, which gained intensity as it crossed the Gulf of Mexico, raked across Florida, pushing sixty tornadoes ahead of it. It packed 109 mile per hour winds, and the barometric pressure registered below twenty-eight inches at some stations along the Atlantic coast. Although it was believed that Muer knew a storm was in the offing, he was surely not aware of the deadly giant that hit him, which in fact was upgraded from a watch to a warning with expectant gale force winds after he left port. His boat carried a life raft, a small Zodiac, a VHF radio, a cellular phone, and an emergency distress radio signal beacon, the type which had to be manually activated. Someone aboard the forty foot sailboat, which was no doubt assaulted by monstrous seas in the middle of the night, gave a hint of Muer's location in the storm through a 911 cellular telephone call at 4:34 a.m. on March 13. After fourteen seconds of static, the line went dead. It was later determined that this call originated within twenty-five miles of shore. *Charlie's Crab* was caught sailing in the Bermuda Triangle in a vicious storm, the severity of which was not foreseen.

After an intensive 110,000-square-mile Coast Guard search, not a single scrap of wreckage or flotsam was found. According to the 7th Coast Guard District at Miami, the final tally included twelve vessels lost in the Gulf of Mexico, one of which was the 205-foot freighter *Fantastico*, and four vessels lost off the Atlantic coast, two of which ran aground. Seventeen lives were lost in the Gulf and four were lost in the Atlantic.

Messages sent from victims before their disappearance add further mystery to the Triangle's fame. The pilot of a DC-3 on approach to Miami on December 28, 1948, with thirty-five people aboard, sent the following transmission: "We are approaching the field . . . . We can see the lights of Miami now . . . . All's well . . . . Will stand by for landing instructions." The aircraft and all aboard vanished.[31]

The *Star Tiger*, a British passenger plane in the air northeast of Bermuda, radioed: "Weather and performance excellent . . . . Expect to arrive on schedule." Two more strange messages were received. One, which spelled out "tiger" in Morse code, was picked up by a ham radio operator and the other, a voice that transmitted the call letters of the aircraft— G A H N P—was received by a Coast Guard base in Newfoundland. There was no assurance the faint messages came from the *Star Tiger,* which would have run out of fuel before the transmissions were received, which further compounded the riddle.[32]

Messages were reportedly still coming from the freighter *Anita* a day after it was believed to have sunk off Norfolk, Virginia on March 21, 1973.[33]

Incredibly strange were the secret navy signals received on a special VLF (very low frequency) channel from the U. S. Navy submarine *Scorpion* after it had disappeared en route to

Norfolk on May 21, 1968. Although the signals pinpointed the location on the ocean bottom from which they came, the sub was not there. The Russian Navy research vessel *Mizar* later found the sub four hundred miles southwest of the Azores, hundreds of miles from the pinpointed location where the signals originated.[34]

After the Japanese freighter *Raifuku Maru* radioed a call for help while steaming between Florida and Cuba in 1925, a second desperate transmission was heard: "Danger like dagger now . . . . Come quickly . . . . We cannot escape."[35]

Because so much has been written revealing the increasingly wide scope of phenomena associated with the Triangle, many former pilots have come forth to relate their strange experiences. One of the strangest is that which took place two years before the famed disappearance of Flight 19. Lt. Robert Ulmer, flying a B-24 in good weather at nine thousand feet over the Bahamas, suddenly found his plane out of control and shaking violently. The aircraft lost four thousand feet of altitude in moments, and, not able to regain any control, the crew bailed out. All but two of the crew survived. The plane, however, instead of diving into the sea, righted itself to fly crewless for an astounding fifteen hundred miles, crossing the Gulf of Mexico, to eventually crash on a mountainside. Stranger still was the fact that before the pilot had bailed out he had set the controls on a northeast course, but a mysterious force that guided the plane changed its course to fly to Mexico in nearly the opposite direction.[36]

Another former pilot, Cmdr. Marcus Billson, relates his unusual experience during a flight from Banana River, Florida, to Grand Bahama in a PBM the night of March 25, 1945:

> We were on a night flight about half way to Grand Bahama when things started to happen. The radio compass started to circle. The magnetic compass was also spinning. Our radio became useless because of static. All our flight instruments went out. The night became very dark. There was no sea, sky, stars, or clouds—only blackness. I experienced very violent vertigo, the only time it ever happened to me during 5000 flying hours. We didn't know where we were going so we turned around and limped back to Banana River, navigating by guesswork. As we approached the Base our instruments came back. I always wondered about this but did not realize the connection until the Bermuda Triangle was made public.

Another mystifying and long-feared region of the oceans is that strange area in the constant turning circle of North Atlantic currents known as the Sargasso sea. The region was believed named by Portuguese sailors, who compared the air bladders that kept the pale brown sea growth afloat with the Portuguese grape called *Sargaco*. Its northern border stretches from Chesapeake Bay to Gibraltar, United Kingdom, while its southern boundary stretches between Haiti and Dakar, Senegal. Encompassing Bermuda and the Bermuda Triangle, the region extends more than halfway across the Atlantic and is nearly as large as the United States!

This two-million-square-mile area of floating primordial sargassum weed terrified ancient mariners, who based their fears on the chronicled dangers supposed lurking in those distant western waters. The early Carthaginian navigator Himilco was said to have been halted by seaweeds and monsters en route to Cornwall, and the medieval St. Amaro was reportedly encompassed by seaweeds in the western Atlantic.[37]

Columbus, it appears, was not shaken by the potential threat, but saw the yellowish-green weed as a sign that land was near, mistakenly calling it "weed from rocks that lie to the west."[38]

The sailors' fears of their ships being trapped in the weeds were aggravated by the fact that the area lies within the horse latitudes, a vast subtropical area of light winds, believed named by mariners who, when becalmed there, slaughtered the horses they carried to conserve water. The Sargasso, forgotten by the winds, was thought to hold an enormous graveyard of ships, from treasure-laden Spanish galleons to countless slavers crammed with human cargo entangled and rotting in a sea of menacing weeds.

As recent as a hundred years ago, steamer captains were warned to avoid the area for fear the weeds would foul their propellers. It is a wonder in itself to imagine that the same weed growth that the ancient seafarers saw is still there and thriving. Strange too is the sea level in the Sargasso, which scientists estimate to be four feet higher than the water level near the Atlantic coast of the United States.[39]

In 1615, the Dutch merchant Jacques Le Maire sent an expedition to the south Atlantic to find a passage to the Pacific better than the Strait of Magellan, the twisting strait monopolized by the Dutch East India Company. The mission, in command of Capt. Willem Schouten, while encamped on the Patagonian coast, nearly met its end. One of their vessels, the schooner *Hoorn*, was destroyed by fire. However, the mission continued with success in the remaining boat, *Unity*, to discover Cape Horn on the afternoon of January 29, 1616. They named the granite spire that pointed the way to the Pacific in honor of the burnt schooner and Le Maire's hometown.

Ever since its discovery, Cape Horn has had the sinister reputation of having the most ruthless weather and the cruelest waves to be found on any part of the earth. One theory of why the region is so dangerous is that the constant howling west winds that encircle the earth in those latitudes encounter no obstacle in their mad race eastward. As these winds assault the Chilean shores, giant waves, which rake along that southernmost landfall, explode like charging elephants into Drake passage.

Another theory is that the heavy seas there are caused by the sudden drop-off of the continental shelf. Estimates of the size of the waves range from thirty-nine feet seen by the crew of the Polish schooner *Gedania* in early 1976, to that of Argentinian fishermen who claim the monster graybeards reach fifty-eight feet.

The fastest passage around the Horn in the days of sail was by the famous clipper *Flying Cloud,* which sailed on her record voyage from New York to San Francisco in eighty-nine days and eight hours in 1854. Other passages were not so lucky. Captain Bligh, the cantankerous, hard-driving master of the *Bounty* in quest of breadfruit seedlings in the Pacific islands, fought fierce weather, hail, snow, and treacherous seas for twenty-nine days before turning back into the Atlantic in the teeth of a gale for his east-around voyage to Tahiti.

The most difficult passage of all was that of the *Edward Seawell,* the four-masted, steel-hulled bark, which was tortured during her labyrinthine course by towering seas, calms, and frequent gales in a sixty-seven-day attempt to round the Horn in 1914.

In a region that has ferocious weather for twenty-six days out of the month, it is rare and perhaps foreboding to witness a dead calm in the usual menacing gray waters.

"A calm in Cape Horn," wrote Herman Melville, "is worse by far than a calm on the equator. There we were 48 hours under the most intense cold. I was surprised to see that the ocean refused to freeze at such a temperature. The clear, cold sky appeared to be a blue-steel cymbal which, if one had been able to tap it, would surely have sounded."[40]

In this sector of the earth can also be found another threatening region of great hazard where giant seas can dwarf a ship. Known as the "roaring forties," the area in the Southern Hemisphere between 40° and 50° south is famous for boisterous westerly force-five winds that blow with great regularity.

In seas of such great magnitude, helmsmen were strictly forbidden to look astern, as the sight of the mountainous waves would often terrorize even the most seasoned sailor and cause him to lose his concentration, which could jeopardize the safety of ship and crew.

Edgar Allan Poe wrote about one of most evil manifestations of the sea in his "Descent into the Maelstrom." He wrote of the maelstrom, or gigantic whirlpools, that exist between the islands of the Lofoten group off the west coast of Norway. Known to have drawn men and boats down into the twirling funnels of water, their existence has been verified in the *Sailing Directions for the Northwest and North Coasts of Norway*:

> Though rumor has greatly exaggerated the importance of the Malstrom, or more properly Moskenstraumen, which runs between Mosken and Lofotodden, it is still the most dangerous tideway in Lofoten, its violence being due, in great measure, to the irregularity of the ground . . . . As the strength of the tide increases, the sea becomes heavier and the current more irregular, forming extensive eddies or whirlpools (Malstrom). During such periods no vessel should enter the Moskenstraumen.
>
> These whirlpools are cavities in the form of an inverted bell, wide and rounded at the mouth and narrower toward the bottom; they are largest when first formed and are carried along with the current, diminishing gradually until they disappear; before the extinction of one, two or three more will appear, following each other like so many pits in the sea . . . . Fishermen affirm that if they are aware of their approach to a whirlpool and have time to throw an oar or any other bulky body into it they will get over it safely; the reason is that when the continuity is broken and the whirling motion of the seas interrupted by something thrown into it the water must rush suddenly in on all sides and fill up the cavity. For the same reason, in strong breezes, when the waves break, though there may be a whirling round, there can be no cavity. In the Salstrom, boats and men have been drawn down by these vortices, and much loss of life has resulted.[41]

Ancient mariners also feared the waters beyond the equator. Many believed that because of the extremely hot climate, one would enter a boiling or burning sea where flames would leap to the sky. It was thought too that one who ventured beyond the equator would turn into a negro.

A crusty saltwater captain once sarcastically asked a Great Lakes captain, "Have you ever sailed 'round the Horn?" The freshwater sailor quickly retorted, "Yes, sir, I sailed the lakes in a November storm."

Long scoffed at, freshwater seamen who sailed on the so-called mill pond inland seas were considered a wimpish and fearful lot compared with their brother mariners who sailed the high seas. Over the years, however, ferocious Great Lakes waters, particularly those sailed during the famed November storms, have finally been recognized and scientifically proven as some of the most treacherous waters in the world.

Three newly constructed trawlers, the *Sebastopol*, *Cerisoles*, and *Inkerman*, built for the French navy, departed Fort William, Ontario, November 11, 1918. The French sailors were said to have laughed at Great Lakes mariners' tales of the "fury of the lakes." Only the *Sebastopol* survived a raging Lake Superior storm.

John A. McGean

In just two storms that raged on the lakes from November 7 to 13, 1913, twelve major vessels were lost with all hands in the "king of storms," which registered one of the lowest barometric pressures (28.61" at Erie, Pennsylvania, November 9) ever over North American landmass.

The Great Lakes have seen twenty-one hurricane-type storms in the last 150 years, the last of which sank the ore carrier *Edmund Fitzgerald* on November 10, 1975.

The ruthlessness of Great Lakes waters was scientifically confirmed when strain gauges installed on the *Edward L. Ryerson* while sailing in Lake Michigan on November 29, 1966, during the same storm that sank the *Daniel J. Morrell* in Lake Huron, recorded a stress of twenty-three thousand pounds per square inch—much more than had ever been recorded on any ocean vessel.[42]

Rescue

One of the strangest rescue stories in the history of sailing occurred on the whaler *Canton* in 1887. It felt good to be alive as the sun glistened with magic wonder on the sea that June 14 when the small blunt ship left New Bedford with sails straining for the open sea. Bound for the Indian Ocean in pursuit of whales she was commanded by Capt. George Lyman Howland, a veteran sailor of thirty-six years.

Under way but just a few days, a mysterious predicament befell the *Canton,* which perplexed all those aboard. The ship would not hold its course. Time and again Howland tried to put his ship back on course, but each time the vessel balked and persisted in sailing its own way, sails slapping against the wind in defiance.

At his wits' end, the captain paced the deck and scratched his head in wonder. Winds were fair and the *Canton* was in Bristol fashion. What could possibly be wrong? Finally, he ordered the ship thoroughly inspected for an explanation as to why his ship would not maintain his course. The inspection, having taken several hours, revealed nothing, and now, with night upon them, Howland stood at the bow under the stars smoking his pipe completely baffled. It was then that several crewmen saw him join his hands in prayer and look to the heavens. Coming closer the men heard him pray: "M'Lord, Ye've seen the sea refuse me passage. None of m' knowledge gives me an answer as t' why this is got t' be." Then he spoke as if enlightened "Have mercy! Forgive me! I should have recognized Ye've chosen the course this good little ship must take." His prayer finished, with a deep sigh and a sense of peace he walked aft past the sailors who watched him. Worried to see their captain so desperate as to give in to prayer, they too thought it best to pray for help.

Back at the wheel, Captain Howland shocked the helmsman by ordering him to let go of the wheel and "let 'er steer the way she will by the Hand of Providence!" Having sailed with the master for many years, the helmsman, whose astonished look was read by the captain in the moonlight, was told again to let go the helm.

Hours passed as the captain peered out to sea in the direction the Lord had willed the ship to sail. Several crewmen approached the captain seeking orders to test his saneness and were kindly directed to their tasks, obeying willingly.

The *Canton* sailed on her own for days until one of the crew spotted something in the distance in the direction the vessel sailed. Looking toward the crewman's sighting with a glass, the captain spotted some small boats filled with people lazily drifting on the sea. The *Canton*, still unsteered, slowly eased up to ravaged survivors from the British trader *Monarch,* which had been abandoned after it caught fire and blew up about seven hundred miles from the Cape of Good Hope. As the desperate and weak seamen were brought aboard, after being adrift for a week without water or food, they found strength to rush to the captain, falling on their knees and hugging him in thanksgiving.

One of the rescued was heard to comment on how "luck" finally shined upon them. "Luck ye call it?" the captain shouted. "Ye faith is mighty weak. The good Lord gave me my orders. Don't dare ye call it luck." Then, so humbled, the survivors fell to their knees in thanks. Thereafter the good ship sailed where she was steered.

On November 13, 1890, with her crew and survivors, the *Canton* came home to New Bedford after the long 3-1/2-year voyage. Living to the fairly ripe age of 70, in 1923, Captain Howland died, but from the time of his strange experience until his death he often told the beautiful story of how he gave up his helm to the greater Captain, who steered him in a very special way.[43]

Notes

1. Berlitz, *Without a Trace*, 50.
2. Berlitz, *The Dragon's Triangle*, 20-21.
3. Ibid.
4. Ibid.
5. Ibid., 24.

6. Ibid.

7. Ibid., 24-25.

8. Ibid., 25.

9. Ibid., 38.

10. Garrett, *Voyage into Mystery*, 30-32.

11. See chap. 10, "Islands."

12. Berlitz, *Without a Trace*, 16.

13. Ibid. 21-33.

14. Ibid., 18-19.

15. Ibid., 19.

16. Ibid.

17. McDonell, "Lost Patrol," in *Naval Aviation News*, 11-16.

18. Berlitz, *Without A Trace*, 45.

19. Ibid., 45.

20. Maine, "The Atlantic's Sinister Triangle," in Canning, ed., *Fifty True Mysteries of the Sea*, 362-63.

21. Ibid., 363-64.

22. Ibid., 364.

23. Ibid., 366.

24. Berlitz, *Without a Trace*, 47-48.

25. Maine, "The Atlantic's Sinister Triangle," 368.

26. Ibid.

27. Ibid.

28. Ibid.

29. Ibid., 372-73.

30. Ibid.

31. Berlitz, *Without a Trace*, 37.

32. Ibid., 38.

33. Ibid.

34. Ibid.

35. Ibid., 39.

36. Ibid., 41.

37. Bassett, *Legends and Superstitions of the Sea and Sailors*, 14.

38. Dor-Ner, *Columbus and the Age of Discovery*, 140.

39. Engel, *The Sea*, 77.

40. Rawson, *Cape Horn Is the Terrible Test*, 54-60.

41. Carson, *The Sea around Us*, 160-61.

42. Clary, *Ladies of the Lakes II*, 124.

43. Compass, *The Unseen Skipper*, 39-40.

19. Saluting

Sea, Sea Monsters, Sickness

Salutes and piping of oldest form,
Giant waves pushed by the storm.
Old proof of monsters in the bay,
Do they still roam the seas today?

Saluting

When a sailor salutes the quarterdeck upon boarding a vessel, he mimics the ancient practice of showing respect to a pagan altar, crucifix, or shrine that was situated in a place of honor on ancient ships. Long after the shrines disappeared, the tradition continued by recognizing the colors, the symbol of state, or the seat of authority, with a brief, dignified removal of the hat or a hand salute.

The junior in the early days of any organized military unit would always uncover his head when meeting or addressing the senior. Although touching one's hat was considered slovenly or disrespectful, the gesture became dignified when, in 1796, Lord St. Vincent issued an order that officers were to remove their hats when receiving orders from superiors, "and not to touch them with an air of negligence."[1]

The American Navy adopted the gesture. An excerpt from *Jones's Sketches of Naval Life*, written on board the USS *Constitution* in 1826, describes the practice during a salute of the day:

> The Captain and First Lieutenant, Mr. Vallette, are now on the deck; they pass around and examine every part of it, each man lifting his hat, as they pass, or, in default of one, catching hold of a lock of hair.[2]

By 1882, the salute in the Royal Navy evolved to the practice of "touching the hat," defined as holding the edge with the forefinger and thumb. Because at the time there were so many different variations of the personal salute, in 1890, Queen Victoria decreed that the salute would be made with the hand only, voicing her displeasure at seeing so many uncovered heads appear before royalty.[3]

Hand saluting in the American Navy was also adopted from the British Navy which borrowed the gesture from the British Army.

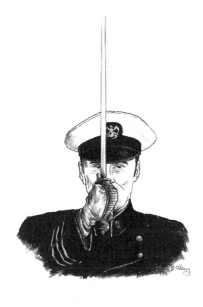

The origin of the British and French Army salute with the palm turned out is believed to have been adapted from the showing of one's palm to indicate that there was nothing hidden in the hand.

The sword salute can be traced to the crusades. In the days of chivalry, it was common for the crucifix to be depicted on the sword near the handle, and it was customary to kiss the hilt of the sword before going into battle. The sword held at arm's length symbolizes the original salute or hail to a superior, and descending the point of a sword to the ground reflects the ancient act of submission. The beginning of both movements—bringing the hilt of the sword up near the mouth or chin—is a remnant of the ancient practice of kissing the cross on the sword.[4]

A old court-martial custom of the British Navy involved pointing an officer's sword toward him on a table if he was found guilty or away from him if he was found not guilty.

Manning the yards and cheering a distinguished personage upon entering a port is a very old form of saluting. According to naval instructions printed in 1824, the people, placed according to their size, would stand together on the ratlines with two or three ratlines between each man. After the three cheers were given, if the commodore returned the same number, it would be answered by one cheer; if he returned but one cheer, no further cheers were given and the men were sent down.[5]

One of he oldest items of personal sea gear is the boatswains's pipe. Greek and Roman galley slaves were said to have kept their stroke with the playing of a flute or pipe, and a pipe summoned English crossbowmen on deck in the crusade of 1248. Just as it was used in the old navy to call sailors aloft, to sweep the decks, heave around, stand by, haul, to pass a word, or pipe down, the boatswain's pipe is still used in today's modern navy to summon men (over loudspeakers) to their tasks, to call them to chow, or to signal lights out.

The pipe was and still is used to salute or pipe aboard distinguished personages, be they military or civilian. In the days of sail, when fleet officers were invited to the flagship for dinner or conference in bad weather, they were often hoisted aboard in boatswain's chairs. The pipe was used to call for "hoist away" or "avast heaving." Crewmen did the hoisting and a number of men were required in tending the side. The custom originated from the aid that was rendered, and in time, it developed into a gesture of courtesy.

It is believed that the design and form of the more elaborate gold pipe worn by upper eschelon officers as a badge of office or honor was adopted to commemorate the defeat and return of the body of the famous Scotch pirate, Andrew Barton.

It is a custom of the British Navy to pipe the corpse of an officer or a man over the side if sent ashore for burial.[6]

Before electric lighting came into use aboard ships, one of the more ostentatious and colorful salutes of the old U.S. Navy was that rendered to officers when coming aboard a vessel at night. The anchor watch would line up holding lanterns to light the way for the guests from the gangway to their quarters. Six lanterns were held for admirals, four for captains, and two for wardroom officers.[7]

Sea

The sea is baffling even in its tiniest form. The total molecules in the interconnected system of oceans, gulfs, and smaller seas is estimated at 60,000,000,000,000,000,000,000,-000,000,000,000,000,000,000. A single glass of water contains so many of them that if they could somehow be colored for identification and poured into the sea, in time (perhaps thousands of years), a glass of water taken from any sea in the world would contain some of those colored molecules. Containing 330 million cubic miles of water, the seas could fill a seventy-five-mile diameter column, 70,000 miles high—about a third of the distance between the earth and the moon.[8]

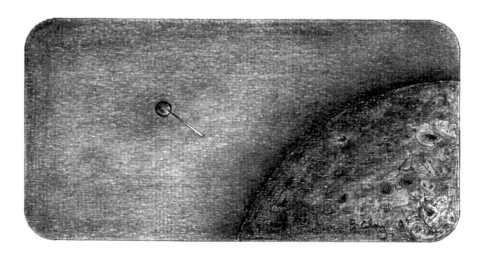

Stronger than the wind or earthquake energy that produces great waves are the forces that create the tides. Every drop of water in the seas, even at the deepest abyss, is affected by these mysterious forces. An example of the masses of water moved by the tides can be brought into focus by the estimated

2 billion tons of water carried twice each day by tidal currents into the small Passamaquoddy Bay on the Atlantic coast.

The tides respond to the waters of the oceans, which are affected by the gravitational pull of the moon and the sun. The moon, because it is closer, has more than twice the gravitational pull of the sun even though the sun has a mass 27 million times that of the moon. The highest tides, called springs, occur twice each month, when there is a sliver of a new moon and when the moon is full. During this time, the sun, moon, and the earth are aligned to combine their pull to cause the highest of the high tides. Conversely, neap tides occur during the quarters of the moon, when the sun, moon, and the earth are positioned at the apexes of a triangle, and the pull of the sun and moon are opposed.

Besides being influenced by the sun and moon, tides are further affected by the position of these bodies in relation to the equator, their distance from the earth, and by periods of oscillation of the water in ocean basins, which is determined by the physical dimensions of those basins. The gravitational force of the moon and sun sets the water in motion, but how far, how fast, or how strong a tide rises is determined by other characteristics, such as the slope, drop-off, and depth of the area.

The Bay of Fundy is home of the world's highest tides; in the Minas Basin near the head of the bay spring tides of fifty feet occur. On the island of Tahiti, because of its location, the sun has more effect on the tide than the moon, and the difference between high and low tide there is usually no more than a foot.

Of all the unusual phenomena created by the tides, the most renowned are the bores, which are born when much of a flood tide enters a river as one to three steep waves. Physical characteristics of the area, such as the range of the tide and obstructions at the mouth of a river, hold off the tide until it gathers enough strength to burst through the barrier. The phenomenal bores of the Amazon have been known to travel two hundred miles upstream with as many as five flood tides pushing their associated bores up the river at one time.

The largest, most famous, and most dangerous bore occurs on the Tsientang River, a tributary of the China sea. Ancient shore inhabitants threw offerings into the river in hope of calming the angry spirit of the bore, which during some spring tides raged twenty-five feet above the river, destroying everything in its path.[9]

The ancients believed that the tides rose because the water swelled from being heated by the moon. Others thought that the winds created by the earth and moon produced pressure on the sea, which caused the tides. Some said that the ebb and flow of the tides were due to the putrefaction of the sea by the air and the air by the sea. A thirteenth-century belief was that the tides moved because of the earth's breathing.[10]

An old-time superstition of those who lived near the sea was the belief that death occurred at ebb tide. Assuming that the ebbing of life was associated with the ebbing tide, it was thought that no one would die until the tide went out. A more absurd belief was that the tides were caused by the breath of a sea monster, who inhaled for six hours to cause a low tide and exhaled for six hours to make the water return.

If a baby was born as the tide came in, it was an omen of good luck for the infant. An old fishermen's belief was that no work should be performed except when the tide was flowing.[11]

The tide was thought able to cure a fever or whooping cough in Ireland. The patient was placed on a sandy shore as the tide came in, and the retreating tide, it was thought, would carry away one's fever. A popular remedy for whooping cough was to have those affected walk up and down the beach at low tide before the flowing waves. Children with the illness were made to drink seawater, causing them to vomit in the sea, which carried away the disease.[12]

The most frightening spectacle of the oceans are those giant, deadly, and unpredictable waves created by the wind on the sea. Traveling in trains of varying frequency, energy, and speed, a wave substantially higher than its parts can occur when two or three of these trains going in the same direction happen to fall "in step" with one another to produce a massive wall of water.

If you have ever seen surfers appear like tiny ants as they glide down the steep face of fifty-foot waves during a high surf warning, you might imagine the immensity of these terrifying waves, which are sometimes over twice this high. Blair Kinsman of the Marine Sciences Research Center on Long Island describes the phenomenon: "Imagine a green-black mass the height of a seven- or eight-story building, maybe half-a-mile long, suddenly rushing before you at 50 miles an hour. You're on a roller coaster plummeting down into its trough. This monster towers above you, alive, shifting, breaking, roaring, hunching. There's no place to hide. Then it's on top of you. The top third breaks off. Thousands of tons of deadweight water hurtles down on you."

The dreaded hazard was noted in Viking times when the phenomenon was referred to as "sea hedges" that appear "as if all the waves and tempests of the ocean have been collected into three heaps, out of which three billows have formed. These hedge in the entire sea, so that no opening can be seen anywhere; they are higher than lofty mountains and resemble steep, overhanging cliffs. In only a few cases have the men been known to escape who were upon the seas when such a thing occurred."[13]

The *Queen Mary*, loaded with fifteen thousand U.S. troops, encountered one of these phenomenal giants while laboring in very heavy seas seven hundred miles west of the English coast in the late winter of 1942. Suddenly the giant towered above the thousand-foot liner and quickly smashed onto her decks, careening her so violently to port that she was within five degrees of going under. She went into such a severe list that her upper decks were awash, and her veteran crew members were convinced that she would never right herself.[14]

Another monster wave came aboard the 44,000-ton liner *Michelangelo* sailing with 775 passengers during an April 1966 storm, eight hundred miles east of New York City. The awesome wave engulfed the entire forward half of the vessel, gouged a huge hole in her curved superstructure, crumpled her flared bow, sheared off forty feet of railing and bulwark, and smashed heavy glass eighty feet above the water line.[15]

Ocean waves called tsunamis are produced by the sudden, wide-spread motion of a portion of the ocean floor or shore, such as through volcanic eruption, earthquake (seaquake if it occurs at sea), or landslide. They are also known as freak, rogue, and rage waves, or seismic sea waves when caused by a submarine earthquake. When a volcanic eruption occurs below the sea, escaping gases push an enormous dome of water upward. A similar disturbance happens when a portion of the ocean floor suddenly rises. As the water rushes back, a wave is born, which travels at high speed across the surface of the sea. Hardly conspicuous in deep water, the wave may be only two or three feet high, stretching over a hundred miles. Its speed, however, in the deep waters of the Pacific, can reach an astounding four hundred knots or more.[16]

The tsunamis that struck the Hawaiian Islands on April 1, 1946, which originated at an epicenter near the Aleutians, traveled at an average speed of 490 miles per hour, and were recorded at fifty feet higher than the high-water level. The waves reached the islands in four hours and thirty-four minutes; lesser waves, traveling some 6,700 miles, reached North and South America and Australia.[17]

In gale winds of sixty-eight knots, the USS *Ramapo* encountered what is considered the official record height of a mountainous wave during a voyage from Manila to San Diego in February 1933. The storm raged in an area that allowed the winds to build the seas in an unbroken fetch of thousands of miles. An officer observed an enormous sea rise astern above an iron strap on the crow's nest on the mainmast while the vessel was on an even keel with her stern in the trough of the sea. This situation allowed an accurate measurement of the 112-foot wave.[18]

Perhaps the most mysterious of all ocean waves are those that are invisible. Down in the deepest caverns of the seas, between a thin layer of fresh and underlying saltwater, exist the largest and most awe-inspiring submarine waves of the ocean. What causes these great waves to perpetually rise and fall, as if on some imaginary shore far below the surface of the sea, is still a mystery. Their turbulence can make a submarine pitch and roll just as a ship is thrown about on the surface. However, these waves, the magnitude of which has never been matched above the sea, can be as high as three hundred feet.[19]

The kinetic energy waves produce is tremendous. It has been estimated that a four-foot wave of ten seconds duration, hitting a coast, delivers more than 35,000 horsepower per mile of shore. The energy created in every fifty-six miles of shoreline equals that produced at Hoover Dam.[20]

The incredible force of waves created by an earthquake off the coast of Chile in 1868 drove a U.S. Navy steamship three miles up the coast and two miles inland to the foot of a cliff. A British three-masted ship, rolled helplessly over and over, anchor chains wound around its hull many times, lay nearby, leaving no survivors.[21]

Captains of vessels fortunate enough to make it through the great November storms of 1913 on the Great Lakes told of a confused sea of waves that attacked their ships from every direction. Mountainous seas driven by near-hurricane-strength winds, which quickly and often changed direction, produced a vicious crosshatched pattern of graybeards unlike those of any ocean.

Many old legendary beliefs are associated with waves. In Ireland, the song of the sea, the moan of the sea, or sighing of the waves was believed to predict the passing of a great man or indicate that the sea wanted someone. An Irish fishermen's legend told of the "avenging wave," the result of a curse for the murder of a mermaid. Although she begged for mercy, a fisherman named Shea killed a mermaid. The next time he put out to fish the bay, a violent storm claimed him and all those aboard his boat. Thereafter, every time one of his descendants sailed in that bay the avenging waves arose.[22]

Mariners in England referred to the ninth wave as the death wave. Others there believed that the ninth or tenth wave, which would reach shore before other waves, was more powerful than all others. Many waves could assault a ship, but the ninth wave was thought of as the fatal one to sink it. English fishermen called it the "death wave;" only by making the sign of the cross over the wave would it break up. Shetland Islands fishermen believed that water collected from the third wave had healing power. Icelandic fishermen would not launch their boats in the three great waves that always followed one another. At sea, when red or blue waves clashed it was called death's clash and foretold a shipwreck.[23]

French sailors thought that the third wave was the most powerful and produced the loudest roar. Scottish seamen believed that every tempest always had three violent waves. Another legend told of waves that appeared as witches that could sink a vessel and drown those aboard with whom they bore a grudge.[24]

A old belief of Chinese seafarers was that when the seas grew mountainous, little black human forms came from the seas onto their ships. Although harmless even in great numbers, they warned of an approaching tempest.[25]

So much salt is in the oceans that if all the valleys, canyons, hills, and mountains of the earth were graded flat, and all the ocean water evaporated, there would be a two hundred-foot thick crust of salt covering the entire earth.[26] It is a strange irony that although many mariners sail in saltwater, the word salt is taboo, never to be spoken at sea.

Acording to a Danish legend, all the salt in the seas comes from the bottom of the ocean. An ancient king of Denmark possessed two huge grinding stones that could grind whatever he wished for, but they were so big that no one could turn them. While visiting Sweden, the king received a gift of two giant women who had been taken prisoners from the land of the giants. He set them to labor turning the giant stones, which then produced gold, silver, peace, and joy. Soon tired of their work, the giants asked for rest, but were ordered to continue day and night. Because of this treatment, the giants began to grind out soldiers, as enemies of the cruel king. When the enemy forces were strong enough, they attacked the king's domain and sailed away with the magic grinding stones and the two giants. Greatly needing salt in their country, the forces that held the stones ordered the giants to grind salt while aboard the ship that carried them to their land. They ground and ground until the ship filled and sank from the weight. All the forces were lost except the two giants, who, under orders not to stop, continue to this day to grind the salt of the sea.[27]

Many virtues are attributed to salty seawater. French sailors beleived that you would never catch a cold if you bathed often in saltwater, or, if you had a head cold, a drink of saltwater in the morning and evening provided an excellent cure. Drinking a glass of seawater was said to cure a sore throat, and bronchitis, and was as well an effective laxitive.[28]

An experience in this regard made a believer out of me. After arriving in Hawaii with one of the worst sinus infections I ever had, I bodysurfed in the waves for many hours the first day there, undoubtedly ingesting much saltwater in the frolic. Surprisingly, the very next day, my sinus infection had abruptly broken up without leaving a trace of the illness.

Sea Monsters

Accustomed as we have become to these take-it-for-granted high tech times of satellite images being flashed around the world in seconds, it is difficult for us to believe in old documented fact without the verifiable proof of a photograph. Volumes are filled with ancient and incredible sea tales lacking proof of their occurrence other than being accompanied with someone's drawing. The older a story is, the easier it is to become entangled in legend or myth.

When compiling the data for this book, I was satisfied to exclude sea monster fables because I found nothing positively factual that I could sink my teeth into. Even the world's most famous sea monster, that of Loch Ness believed to have been captured in several photographs and on sonar since 1934, lacks credibility, sighted but by a chosen few.

Sea monster stories, I thought, were truly the stuff legends were made of. Then I came across the factual accounts that follow, an all but hidden saga of a strange sea creature indisputably sighted by hundreds of people at one time.

This is the story of the famous "Sea Serpent of Gloucester," which appeared off the coast of Massachusetts near Cape Ann for nearly seventy years. Contrary to the look people give you today when you speak of sea monsters, back then it was difficult to find a disbeliever in that area where hundreds of reputable citizens, scientists, and naturalists identified the creature and documented their testimonies.

The serpent was first observed one August morning in 1817 on the surface of the sea in a vertical undulating movement. It was said that the creature appeared to be pursuing a school of fish that swam ahead of it and was oblivious to those who quickly gathered to view it. It cavorted about daily for two solid weeks, attracting spectators from as far as a thousand miles away. Science scholars heretofore indifferent to such tales of the sea, their interest aroused by the persistent sightings, finally came to Cape Ann to see the phenomenon firsthand and join the ranks of the believers.

In a published report issued after a scientific investigation by the reserved Linnean Society, the creature was acknowledged as an unknown marine animal with a serpent's head, about a hundred feet long.

Depositions given by people of unimpeachable integrity were offered in the booklet, *The Sea Serpent of Gloucester*, compiled by Irma C. Kierman after two years of research. Col. Thomas H. Perkins, a leading Boston citizen, described his observance:

> I went down with Joseph Lee to Gloucester . . . and found the town alerted. There was hardly anyone who had not seen the serpent. We sat on a promontory on a point that projects into the harbor 50 or 60 feet above the water. I first saw agitation in the water like that following a small vessel. I assumed it was the serpent swimming under water in pursuit of small fish. Almost at once it appeared on the western shore. As he came along, it was easy to see its motion was not like a common

Superstitions of the Sea

snake, but a caterpillar. Almost 40 feet of the body was visible. I had a very fine spy glass. I saw a single horn nine to 12 inches long on the front part of the head. I left Glousester fully certain that the reports were correct.

Another steadfast observer declared:

> I, Solomon Allen, of Gloucester, depose and say that I have seen a strange marine animal that I believe to be a serpent in the harbor of Gloucester. I should judge him to be between 80 and 90 feet in length, apparently having joints from his head to his tail. I was about 150 yards from him when I judged him to be the size of a half-barrel.

Then there came scores of hunters who tried in vain to shoot, harpoon, or capture the serpent. Even experienced whalers from Nantucket, who appeared to be the most adept in the hunt, failed to take the beast. Robert Bragg, a sailor on a becalmed vessel near Eastern Point, was one of the last to see the serpent in that area during the two weeks of excitement. Bragg stated:

> He made no noise. He was much swifter than a whale; his motion was up and down. It had a head like a serpent and when it passed astern of the vessel it threw out several feet of tongue, resembling a fisherman's harpoon, several times, perpendicularly, and let it fall again.

The serpent or one like it was sighted off the coast for many years, last appearing off Rockport, Massachusetts, in July 1886. Descriptions from hundreds of later accounts of persons who observed the serpent all reflect those given by those who first sighted the creature. In general they describe a strange, smooth-skin serpentlike creature with humps on its back that moved in an up-and-down caterpillar undulation on the water at fifteen knots, and could turn in a U.

A similar sighting of unquestionable veracity was that by Capt. Peter M'Quhae and crew of the British frigate *Daedalus,* sailing between the Cape of Good Hope and Saint

Helena in 1852. Watching the serpent for twenty minutes until it passed under the ship's quarter, crewmen related that the creature opened its jaws, which had many, large and jagged teeth, and "seemingly sufficiently capacious to admit of a tall man standing upright between them."

Captain M'Quhae dutifully documented his observance in a report to the Admiralty:

> In reply to your request that I provide information as to the truth of my statement about sighting a sea serpent of extraordinary dimensions, from her Majesty's ship *Daedalus*, under my command, on her passage from the East Indies, I have the honor to acquaint you, for the information of my lords commissioners of the admiralty, that at 5 o'clock PM in latitude 24 degrees, 44 minutes south, and longitude 9 degrees, 22 minutes east, wind fresh from the northeast, with a long ocean swell from the southwest, the ship on the port tack heading northeast, by north, something very unusual was seen by Mr. Saroris, midshipman, rapidly approaching the ship from before the beam. The circumstance immediately reported by him to the officer of the watch, Lieutenant Edgar Drummond, with whom, and Mr. William Barret, the master, I was at the time walking the quarter-deck. The ship's company were at supper.
>
> On our attention being called to the object, it was discovered to be an enormous serpent, with head and shoulders kept about four feet constantly above the surface of the sea; and as nearly as we could approximate by comparing it with the length of what our maintopsail-yard would show in the water, there was at the very least sixty feet of the animal a *fleur d'eau*, no portion of which was, to our perception, used in propelling it through the water, either by vertical or horizontal undulation. It passed rapidly, but so close under our lee quarter that had it been a man of my acquaintance I should have easily recognized the features with the naked eye; and it did not, either in

approaching the ship, or after it had passed our wake, deviate in the slightest degree from its course to the southwest, which it held on at the pace of from twelve to fifteen miles per hour, apparently on some determined purpose.

The diameter of the serpent was about fifteen or sixteen inches behind the head, which was, without any doubt, that of a snake; and it was never, during the twenty minutes that it continued in sight of our glasses, once below the surface of the water—its color a dark brown, with yellowish-white about the throat. It had no fins, but something like the mane of a horse, or rather a bunch of seaweed, washed about its back. It was seen by the quartermaster, the boatswain's mate, and the man at the wheel, in addition to myself and officers above mentioned.

I am having drawings of the serpent made from a sketch taken immediately after it was seen, which I hope to have ready for transmission to my lords commissioners of the admiralty by to-morrow's post.[29]

In the old testament Isaiah tells of Leviathan the serpent: "In that day the Lord will punish with his sword, His fierce, great and powerful sword, Leviathan the gliding serpent, Leviathan the coiling serpent; He will slay the monster of the sea."[30]

Every so often we are given a glimpse of the deep and mysterious secrets the oceans hold when a previously unheard of or presumed extinct sea creature makes its appearance. Heavily documented sightings, such as the Gloucester serpent and even those of lesser credibility, undeniably point to the existence of these unexplained phenomena of the seas.

Sickness

A thirteen-year-old apprentice serving under Captain Woodget on the clipper Cutty Sark approached the captain one day, feeling rather puny. His mates told him to tough it, but he went before the master anyway. "I'm sick, Sir." "Sick? How sick?" "Just sick, Sir. Just sort of sick all over. There's no particular pain anywhere."

The piercing blue eyes of the captain penetrated the boy and his friendly collie there in the cabin looked him over too. "What you need, my boy, is a good cleaning out," the old master finally said. "We'll fix that. Run along to the galley and tell the doctor [cook] to hot up some water. Then come back here."

When the boy returned he saw the captain tying line to each end of a long-handled, wire bottle brush. When cookie brought in the basin of hot water, he hung around and watched with a smile on his face. "What are you going to do with me, Sir?" he asked timidly. "We'll clean you out fore and aft with this," the captain said, waving the bottle brush at the boy. "I'll reeve the fore-part down your throat and the doctor will haul the after-part out through your stern. Come here now. It's going to do you the world of good!" With that the lad was gone like a shot, off to his work, any work that put a good distance between him and the captain's quarters. For the rest of the voyage or through the remainder of his apprenticeship, he was never "sick" again.[31]

Treatment of common illnesses in the early naval days involved an attempt to counteract the symptoms of the patient by purging the body of that which was determined to cause the sickness. Castor oil to rid the body of disease was given for all disorders, especially of the gastrointestinal tract; laudanum was prescribed to slow bowel movement for severe diarrhea or pain; Peruvian bark, which contained quinine, was administered to fight all fevers and heal diseased tissue; a tonic of acidulated wine was offered to strengthen the body during consumption; vomiting was induced or a blister was raised on the skin to facilitate the loss of disease-producing matter for any severe illness; and pearl barley was used as a refrigerant to cool fevers or soothe inflammation.[32]

The miseries of severe seasickness created by the constant motion of a ship in a storm or even in a mild swell caused inevitable hardships not only for first-time voyagers or greenhorns but also for some well-seasoned veterans. The warm and "greasy" galley of many vessels had few hungry hands except for the most senior shellbacks, when rough weather "heaved" a vessel for long periods.

Admiral Lord Horatio Nelson, Britain's greatest sailor, was known as a chronic seasickness sufferer. He braved five months of the illness on his first voyage, and thirty years later, in 1801, he complained of "a heavy sea, sick to death . . . . I shall never get over [it]."[33]

Sailing Forever

It has been said that no seafarer with any depth of experience really loves the sea; love of the sea is a fantasy of romantic poets. It is his imaginary dominance over an unknown element, his survival in that harsh environment, or his experiences at sea that he loves rather than the sea itself—which is mysterious, unpredictable, perilous, and without compassion.

Notes

1. Lovette, *Naval Customs, Traditions, and Usage,* 23.
2. Ibid.
3. Ibid., 25.
4. Ibid., 25-26.
5. Ibid., 29-30.
6. Ibid., 32-34.
7. Baker, *The Folklore of the Sea,* 121.
8. Engel, *The Sea,* 11.
9. Carson, *The Sea around Us,* 151-66.
10. Bassett, *Legends and Superstitions of the Sea and Sailors,* 28.
11. Lys, *A Treasury of American Superstitions,* 398-99.
12. Opie and Tatem, *A Dictionary of Superstitions,* 407.
13. Wernick, (Time-Life) *The Vikings,* 147.
14. *Detroit News,* July 21, 1980.
15. Ibid.
16. Bowditch, *Waves, Wind, and Weather,* 12.
17. Ibid., 13.
18. Carson, *The Sea around Us,* 122.
19. Ibid., 132-33.
20. Bowditch, *Waves, Wind, and Weather,* 10.
21. *Did You Know?* Reader's Digest Assoc., 72.
22. Rappoport, *Superstitions of Sailors,* 197.
23. Bassett, *Legends and Superstitions of the Sea and Sailors,* 26-27.
24. Rappoport, *Superstitions of Sailors,* 34-35.
25. Ibid., 73-74.
26. Cousteau, *The Ocean World,* 223.
27. Ibid., 275-76.
28. Rappoport, *Superstitions of Sailors,* 30-31.
29. Information in this section taken from Estes, "Serpents of the Sea", ed., *Yankees Under Sail,* 148-59.
30. Isa. 27:1.
31. Villiers, *The Way of a Ship,* 238-39.
32. Fowler, *Jack Tars & Commodores,* 134.
33. *Did You Know?* Reader's Digest Assoc., 275.

20. Tattoos

Traditions

A symbol of love or luck they wore,
The true salt flaunted many more.
Patriot's valor, customs of yore,
Traditions of honor, and esprit de corps.

Tattoos

Tattooing became popular with sailors about the late fifteenth century when European vessels reached the East Indies. Until recently, the skill was thought to have originated with the early South Pacific islanders or with the Central American Indians, who also practiced tattooing and body painting. But then came the amazing discovery of the five thousand-year-old mummified corpse of an iceman found in the Italian Alps in 1991. On the incredibly preserved skin of this man, who froze to death about 3000 B.C., were markings of a cross behind his left knee and several sets of parallel blue lines on his lower back and right ankle, which are believed to be tattoos.[1] Evidently, the art of tattooing is far older than expected.

Now associated almost exclusively with seafarers, tattoos have been in vogue as a distinguishing mark of their profession ever since the sailor became acquainted with the customs of those who practiced the art form. Seaman Robert Stainsby, a crew member on Captain Cook's first voyage to Tahiti in 1768, is believed to have been the first westerner to wear a tattoo.[2] The popularity of tattooing among seamen soon became widespread. According to a description of the men wanted for the famed mutiny on the *Bounty* (April 28, 1789), twenty-one out of the twenty-five men wore tattoos, many of whom were listed as being "much tattooed."[3]

Some sailors wore a tattoo for protection. A tattoo of a pig on the instep or knee was considered a guard against drowning; pig and chicken tattoos gave one the assurance of never being without "ham and eggs"; a star between the finger and thumb was believed to help bring a sailor safely home; Protestant sailors bore a tattooed cross on their arms so that if they perished in a Catholic country they might receive a proper burial; a crucifix or an image of Christ on the back offered the chance of a lighter flogging; and a wide and handsome display of tattoos was thought to be an effective guard against venereal disease.[4]

Nude women, cats, horseshoes, four-leafed clovers, fouled anchors, and the four playing-card suit symbols were all considered good luck tattoos.

Because all human orifices were considered a temptation to evil spirits, adjacent areas of the mouth, ears, eyes, nose, and sexual organs were sometimes tattooed as a guard against entry by the devil.[5]

Although a tattooed heart on a sailor might be thought of as a symbol of his sweetheart's love, an older belief was that the heart represented the center of one's courage and intelligence.

Some sailors believed that the more tattoos they had, the saltier they appeared. These walking advertisements for tattoo parlors were undoubtedly much sought after by the carnival trade upon separation from their service.

After a sailor subjected himself to the painful decorative practice, he could expect swelling, fever, and possibly even death from septicemia. No sailor was considered exceptionally salty or fully initiated by his peers unless he was adorned with a tattoo.

One fourteen-year-old greenhorn signed on a Scottish fishing boat with a crew of eleven of which ten bore elaborate tattoos. Having little experience, he had fallen overboard twice before settling into the routine of his apprenticeship. Because he refused to be tattooed, he was told that he would never make it as a sailor. As he was the target of much scorn and ridicule, the entire group further assured him that his clumsiness was caused by his refusal to be decorated with the mark of a true salt.[6]

Courtesy Todd Clary

I once visited a tattoo parlor in Halifax where one could choose from over 340 different designs including variations of nude women, panthers, serpents, flags, cartoon characters, birds, the grim reaper, dripping daggers, cannons, crossed harpoons, ships, religious pictures, and selected scrollwork with names or initials.

In the obscene category, one could choose the portrayal of an innocent-looking woman with a broad hat that the bearer could transform into a naked women with her legs apart by raising his arm. Her buttocks wiggled with the flexing of muscles. Sleazy tattoos of flies or bees on the genitals were also available for those brave enough to undergo the torture and threat of infection.

One of the more elaborate full torso designs was the complete and highly detailed version of a fox hunt. Colorful horsemen dashing through the green, jumping fences, chased a goodly number of hounds hot on the trail of a fox, of which only the tail was visible and protruding from the bearer's bottom. A tattoo of this caliber might have taken up to three years to complete.

Traditions

The custom of burning the "dead horse," marking the day when a crew "stopped working for nothing," was a much heralded ceremony in the days of sail in the navy and in the merchant marine.[7] Each seaman received about a month's pay in advance, which more often than not was spent on high living before shipping out. After four weeks at sea, or at whatever time the advance had been worked off "flogging a dead horse," the crew would fashion a horse of canvas stuffed with waste material, complete with mane and tail. Permission was then granted to burn the horse (at night for a more spectacular event) hoisted to the end of a yardarm. From then on the men began to accrue wages "on the books," and plans could be made for activities at the next port. All watches happily joined in singing the chorus:

Now, old horse your time has come,
And we say so, for we know so!
Altho' many a race you've won,
Oh! poor old man,
You're going now to say good-bye,
And we say so, for we know so;
Poor old horse, you're going to die.

During the 1976 Tall Ships meet in New York Harbor, the crew of the brigantine *Phoenix* sent overboard their "horse" stuffed with burlap and scrap chafing material in reenactment of the old custom at least in gesture, for the crew had not worked a "dead horse."

Dueling, the practice of settling "affairs of honor among gentlemen," was a custom relegated to the extinct section of the code of an officer and a gentleman. This method of redress was not only confined to senior officers, but also to juniors and midshipmen. It has been estimated that in the first half century of the U.S. Navy, more officers were killed in duels than in battle. One of the most famous duels in naval history took place between Commodores James Barron and Stephen Decatur because of a heated dispute surrounding Barron's restoration to duty after five years' suspension of rank and pay.

Just before the duel, on the morning of March 22, 1820, Barron related to Decatur the hope that "on meeting in another world [they] would be better friends than in this." Decatur replied, "I have never been your enemy, Sir." At the short count of two, both officers fired and both fell. Decatur was shot in the abdomen and Barron was wounded in the thigh. Decatur died twelve hours later at his home in Lafayette Square,

Washington, at the age of 41. Barron was restored to active service, later to become senior commodore of the navy.

Burning the dead horse, the initiation of greenhorns, the gesture of saluting, the firing of three volleys at funerals, and hundreds of other solemn ceremonies and customs, including even the practice of dueling, were all steeped in the traditions of honor inherent in the navy and in the brotherhood of seamen of all nations.

Tradition is the foundation of such customs as which side of the ship will be the ceremonial side, whether taps should be sounded at a funeral, or what side of the quarterdeck is the captain's. The significance of tradition, however, has a far deeper meaning and value than as a guide for proper protocol. An excerpt from an essay, "Military Rule of Obedience," describes its value:

> The value of tradition to the social body is immense. The veneration for practices, or for authority, consecrated by long acceptance, has a reserve of strength which cannot be obtained by any novel device. Respect for the old customs is planted deep in the hearts, as well as in the intelligence, of all inheritors of English speaking polity.

A great tradition was given to us when that first frigate of the dominating and invincible Royal Navy, the *Serapis,* was engaged and defeated by our infant navy and John Paul Jones in the *Bonhomme Richard* on September 23, 1779. When the captain of the *Serapis* hailed to ask if he had surrendered, Jones shouted those most famous words, "We have not yet begun to fight." After the victory that inspired our tiny navy and gave hope to the American cause, the tradition of honor continued when the British captain presented his sword to Jones, who returned it saying, "You have fought gallantly, Sir, and I hope your king will give you a better ship."

Both sides of the Atlantic were shocked, our young navy received another boost of confidence, and tradition was broadened when Isaac Hull defeated HMS *Guerriere* in the *Constitution* during the War of 1812. The brave exploits of the "Yankee sailors" and their frigates gained attention in the *London Times*:

It is not merely that an English frigate has been taken, after what, we are free to confess, may be called a brave resistance, but that it has been taken by a new enemy, an enemy unaccustomed to such triumphs, and likely to be rendered insolent and confident by them.

The Naming of Old Ironsides

The victory indeed enkindled the spirit of confidence that led to the subsequent victories of Decatur's capture of the *Macedonian,* the *Constitution*'s mutilation of the frigate *Java,* the capture of the *Cyane* and *Levant,* and later the defeat of the British on Lake Erie by Oliver Hazard Perry in 1813.

It was a time when famous fighting slogans were coined and never forgotten. Capt. James Lawrence's dying words in the battle between the *Shannon* and the *Chesapeake* resound to this day: "Fight her till she sinks and don't give up the ship." On Lake Erie Perry flew on a flag of the *Lawrence* the last words of Capt. Lawrence: "Don't give up the ship."

After his glorious victory there, Perry would dispatch the famous words, "We have met the enemy and they are ours, two ships, two brigs, one schooner, and one sloop."

Lake Erie Battle

Deeds, actions, and victories such as these would add impetus and honored tradition to American sea power forever.

The memory of great traditions enhances and toughens the fiber and character of men. It has always been the objective of the navy to maintain and cultivate not only the traditions of the service but also the traditions of the sea. Those who know and follow those traditions share a brotherhood with the seamen of all nations. The pride of profession, of striving to be courageous in the face of peril and adversity, emanating the famous patriots, is perhaps best characterized in the words of Joseph Conrad:

> The mysteriously born tradition of sea craft commands unity in an occupation in which men have to depend on each other. It raises them so to speak above the frailties of their dead selves.

Bravery in battle was epitomized by the words of Admiral Nelson at Copenhagen when a cannonball smashed splinters off the mainmast close to where he stood. With a smile he said, "It is warm work, and this may be the last of us at any moment."

The sea has been the stage for some of the most daring and noble deeds of man, and stout courage amid battle, peril, or storm has inspired the documentation of sagas that thrill mankind. From the days of the first seafarers, to the thunderous sea battles, to the perils known in great tempests, the heroic and honored actions of those at sea become the golden pages of tradition.

Notes

1. "The Iceman," *National Geographic*, June 1993, 36-47.
2. Baker, *The Folklore of the Sea*, 80.
3. Thrower, *Life at Sea in the Age of Sail*, 68-71.
4. Baker, *The Folklore of the Sea*, 81.
5. *Encyclopedia of Magic & Superstition*, 187.
6. Beck, *Folklore & the Sea*, 197.
7. Information in this section taken from Lovette, *Naval Customs, Traditions, and Usage*, 3-51.

21. Unlucky Ships

Vessels cursed and Jonah ships marked,
Death ships with the devil so embarked.
Many that sailed them heard the siren's call,
But one ship was the unluckiest of all.

There have been thousands of unlucky ships. There were those that through some misfortune during building or launch, through some indifference to ceremony, or some taboo deviation from custom met their untimely demise, the loss quickly blamed on the stigma the vessel carried because of the misfortune. There were those famous ones such as the great *Titanic*, lost on her maiden voyage with but a few unlucky blemishes on her record. There were those Jonah ships, tainted with many misfortunes of one kind or another during their long careers, which were finally but tragically lost, it was said, because of the indelibly unlucky marks upon them. There were those whimsical unlucky ships that had the reputation of ramming everything in their path, and those unlucky "death ships" that claimed a life nearly every time they sailed. But there was one ship, probably the most unlucky of them all, whose dark and stained career was filled with nearly every conceivable misfortune possible.

This is the story of the infamous four-masted barque *Wanderer*, built by W. H. Potter and Company at Queen's Dock, Liverpool, and sent down the ways Saturday, August 20, 1891.[1] The 309-foot long, 46-foot beam beauty had two sister ships, the *Wayfarer* and the *Seafarer*, built by the same firm in 1886 and 1888 respectively. Contrary to rumors that no doubt circulated because of her misfortunes, her launch was without mishap and it was not on a Friday.

The strongly constructed vessel had steel frames, beams, and shell plating; living quarters were built into a central bridge amidships, which stretched completely across the main deck. Although this structure added greater strength to the hull and provided accommodations where the least motion was likely, there were distasteful disadvantages as well. Crewmen constantly grumbled at the aggravation of having to climb to the top of this deckhouse to reach lines at the mainmast fiferails or to simply pass from one end of the ship to the other. When the vessel took big seas, rather than wash away, they flooded the forecastles and deck forward of the house, making the crew's bunks perpetually sodden. Further, the length of steering chains attached to the steering wheel drum on top of the house resulted in difficulty in steering the vessel from amidships.

With stout yet handsome rigging, remarkable sheer, graceful lines, tastefully painted yellow masts, and black, white, and light blue hull, she presented a breathtaking and svelte appearance. Her figurehead of a beautiful woman peering forward from beneath her right hand that shaded her brow added the final touch to her sleek appearance. The carving was modeled after the face and figure of Mrs. W. H. Potter, wife of the builder, who, it was said, was a lady of unmatched beauty and sweetness. Sailors long remembered the figurehead as one of the most beautiful of the time, and many an amorous seaman fell strangely in love with the cold, gazing beauty. As often happened, the figurehead became the personality of the ship, and this ship, this mysteriously fatal ship, would, like a siren, lure many to their doom.

On Saturday, October 17, 1891, with a cargo of coal for San Francisco, the *Wanderer*, under command of Capt. George Currie, a fifty-two-year-old native Nova Scotian, known as "genial Captain Currie," departed in tow of the tug *Wrestler*. The region was being wracked by violent gales that had assaulted the area for several days. At tea the day before sailing, Mr. Potter recommended that Captain Currie postpone sailing until Monday. Currie, however, insisted on the Saturday departure because it was the anniversary of his bringing-out of the *Wayfarer*, which he had previously commanded for five years. He considered it his lucky day. So, with a crew of thirty-seven men and boys, only three of which were sober, the pristine vessel, seemingly anxious for its maiden jaunt, was towed out of her slip toward the sea. On the way, an able-bodied seaman joined on through the acrobatics of a "pierhead jump" as the vessel slowly passed a pier. As she glided by in all her splendor, stevedores, crewmen from other vessels, and throngs of other awed spectators three-cheered and bade her farewell.

By evening the next day, after her pilot had been discharged, the tug, still laboring with her tow in the growing tempest, signaled if they should not run for shelter. Currie answered, "Keep towing: we will not put in," and the pair pushed on together in the teeth of the coming storm.

On they struggled, as the seas grew mountainous and roared upon them from the blackness of the night. Without warning and unbeknown to all, the towing hawser snapped like thread, and the proud *Wanderer* wallowed out of control while the tug was dashed away nearly on her beam ends, each vessel left to fend for itself.

Soon aware of the calamity, Currie desperately called for the men to set sail, but the ruthless storm laughed as the drunken, half asleep, and inexperienced lot were driven aloft to wrestle with sails that thundered and blew to rags like cheap cloth. Those on deck, awash in flooded footing and braced against the onslaught of the raging seas coming aboard, dodged heavy gear falling from above.

In the madness three lower topsails were set, but Currie, afraid he would be blown ashore, wore ship in the roaring gale, his ship finally responding with a gallop after plunging and rolling in the trough of the sea. As she came to windward all three topsails were quickly blown to torn ribbons of rag.

As intense lightning illuminated the black night, the fore topgallant mast suddenly snapped and fell but was snared by its rigging, sending an awful rain of more heavy gear to the deck. After a crewman finally succeeded in hoisting distress lights after three attempts, the lanterns came crashing down when the spanker gaff tore away and was blown overboard. With the ship still out of control, efforts to set the inner jib and stay foresail began but was halted with a jam of the rigging aloft. Through the brave work of the oldest apprentice, the jam was freed when he climbed to the foremast crosstrees, dodging sure death from the windblown and madly swinging tackle. His gallant work enabled the staysail to be hoisted, but it too was ripped to rags by the screaming winds, and the lad was knocked senseless when hit by heavy tackle as he returned to the deck. When the main topgallant collapsed in its rigging, many of those on deck scurried for cover and remained in hiding because the dreaded darkness, except for intermittent flashes of lightning, concealed the wildly swinging maze of deadly spars, chains, and blocks. The few stout hands that stood by were sent to rout the mutinous and cowering drunks.

Now the captain himself tried to signal distress with blue lights above the deckhouse amidships but was struck on the head by one of the swinging pendulums of death. He was carried below and stretched out beside six others badly hurt. The mate succeeded in rigging distress lights and the sending off of rockets, which was soon followed by the further torrent of falling gear from the collapse of the mizen topgallant.

Captain Currie died during the night, and before dawn, the winds still shrieking, the small steamer *Merannio* had answered the distress calls and was standing by to take the ravaged *Wanderer* in tow and bring her into Kingstown, where she was finally moored the following morning. She had survived the worst storm to hit that area in eighteen years.

Already she had a bad name. The superstitious said she would never come to any good at sea. As beautiful as she was, she had killed her captain and her maiden voyage was a disaster. This incident was the first of *Wanderer*'s misfortunes. The succeeding mishaps follow in order of their occurrence.

(2) During her next putting-forth, a voyage (which really was her first) from Liverpool to San Francisco, November 21, 1891, the crew believed the ship was haunted by the ghost of Captain Currie. About a thousand miles from her destination, her cargo of coal was found to be on fire. The vessel made port and the fire was extinguished without major damage.

(3) After unloading her cargo she was stranded on the mud at Saucalito without damage. A man fell overboard from aloft while at this station without major injury.

(4) Also while at Saucalito, another man fell from aloft onto a teak spreader, which broke his fall to the deck where he broke both legs.

(5) After sailing from San Francisco August 18, 1892, for Queenstown, a newly assigned seaman, refusing to take orders, became violent and jumped overboard. The vessel was becalmed at the time, and the man being ordered aboard declared that he intended to swim home. He eventually returned to the ship and was brought aboard with great difficulty.

(6) During the same voyage, seaman Robert Jackson fell overboard and was never seen again. He was suspected of hitting his head in the fall; all that was found was his cap. The "rowdy scoundrel" that had jumped ship to swim home was sent to prison for six weeks and another mutinous seaman was fined fifty shillings and paid off.

(7) While on her second voyage, sailing from Liverpool to Philadelphia May-June 1893, two men were put in irons after an ax-throwing incident that occurred after a fall said to have been caused by a man being made to wear oilskins while doing dangerous work aloft.

(8) After reaching her destination, she was involved in a mishap in the Delaware River when she snapped her towing hawsers and dragged a tug downriver and into a pier. Running free, she struck another pier, holed and smashed the superstructure of the ferry *Cooper's Point,* and damaged her rudder before being brought under control.

(9) After departing Philadelphia in July 1893, she encountered a hurricane and survived with remarkably slight damage. A heavy sea came aboard and washed a man into some spare spars that were lifted from their lashings to gently settle down and pin the man's head beneath them. With some difficulty the spars were raised but they nearly caused the man to drown.

(10) Many of the crew were injured after surviving a vicious cyclone in the Bay of Begal while on a voyage to Calcutta, the likes of which her veteran crewmen described as the most terrible weather they ever knew.

(11) On the same voyage one seaman died of apoplexy and another died of cholera.

(12) Four crewmen who refused to work were imprisoned for ten days.

(13) In November 1896, after leaving Philadelphia, she once again took charge of her tug and went aground on shallow sands. After refloating she grounded again.

(14) On a trip to Calcutta in June 1899, an old sailor took sick and died from what was thought to be old age.

(15) Between the Cape of Good Hope and Ascension

Island on the same trip, another sailor became sick and died from what the captain called "eating diabetes." After the man had been locked up and put on a diet of soft foods for several days, he broke into the food stores and stuffed himself with peasoup and biscuits and was found dead on deck by the watch. The captain was accused of starving the men to death.

(16) In October 1899, the *Wanderer*'s hull color was changed from black to gray, which most of the men considered a bad omen. The day after Christmas the captain fell into a lower hold and broke a leg and ribs.

(17) In May 1900, she shipped one of the biggest seas she ever encountered. The cook was badly scalded when water burst in the galley, smashed skylights, and flooded the cabins.

(18) Much fighting occurred between the steward and the carpenter at this time.

(19) Renewed fighting in July resulted in the steward and carpenter being unfit for duty.

(20) Fever visited the ship while in Shanghai and two weeks later claimed the third mate, who was buried at sea.

(21) Many of the crew deserted the ship, resulting in shipping an inexperienced crew.

(22) The *Wanderer* encounters severe weather, which plays havoc with the green crew.

(23) On March 13, 1901, the tug *Royal Briton* slipped her towrope and disappeared, leaving the *Wanderer* to drift

helpless in a fog, but rejoined the vessel after the fog lifted. Upon arrival in Bristol, her crew related that she was an unfortunate ship.

(24) While the *Wanderer* was being towed from Bristol to begin a voyage to New York, April 1901, a woman was seen running on the road abreast of the vessel and waving to one of the few white men aboard. The man was said to have murdered the woman's husband for her love. The crew thought this incident to be an omen of bad luck.

(25) During the voyage the ballast shifted.

(26) Because of illness, the captain was confined to his quarters, and the second mate was unable to work for most of the trip.

(27) On October 10, 1901, seaman C. Christiansen fell overboard while reefing the fore upper topsail and was not seen again.

(28) At Shanghai many of the crew were unable to work after drinking native liquor.

(29) While lying at Tacoma, Washington, in June 1903, the ship was robbed of her compasses. The burglar, who was later captured, acted in concert with one of the crew.

(30) After a seaman deserted, he was returned to the ship by paying blood money to a crimp who had lured him ashore. This man later made a brutal assault on the captain.

(31) Much fighting aboard.

(32) In December, 1903, The *Wanderer* again took charge of her tug and collided with the steamer *Strathmore*.

(33.) A few days before reaching San Francisco, after an unusually bad-luck voyage in 1906, twenty-five of her crew mutinied, refusing to work.

(34) Homeward bound from San Francisco near the equator, she lost her fore-topgallant mast and splintered her main topgallant mast as well. An "incompetent slacker," who was aloft trying to clear the resulting tangle, fell along with the mass of gear into the sea when he cut the line that held the mass in place. He came through the harrowing ordeal without a scratch.

(35) Later in the voyage the topgallant mast snapped again.

(36) On the clear early morning of April 14, 1907, while lying at anchor at the mouth of the Elbe River, near Cuxhaven, Germany, she was struck on the port bow by the steamer *Gertrud Woermann*. Some said that her riding lights were not bright enough to be seen. The *Wanderer* heeled over and sank, quickly settling into quicksand and becoming a total loss. No lives were lost. Her hulk, because of a navigational hazard, was eventually blown up.

An incident offers a strange footnote to the story of the unlucky ship. On the night of the sinking, Captain Brander, one of her old masters, awoke from a dead sleep and aroused his entire household to relate an unusual vision he had had of his old ship being run into and sunk by a steamer. The dream was so clear in his mind that he envisioned the crew leaving the ship before she slowly rolled over and sank. The captain had no idea where the ship was at the time, but the next day, when he read an account in the papers, the facts surrounding the loss matched those of his dream even to the hour of the sinking.

John Masefield wrote this epitaph about the *Wanderer*:

Since nothing could save her, men blasted the wreck from the stream
And left her dead bones in the quicksand full fathom five down,
She lies there deep sunken, unminded, sea-creatures encrust her,
White shells, such as cover the *Siren*, red frond-waving weeds.
Herself is not there, being beauty Eternal, alive,
She wanders the waters of thought, past disasters, past hates,
Past the world's disapproval, across the black seas of despair,
And on, beyond anguish to havens of peace whence she brings
Hope, Mercy and Courage, all gentle and beautiful things.
She shines on the waters, in summer's mid-daylight she shines
For the hand-shielded brow of her gazer is crowned with a star
And gently and surely she sweeps through the waters of thought
Up, over the curve of the planet, uplifting a song:

"Adventure on, companions, the attempt
At high adventure brings reward undreamt.
The raging sea is grim with reefs unconn'd:
There is a way, a haven is beyond.
Way for yourself, a harbourage for you,
Where every quarry spirit can pursue
Is, in the glory of the dream come true."

So singing, she wanders the waters with white wing on wing
Star-lighted, starguided, the sea-gleaming beautiful thing.[2]

Notes

1. Information in this section is from Masefield, *The Wanderer of Liverpool*.
2. Ibid., 103.

22. Vikings

Out of the north the warriors sailed,
And over the land the innocents wailed,
Deliver us, from the Norsemen's fury,
Let us sleep tonight without a worry.

Vikings

From the villages, from the meadows, from churches and monasteries across the land, the pitiful cry was heard. *A furore Normannorum libera nos, Domine*—"From the fury of the Northmen deliver us, O Lord."

No one really knows why the Scandinavians chose to plunder rather than seek peaceful settlement, especially when many of their population were thought to be peaceful settlers. Historians have theorized that it was because of overpopulation of their barren homeland. Regardless, the Scandinavian Vikings, also known as the Norsemen, Northmen, or Danes (as Ashmen by the Germans, *Gaill* by the Irish, *Majus* by the Spanish Arabs, and Rus or Ros by the Swedes, Slavs, Arabs, and Greeks) incessantly plagued and profitably plundered the coasts of Europe and the British Isles for nearly three centuries with a vivacity and purpose unmatched but by the Roman Empire. They sacked cities in England, Scotland, Ireland, and the North sea islands. They sailed south to pillage towns along the German and French coasts, and from the Baltic they sailed east and through the rivers Dvina, Volga, and Dnieper, where the Swedish Vikings, known as the Rus, settled and gave their name in founding modern Russia. In 912 they raided the regions around the Caspian sea. Venturing west across the

Atlantic they discovered Iceland about A.D. 860, Greenland in 982, and Newfoundland about 1000, five hundred years before Columbus came to the Americas.

Beginning with blitzlike, hit-and-run tactics, small unorganized bands of brawny seaborne warriors in their sleek long boats swept across the North sea to raid, plunder, and kill. The Vikings' first attack on the south coast of England in A.D. 789 was marked by the murder of the king's representative in that region.[1]

According to Anglo-Saxon Chronicles, for nearly fifty years from 835 onward, hardly a year went by in which the shores of England were not attacked. In 866, with a force of a thousand sea warriors, the Dane Viking, Ivar the Boneless, ignored the offer of inhabitants of Kent to buy peace and instead crept inland by night and plundered more treasure than he would have gained through peace. The attacks continued until 886, when a treaty allowed the Scandinavians to settle in northern England. By then the Vikings had conquered more than half of that country[2].

A favored early target of the Viking forays was monasteries. The pagan attackers from the sea had no love or respect for Christendom, little regard for human life, and certainly no qualms about attacking Christian sanctuaries. For generations these institutions served as repositories of the bequeathed riches of both the holy and the wicked flocks they served. Furnishings and ornaments of gold, silver, ivory, silk, and precious gems were there for the taking and were unguarded except for a few timid priests or monks who were viciously murdered on their altars.

In 793, an attack on the small island of Lindisfarne off the coast of Northumbria and the plunder of the monastery of Saint Cuthbert there was chronicled by the English scholar Alcuin:

> Never before has such terror appeared in Britain as we have now suffered from a pagan race, nor was it thought that such an inroad from the sea could be made. Behold, the church of St. Cuthbert spattered with the blood of the priests of God, despoiled of all its ornaments; a place more venerable than all in Britain is given as prey to pagan peoples.[3]

When the Irish monastery on the small island of Iona was attacked in 806, for the third time in eleven years, the crazed marauders massacred sixty-eight monks.[4] The Irish monastery of Armagh was attacked five times, three raids coming in a single month in 832.[5] One of these attacks was staged by the Norwegian Viking Thorgils, who commanded a fleet of 120 ships and ten thousand warriors.[6]

An example of the Vikings' savage behavior can be imagined through the writings of eleventh-century chroniclers who related the mass killings that commonly took place during a Viking yule festival. The event was celebrated in January, "by sacrificing ninety-nine humans and as many horses to their gods." Honoring Freya and Thor, they made sacrifices every nine years. The bodies of men, women, and animals were hung in holy effigy in a sacred ash grove where "of all living things that are male and female, they offer nine heads."[7]

One frenzied Viking slaughter was recorded in 867 when King Ella of Northumbia was killed. In a sadistic ritual called "carving the blood eagle," they cut open his rib cage and tore his lungs out through his back, the organs apparently quivering during the victim's dying breaths.[8] No one was spared. Innocent clergy, the elderly, women, and even babies fell to their wanton killing. Word of such atrocities spread like wildfire and carried with it the terror one might expect if they did not yield to the Norsemen's invasions.

They had wild rolling eyes and were known to make guttural animal sounds. Often without armor, they would bite the edges of their shields as they stormed their adversaries. A Viking displaying these shock tactics came to be known as a *berserkr*, an Old Norse term thought to mean "bare skin," or without shirt, possibly referring to the omission of the protective coats-of-mail shirts worn over leather tunics, which repelled their foes' weapons. The word *berserk* came to characterize the violent battle fury of the Vikings.[9]

The favored weapons of the Vikings were the double-edged sword, the spear, and later the ax, which was recognized as the standard weapon of these warriors. Sometimes a single-edged sword called a *sax* and bows and arrows were also used. Some Vikings believed that if a sword was quenched in blood, or "hardened in blood," it would be especially effective.[10] Many swords, particularly those of chieftains, received a special name, such as Odin's Flame, Fires of Odin, Battle Snake, or Sea-King's Fire.

Axes were sometimes named after forests, timber, or after blood or wounds.[11]

The meaning of the word *Viking* has been long disputed. Many say it is derived from the Old Norse words *vik,* meaning inlet, bay, or creek, which could be associated with the maze of fjords in the Vikings' homeland. Others say it is derived from *vig,* meaning battle or warlike, or from *vikja,* to turn aside or deviate. In medieval Scandinavian languages a *vikingr* was a pirate or sea raider; the word was most likely adopted during or after the Viking invasions began. Another theory suggests that *ing* means "son of," indicating that *Viking* stands for "son of fjords."

What the Vikings gave up in battle strategy they made up for in their cunning and guerrilla-type tactics. The stealthy attack at Nantes, France, in June 842 saw the Vikings row a hundred miles up the Loire River to sack the city on the night of the celebration of Saint John's Eve, when all were preoccupied with the festivities that marked the beginning of summer. The warriors dashed into the crowds, killed countless merrymakers, and burnt the town.[12]

The Norwegian Viking Olaf the Stout and his force met with stiff resistance on the Thames in 1009, when his boats were stoned by opposing forces as they tried to pass beneath London Bridge. Expecting a fight, Olaf constructed heavy mat roofs over his boats for protection, but many had to withdraw from the heavy pelting of stones. Not to be outdone, the Vikings managed to get beneath the bridge, affix grappling hooks to the timbers, then row downstream to weaken the pilings, which caused the bridge to tumble down. From this escapade is the origin of the old nursery rhyme, *"London Bridge Is Falling Down"*.[13]

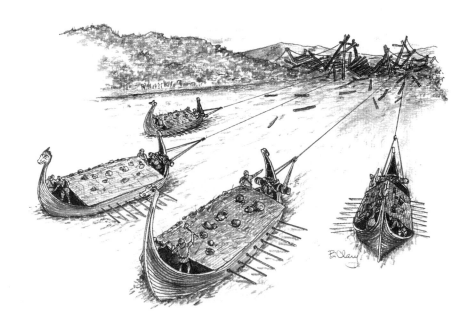

The Vikings were masters at seamanship, but their ancestors, it appears, had perfected their craft long before the Viking age. The design characteristics of the unique, sturdy, and seaworthy Viking boats were handed down from the Bronze Age (4000 to 3000 B.C.) in Scandinavia. Images of boats in rock carvings at Kalnes, Tune, in southeast Norway bear a profound resemblance to the Hjortspring boat of the fourth/third century B.C., which is the oldest Scandinavian plank-built boat found. In other words, the Viking boats possessed many of the same features as the Bronze Age boats, which underscores a remarkable continuity of Scandinavian boat design down through the ages.[14] Bronze Age rock carvings also depict animal or reptile heads on the tops of long stem posts like those later frightening carvings on the prows of Viking boats.[15]

Built with handed down knowledge rather than exact plans, though all Viking boats were similar, no two were exactly alike. The largest Viking vessel, the flagship of the fleets, was the *drakar,* or dragon ship, which measured over 160 feet long with a 25-foot beam. With as many as 72 oars and a crew of 300 men, the vessels high freeboard offered ample protection during battle. The long ship, or *langskip,* the most versatile of all Viking boats, used for trading or raiding, could carry 200 men or 20 tons of cargo. This 100-foot long, 20-foot beam vessel carried about 50 oars. The 70-foot long vessel known as the *karfi* was used as a fleet utility vessel or pleasure craft, carried 16 oars, and had a draft of less than three feet, which allowed travel in shallow waters. The 54-foot boat called the *knarr,* used principally for trading and exploring, was propelled by sail alone, and could transport 15 tons of cargo.[16]

These boats were built of oak and were double-ended to facilitate the ease of landings and departures. The larger vessels carried one 40-foot mast and a single large rectangular woolen sail reinforced with rope or leather strips.

The boats were steered with a tiller bar attached to a rudder or large oar on the starboard side that could be drawn aboard to enable the vessel to sail into shallow water or to run ashore The origin of the word *starboard* is from the Norse word *stjornbordi*, the name given this ingenious steering board on the right side of the boat.[17]

Planking was nailed lapstreak fashion, or each row of planks overlapping the one below. These planks were nailed to the keel and to each other, but were lashed to the framework of ribs, giving the hull both strength and flexibility.

One of the most remarkable achievements of the Viking mariners was their ability to navigate distant waters without the aid of a compass. On voyages within sight of shore, they steered by established landmarks, the flights of birds, cloud formations, sea color, whales, and sea soundings.

It is generally accepted that the discovery of new lands— Iceland, Greenland, North America—was through the accidental sightings of these landfalls after being driven off their course during a storm or in a fog. It is amazing how later voyages, across great expanses of water to these lands, were able to find their way even though landmarks and other sightings still rendered aid, as this medieval guide to Greenland relates:

> From Hernar in Norway set sail due west for Hvarf in Greenland. You are to sail to the north of Shetland in such a way that you can just sight it in clear weather; but to the south of the Faroes, in such a way that the sea seems to be half way up the mountain slopes; and steer south of Iceland, in such a way that you can sight birds and whales from there.[18]

To obtain the most efficient angle of their sails, eleventh-century Vikings closely watched a weather vane, embellished with monsters and serpents, mounted on the masthead or the bow.[19]

Believed used at first in Norse jewelry, a major advancement in Viking navigation was the sunstone, an amazing calcite mineral crystal called cordierite, discovered in Scandinavia and Iceland. When this remarkable crystal was positioned at a right angle to polarized sunlight, the crystal quickly changed from yellow to a dark blue; by postitioning the crystal until it turned dark, a mariner could determine the exact position of the sun. Because the color change was evident even in fog, with overcast skies, or when the sun was below the horizon, it proved to be a crude but invaluable navigating instrument.[20]

Vikings feared dwarfs, trolls, and elves, believing them to be visitations of the spirits of the dead. Little house spirits seen as old men with pointed hoods were thought of as friendly unless upset or ignored. By setting out scraps of food and bowls of milk, the Vikings thought they could be enlisted to help with household chores. If angered they were blamed for the breakage of tableware and cooking basins or for cuts, bruises, and burns. As a guard against the spirits, Vikings wore a necklace with ivory or metal lucky charms in the form of little hammers symbolizing Thor.[21]

Luck was considered the most valuable possession a man could have. If he was lucky, a man was looked up to even if he lacked skill or wisdom. Some Vikings were widely known for having women-luck, weapon-luck, weather-luck, or victory-luck. Those going into battle sought out the famous chieftains who had victory-luck. Those unfortunates known for not having weather-luck might have been thrown into the sea at the approach of stormy weather.[22]

Although void of Christian beliefs, Viking traders were said to fall to the ground in adoration of wooden carvings. At the homestead, sacrificed animals affixed to poles outside one's dwelling were proof of homage paid to the gods.[23]

The Norsemen also made thank-offerings of live birds or of food and drink after surviving the perils of battle, after passing through menacing rapids or other sea hazards. They would go to an island where a giant tree grew (their symbol of the world) and stick spears in a circle in the ground, which contained birds.[24]

Some were real, some were imagined, but many were the perils faced by seagoing Vikings. They braved great whirlpools (which they may have indeed encountered off Norway[25]), giant waves, or the so-called sea hedges, polar ice, icebergs, and polar bears. Of the more imaginary nature they feared giant whales that could swallow their ships whole. In this category was the sea ogress, a terrifying sea monster with the upper body of a horse and the lower body of a serpent with a coiling broad tail. By attaching itself to one side of a vessel with its long tail underneath to the other side, the monster was thought capable of capsizing boats.[26]

According to legend, the runic alphabet was believed by Vikings to be a gift from Odin. The Old Norse word *run* defines "mystery," which in turn describes the vagueness of the alphabet's origin. However, rune symbols discovered in the dolomite region of northern Italy were thought to have come from an unknown group of Alpine people in the first century B.C. From there they were used by nomadic Germanic tribes in the Christian era, worked gradually into the Teutonic language, and eventually were taken north to Scandinavia about the third century.

The Viking sixteen-letter runic alphabet was in use about the ninth century. The runes, inscribed in wood, stone, and metal, documented special events and important places in the daily life of the Viking. Because they wrote only in runes, they represent practically the only source of the Norsemen's written records. These mystical and ancient letters from the gods were carved into gravestones, trail markers, charms, and weapons.

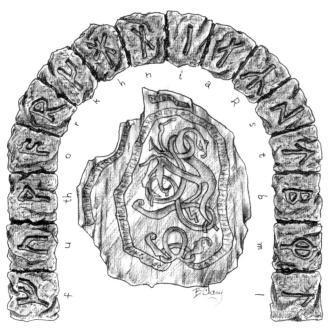

Each letter of the alphabet had a twofold meaning: a means of spelling and an icon representing an object or an idea. In other words, the first letter of the alphabet, *F*, used alone meant "cattle," but it could also be used along with other letters to form a word. The other fifteen letters represented: manly strength, giant, god, journey, torch, hail, need, ice, year, bow of yew wood, sun, the god Tiw of war, birch twig, man, and water.

Being a gift from Odin, runes were believed to possess great magic, and runic letters carved into small sticks were used for spells, curses, and prayer.[27]

Notes

1. Wilson, *The Vikings and Their Origins*, 72.
2. Ibid.
3. Ibid.
4. La Fay, *The Vikings*, 74.
5. Wernick, *The Vikings*, 16.
6. Ibid., 82.
7. Ashley, *The Amazing World of Superstition, Prophecy, Luck, Magic, & Witchcraft*, 173.
8. Wernick, *The Vikings*, 27.
9. Ibid.
10. Simpson, *Everyday Life in the Viking Age*, 121-25.
11. Ibid.
12. Wernick, *The Vikings*, 69.
13. Gibson, *The Vikings*, 72-73.
14. Christensen, *"Scandinavian Ships from Earliest Times to the Vikings,"* 168.
15. Norton, *Ships' Figureheads*, 35.
16. Wernick, *The Vikings*, 44-45.
17. Ibid., 44.
18. Simpson, *Everyday Life in the Viking Age*, 92.
19. Wernick, *The Vikings*, 55.
20. Ibid., 54.
21. Gibson, *The Vikings*, 49.
22. LaFay, *The Vikings*, 21.
23. *Everyday Life through the Ages*, Reader's Digest Assoc., 130-32.
24. Simpson, *Everyday Life in the Viking Age*, 110.
25. See chap. 18, pg.
26. Wernick, *The Vikings*, 52.
27. Ibid., 107.

23. Weather

Women

The wind gods blew their fearful might,
Blackened skies turned day into night.
'Tho unlucky for your ship and me,
There was a lady who mastered the sea.

Weather

Storms have threatened man since ancient times when he first ventured on the water in rafts. One might imagine that the horrifying black clouds, the shrieking winds, and the violent streaks of lightning believed sent by the gods were probably a hundred times more frightening to the ancients, because of the unpredictability of those storm forces and the ignorance of the people.

Australian aborigines feared Wala-undayua, the Lightning-man, who rose to ride the lofty clouds, striking the earth with lightning bolts from his arms and legs. Indra, the Indian god "of a hundred powers," created tempests and other phenomena. Aeolus was the barrel-chested god of wind in Greek mythology. The wind devil Fujin and the thunder spirit Raijin were Japanese deities that created typhoons and thunder. Hung Kong, the god of wind, depicted as a bird, caused raging typhoons in the China sea. The mighty blows of the Norse god Thor's hammer on the giants who attacked him were preceded by thunder and lightning.[1]

Polynesians worshiped the brother and sister wind gods Voromatautoru and Tairibu. Their abode was near a giant rock, the foundation of the world, where storms, hurricanes, and all terrible winds were confined.

Norsemen thought of the winds as the mighty Odin on his horse at a full gallop or as the souls of women driven by him and screeching before a storm. A Scandinavian belief figured the wind as a giant eagle that issued the winds from beneath its wings as it took flight.[2]

A French legend tells of a brave captain dispatched to a far-off land to capture the winds and bring them back to blow upon the ocean. At the time there were no winds, so mariners had to rely on oarsmen to move their ships. Arriving in the land of the winds, the captain secured them in watertight bags, stored them in his vessel, and forbade his crew to touch them. When one of the men, curious of the strange cargo, opened one of the bags, the southwest wind escaped and blew into a tempest, which destroyed the ship and its crew. The gale burst the other bags of wind too, which also escaped, and together they have blown over the oceans ever since.[3]

Within each hemisphere, centered about 30-35° north and 30-35° south, there exists a series of anticyclonic cells from which the trade winds blow outward. Because of the rotation of the earth, these winds are deflected to the right in the Northern Hemisphere (northeast trade winds) and to the left in the Southern Hemisphere (southeast trade winds).[4]

The trade winds were believed named after the benefit they rendered to sailing ship trade vessels. The fifteen hundred-mile wide area of sun-drenched seas and fair-weather sailing within the reliable trades were the boon of the China tea trade. Sailing in trades, the tea clipper *James Baines* is believed to have attained the greatest speed of any sailing ship when in her log was recorded: ship going 21 knots with main skysail set.[5] Old sailors believed that fair winds would come by scratching the mast with their fingernails.

The ancient Greeks believed that lightning was a weapon of Zeus, the father of all gods, who sent thunderbolts borne by his favorite bird, the eagle. The Romans revered areas struck by lightning thought created by Jupiter, their equivalent of Zeus. Thunder on the right side was considered a good omen to the Greeks; thunder on the left was a favored sign to the Romans.[6]

Early native Americans believed that lightning and thunder came from the thunderbird, whose winking eye caused the lightning's flash. The Navaho believed in the healing power of their war god, Slayer of the Enemy Gods. To heal the sick, sand paintings were made of the god with lightning in his hands.[7]

There are no records of lightning damage sustained by vessels until the 1700s, when many vessels reported this phenomenon. Striking and traveling down the masts, lightning undoubtedly burst through hulls and sank many a ship. To safeguard their ships, seafarers quickly adopted Benjamin Franklin's principle of the lightning rod.[8]

A lightning-arresting device was carried and worked with some success on the *Endeavour* during Capt. James Cook's Pacific expedition in 1768. When a storm approached, "an electrical chain" of quarter-inch copper links was hoisted from the masthead and dangled into the sea. The "electrical chain," as Cook reported, "which we had just got up . . . conducted the lightning over the side of the Ship; but though we escaped the Lightning, the Explosion shook us like an Earthquake; the chain at the same time appeared like a Line of Fire." A Dutch ship, a short distance away, without the protection of a chain, was hit by lightning and consequently had its mainmast split and its gallant masts "shivered all to pieces."[9]

Although the device was recommended for all ships at the time, it proved impractical because of the poor conductivity of the chain and because of the dangers involved in carrying the apparatus aloft near a storm. Rigging was often damaged, and on an American ship three men were killed by lightning while trying to hoist and rig the gear.[10]

Despite use of the electric chain, the damage on many British ships continued. From 1810 to 1815, thirty-five ships of the line, thirteen frigates, and ten sloops sustained lightning damage. A Royal Navy study in 1847 recorded 220 ships being struck by lightning. One ship was hit five times in one hour, fifty ships had been set afire, ninety sailors had been killed, and nearly two hundred were wounded.[11]

When all-metal ships with metal masts came into use, lightning damage at sea ceased to be a problem.

Waterspouts, whirling storms over ocean or inland waters, are common in tropical seas, and are sometimes seen in higher latitudes. Their rotation is usually counterclockwise in the Northern Hemisphere and clockwise in the Southern Hemisphere; however, rotation in the opposite direction in relation to their respective hemispheres is sometimes recorded. These strange phenomena often assume fantastic shapes and can even appear to coil about themselves, which no doubt led early mariners to believe they were associated with deadly serpents. The giant, lofty, and sometimes snaking columns of water brought superstitious terror to the early mariners who saw them.

In the Middle Ages the Greeks called them *Prester* and referred to them as a fiery fluid because lightning and the smell of sulphur often accompanied them. Chinese and Japanese mariners believed they were caused by dragons, which they said could be seen moving up and down within them. The Japanese called them *tatsmaki,* or spouting dragons. Some ancients believed the spouts were rising columns of current from the bottom of the sea; others said they were black serpents that had come from the desert into the sea.[12]

Trying to dissipate the waterspouts, early sailors discharged artillery at them, cut the air with a black-handled knife while reciting prayers, sprinkled the winds with vinegar, or simulated a sword fight while making the sign of the cross between blows. Columbus was said to have read the "Evangelist" in hope of stopping one.[13]

Although waterspouts are created through the same processes that cause tornadoes, they are usually weaker, because the radical temperature differences that affect the mechanics of tornadoes do not exist at sea. Tornado winds could reach 300 MPH, while waterspout winds usually do not exceed 50 MPH and rarely last more than fifteen minutes.[14] There have been, however, a few recorded incidents of waterspouts powerful enough to seriously damage and even sink ships.

The whaleship *Alice Knowles* was engulfed and lost in a giant waterspout in the Atlantic near Cape Hatteras in 1915. "About noon a huge funnel-shaped cloud even blacker that the sky itself was sighted four or five miles from the ship." The sea moderated at midnight, but "at two o'clock a terrific roar came out of the blackness. No man could hear another's shouts. The waterspout enveloped the ship, dragging her onto her beams end." Only one of the crew lived to tell of the devastation.[15]

The schooner *George C. Finney* met with a waterspout off Port Colborne, Ontario, in Lake Erie on October 1, 1889. Barely afloat after the encounter, the foremast snapped at the deck and was lost, the mainmast was broken off halfway down, and the jibboom was shattered. The only sail that survived the storm was the mainsail, which was furled at the time. The crew reported dodging four waterspouts on that day, but the fifth one caught the ship and tossed it about like a tiny cork.[16]

Hurricanes derive their name from the Carib god Huracan, whose frown, according to legend, blackened the sky and created the circular tempest by blowing through his pursed lips.[17]

During his voyages to the New World, Columbus noted that the tropical storms of the Caribbean were different from those in the Mediterranean. He was the first to identify the characteristics of the super tropical storms when his fleet of four ships encountered a hurricane on the night of July 10, 1502. Columbus described his experience:

> The storm was terrible and on that night the ships were parted from me. Each one of them was reduced to an extremity, expecting nothing save death; each one of them was certain the others were lost.[18]

Through the study of storms south of the equator and the remarkable voyage of the brig *Charles Heddles* in 1845, Capt.

Henry Piddington, a veteran of the Indian Ocean merchant trade, pieced together the unusual meteorological data that created what he coined a "cyclone," the name meaning the "coil of a snake." The *Charles Heddles* was bound for Madagascar from Mauritius with a load of cattle on February 22, 1845, when she was engulfed in a terrific storm one day after leaving port. Hard-driving Captain Finck was in command of the brig, which was known as a fast runner. The seasoned master saw that his only chance for survival was to run before the ferocious winds. As the hours passed, the intensity of the storm only increased so that by February 25, in serious danger of foundering, the ravaged vessel lay wallowing under bare masts, her sails ripped to shreds. On February 27, after nearly a week of dashing hopelessly before the screeching winds, miraculously the little vessel was still afloat. When the sky cleared, Finck took his bearings and was shocked to discover that his vessel was but a few miles from where he began his voyage! The circulating winds of the tempest had driven his vessel in a wild and enormous circle. The *Charles Heddles* had for sure been caught in the "coil of a snake."[19]

The name "typhoon" is believed to have been derived from the Chinese *tai fung*, "wind which strikes," from the ancient Egyptian representation of a demon as Typhon, or from the mythical Greek monster Typhoeus, the father of storm winds.

Tropical cyclones in different regions are known by several different names. In the North Atlantic region, which includes the West Indies, Caribbean Sea, Gulf of Mexico, and the waters off the eastern coast of the United States, and in the north Pacific waters off the west coast of Mexico and Central America, a storm system with winds of 64 knots or more is called a hurricane. In the eastern Pacific regions, South Indian Ocean, Arabian sea, and the Bay of Bengal, hurricanes are called cyclones, except those near Australia, which may be called hurricanes or willy-willys. In the Pacific waters west of the Mariana and Caroline islands, across the Philippines and the China sea, and northeast to China and Japan, a storm of 60 knots or more is called a typhoon or by the local Philippine name of baguio. A tropical cyclone has never been encountered in the south Atlantic.[20]

Hurricanes in the Atlantic usually occur from June 1 to November 15, although there have been a few storms that began in late November. An 1888 hurricane stirred the western Atlantic from November 17 to December 2. Hurricane Alice, which blew from December 30, 1954, to January 5, 1955, has the distinction of being the earliest and the latest hurricane on record. The earliest hurricane to touch the United States coast was Alma, which hit northwest Florida on June 9, 1966.[21]

Eastern Pacific cyclones occur from June 1 through November 15, the central Pacific cyclone season is from June 1 to October 31. Western north Pacific typhoons can occur during every month of the year.[22]

The most deadly hurricane is believed to be the one that struck Galveston, Texas, on September 8-9, 1900, when from 6,000 to 7,200 people of the 38,000 population perished.[23]

The lowest barometric pressure ever recorded was 25.69 inches during Typhoon Tip, which occurred in the Pacific, October 12, 1979. This monster storm had a diameter of 1,400 miles and packed winds of 190 MPH.[24]

The longest-lasting hurricane was the Atlantic's Hurricane Ginger, which lasted from September 5 to October 5, 1971. The storm was classified as a hurricane for 20 of the storm's 31-day duration.[25]

The mariners who first encountered an "eye" of a cyclone must surely have been struck with awe and fear. Imagine sailing amid a great storm, with ferocious winds from one direction, into a calm where sometimes even blue skies appeared, and then back into the violent and screeching winds that came from a different direction—all within a short time. The diameter of a cyclone's eye is usually about fifteen nautical miles, but the eye of the monster Typhoon Carmen, which passed over Okinawa on August 20, 1960, was verified by radar as having an eye with a diameter of two hundred nautical miles![26]

By knowing the mighty energy associated with the great cyclones, one might better understand why these superstorms wreak such mass devastation and claim so many lives. The average thunderstorm can produce the energy to equal thirteen 20-kiloton atomic bombs. However, the tremendous energy created by just a small hurricane, which could release about 20 billion tons of water, equals nearly 500,000 atomic bombs, or the detonation of six atomic bombs a second![27]

This same small hurricane could release enough heat energy to roughly equal a thousand times the total electrical power output generated in the United States in a single day.[28]

The superstitious and credulous mariner, cut off from the outside world in a heavy and sound muffling fog bank or mist often perceived demons, spirits, or specter ships materialize in the haze. Phantom ships, ghosts of the deceased, patron saints, and many of the strange experiences reported in the Bermuda Triangle were attended by a fog or mist.

"Are We Glad To See You"

The ancient Chinese were said to have visited enshrouded palaces in the fog, which they called the "Sea Market." A Japanese legend relates that the fog is the breath of Shin-Kiro, a clam that lies on the sea bottom, which through the fog, offers a vision of the palace of the god of the bottom of the sea. An old Icelandic belief was that the fog was the bewitched daughter of the king. Human forms called specter-water were thought to ascend in the fog from a lake in Sweden.[29]

The foggiest area in the United States is at the aptly named Cape Disappointment, Washington, near the mouth of the Columbia River, where an average of 106 twenty-four-hour days of fog occurs each year. On the East Coast, the Moose Peak Lighthouse on Mistake Island (again aptly named) off the coast of Maine sees on the average of 66 complete days of fog.[30]

One of the worst maritime disasters blamed on fog was the sinking of the Canadian Pacific liner *Empress of Ireland* after collision with the Norwegian collier *Storstad* in the St. Lawrence River on May 29, 1914, during which 1,024 souls were lost.[31]

Along the New England coast, mariners have their own expressions when referring to the varying thickness of fog. A light fog would be termed "a mite thick." After that is a "thick o' fog," "a dungeon o' fog," and the heaviest, "a thick dungeon o' fog."[32]

The most famous and descriptive words written about fog are those of Carl Sandburg:

> The fog comes
> on little cat feet.
> It sits looking
> over the harbor and city
> on silent haunches
> and then moves on.[33]

Women

The origin of the tradition of referring to a ship as "she" can be traced to the Bible account that describes the ideal wife: Like merchant ships, she secures her provisions from afar.[34] There are, however, many whimsical theories why a ship is called "she." A long-held belief was that because a ship often carried a female figurehead on its bows, the vessel was naturally considered a she. Some smart-aleck old salt said it was because "there's not a straight line in 'em—they're all curves." Chauvinistic sailors said it was because "it takes a man to handle her." Others said it was "because it takes so much paint to keep her trim." Then there were the sailors who noted "that a ship is called 'she' because when 'she' comes into port 'she' is always looking for the buoys."

Throughout this book are many accounts of how women were considered woefully unlucky to have around ships or at sea when they joined their husbands. But in the myriad of all the unlucky incidents and circumstances involving women and ships is a most notable story of the brave and lucky Mary Ann Patten, who sailed with her husband, Joshua A. Patten, on the beautiful clipper *Neptune's Car* in 1866.

Not just any captain would be offered the command of a clipper. The great honor was bestowed only upon men who held the credentials of superior seamanship. Joshua Patten was such a captain. So much in demand were his services that when a sudden illness attacked the first captain of the *Car* just before a scheduled around-the-world voyage, Patten was quickly offered the command along with permission to take his wife with him.

And yes, misfortunes did happen on this voyage the Pattens called their second honeymoon, which undoubtedly were attributed to the presence of the young lady. One seaman fell from the upper deck and was badly injured, and another fell overboard and drowned; many hours were lost in searching for the man. But it was during the *Car*'s 1856 voyage from New York around Cape Horn to the West Coast that Mary Patten would earn her mark in history.

Neptune's Car, with all her white wings of canvas spread, dashed in splendor through the sparkling blue waters in an unofficial race with two other fast clippers, the *Intrepid* and the *Romance of the Seas*, which she was bent on beating to San Francisco.

For whatever reason, the first mate, against the captain's wish for maximum speed, began to belligerently and purposely step in the way of this progress. When the captain slept, the first mate on more than one occasion shortened sail in good weather. To add to the strained relations between him and his captain, he was found asleep on watch several times. Finally, because of his outright insubordination he was relieved of duty.

On one hand this maneuver relieved some stress, but then the young captain was left with the sole burden of around the clock navigation, for the second mate, or any of the other crewmen was unlearned in those procedures. Stress and fatigue took its toll on Patten as the clipper sped on nearing Cape Horn. He soon became ill and then delirious with "brain-fever," thereby unable to command his ship.

As the horrifying westerlies and the mountainous graybeards of the Horn attacked the ship, Mary Patten, nineteen years old and pregnant, calmly took over command of the great *Neptune's Car*. Luckily, she had studied navigation as a hobby during the long hours of boredom at sea when her husband was in command. Although she was greatly tempted to run to the nearest port to seek aid, she firmly stayed her course under the promise to her husband to take the ship to San Francisco. The disgruntled and disgraced mate voiced his strong disapproval and most probably excited the crew to the verge of mutiny by insisting that the clipper seek the closest port for the safety of the ship.

It is hard to believe how the young girl in this distressful and dark situation overcame the obstacles of an alarmed ruffian crew close to mutiny and still portray the confidence necessary to assure the cooperation and discipline required to command and navigate the vessel. Something made the crew's attitude change. Whether they felt sorry for the frail and expectant mother or whether they felt the situation was their last resort, no one knows. At any rate, through the worst they stood by her. For eighteen solid days of bitter cold, howling gales, and monstrous seas, *Neptunes's Car* fought the Horn's wrath. The sails were tattered to ribbons and the crew faced death in the desperate fight aloft. Mary Patten spent a grueling fifty days and nights either on deck, beside her sick husband, or at the chart table continually calculating her course or studying the accuracy of her position.

Past the dreaded waters of the Horn, the clipper sped north. She had survived the worst, but suddenly her husband went deaf and lost his sight. According to the medical terms of the time, persons attacked with this so-called new epidemic soon became insane. But she stood by him, braved the dilemma, and the crew stood by her.

Nearing San Francisco, the clipper was engulfed in heavy fog for days on end—a final test of her endurance and patience. Approaching the harbor as the fog finally lifted, she brushed aside the advice to wait for a pilot and took the helm herself, relying on her self-taught experience to steer the vessel safely and smartly into port.

After a voyage of 136 days, *Neptune's Car* docked on November 15, 1856, beating the clipper *Intrepid* by eleven days.

Mary Patten received one thousand dollars from the underwriters of the clipper for her valiant and renowned voyage. She became known as the "Heroine of Cape Horn" and the "Florence Nightingale of the Ocean." She became the ideal of the newly formed women's rights movement, who "used her as the star example of woman's ability to compete successfully in the pursuits and avocations of man."

Capt. Joshua Patten died in a lunatic asylum in 1857. Mary Patten, at age twenty-four, died a few years later, having played the major role in one of the most daring epics of the sea.[35]

Notes

1. Whipple, *Storm* , 43-45.
2. Rappoport, *Superstitions of Sailors*, 66-68.
3. Ibid., 99-100.
4. Kotsch and Henderson, *Heavy Weather Guide*, 68.
5. Baker, *The Folklore of the Sea*, 183.
6. Viemeister, *The Lightning Book*, 23-27.
7. Ibid.
8. Ibid., 236-41.
9. Ibid.
10. Ibid.
11. Ibid.
12. Bassett, *Legends and Superstitions of the Sea and Sailors*, 30-33.
13. Ibid.
14. Whipple, *Storm*, 133.
15. DeGrasse, *"Few Have, But He Survived a Water Spout,"* 146-47.
16. Beers, *History of the Great Lakes*, 753.
17. Kotsch and Henderson, *Heavy Weather Guide*, 315.
18. Ibid., 133.
19. Whipple, *Storm*, 53.
20. Bowditch, *Waves, Wind, and Weather*, 149-50.
21. Ludlum, *The American Weather Book*, 252.

22. Kotsch and Henderson, *Heavy Weather Guide,* 169.
23. Ludlum, *The American Weather Book,* 202.
24. Ibid., 17.
25. Ibid., 200.
26. Kotsch and Henderson, *Heavy Weather Guide,* 103.
27. Ibid., 113.
28. Gribbin et al., *The Weather Book,* 103.
29. Bassett, *Legends and Superstitions of the Sea and Sailors,* 297.
30. Ludlum, *The American Weather Guide,* 251-52.
31. Ibid., 256.
32. Leavitt, *Wake of the Coasters,* 117.
33. Ludlum, *The American Weather Guide,* 251.
34. Prov. 31:14.
35. Webb, *When Mary Met the Cape Horn Greybeards,* 21-25.

Bibliography

Allen, Oliver E. *The Windjammers*. Alexandria, Va: Time-Life Books, 1978.

Ashley, Clifford W. *The Ashley Book of Knots*. New York: Doubleday & Co., Inc., 1946.

Ashley, Leonard R. N. *Superstition, Prophecy, Luck, Magic & Witch-craft*. New York: Bell Publishing Co., 1984.

Backus, R., and T. Lineweaver. *The Natural History of Sharks*. New York: Lyons & Burford, 1969.

Baker, Margaret. *The Folklore of the Sea*. London: David & Charles, 1979.

Bassett, Fletcher S. *Legends and Superstitions of the Sea and of Sailors*. Chicago: Belford, Clarke & Co., 1885.

Beavis, B., and R. McCloskey. *Salty Dog Talk*. London: Adlard Coles Limited, 1983.

Beck, Horace. *Folklore and the Sea*. Middletown, Conn: Wesleyan University Press, 1973.

Beesley, Lawrence. "The Loss of the S. S. Titanic: Its Story and Its Lessons." In Winocour, J., ed. *The Story of the Titanic*. New York: Dover Publications, Inc., 1960.

Benwall, G., and A. Waugh. *Sea Enchantress*. London: Hutchinson & Co., 1961.

Berlitz, Charles. *The Dragon's Triangle*. New York: Fawcett Publishers, 1991.

____. *Without a Trace*. New York: Doubleday & Co., 1977.

Bodmer, Rudolph J., ed. *The Book of Wonders*. Washington, D.C.: Bureau of Industrial Education, Inc., 1916.

Bowditch, Nathaniel. *Waves, Wind, and Weather*. New York: David McKay Co., Inc., 1977.

Brewington, M. V. *Shipcarvers of North America*. New York: Dover Publications, Inc., 1962.

Brock, Paul. "Floating Phantom of the Icy North." *The Compass*. Winter 1973.

Brown, Raymond Lamont. *A Book of Superstitions*. New York: Taplinger Publishing Co., 1970.

____. *Phantoms of the Sea*. New York: Taplinger Publishing Co., 1972.

Callahan, Steven. *Adrift*. New York: Ballantine Books, 1986.

Carson, Rachel L. *The Sea around Us*. New York: Oxford University Press, 1951.

Gosse, Philip. *The Pirates' Who's Who*. New York: Burt Franklin,

Christensen, Arne Emil. "Scandinavian Ships from Earliest Times to the Vikings." In Bass, G., ed. *A History of Seafaring.* New York: Walker and Co., 1972.

Clary, James. *Ladies of the Lakes II.* West Bloomfield, Mich.: A & M Publishing, 1992.

Clemans, Martin. "Ye Olde Shippe Swallower." *The Compass.* Winter 1971.

Columbus Citizen, April 19, 1912.

Cornwell, E. L., ed. *The Illustrated History of Ships.* New York: Crescent Books, 1979.

Cousteau, J., and P. Diole. *Dolphins.* New York: Doubleday & Co., 1975.

Cousteau, J., and M. Richards. *Cousteau's Great White Shark.* New York: Harry N. Abrams, Inc., 1992.

DeGrasse, Quentin. "Few Have, But He Survived a Water Spout." In Heckman, R., ed., *Yankees Under Sail.* Dublin, N.H.: Yankee, Inc., 1968.

De Lys, Claudia. *A Treasury of American Superstition.* New York: Bonanza Books, 1947.

DeWire, Elinor. "Wreckers and Mooncussers." *The Compass.* 1989, no. 3.

Did You Know? New York: Reader's Digest Assoc., 1990.

Dor-Ner, Zvi. *Columbus and the Age of Discovery.* New York: William Morrow and Co., 1991.

Eaton, J., and C. Haas. *Titanic Triumph and Tragedy.* New York: W. W. Norton & Co., 1986.

Edsall, Margaret Horton. "A Place Called The Yard." In *Guide to the U.S. Naval Academy.* n.p.,n.d.

Encyclopedia of Magic and Superstition. London: Octopus Books Limited, 1974.

Engel, Leonard. *The Sea.* New York: Time Incorporated, 1961.

Estes, Richard D.."Serpents of the Sea." In Heckman, R., ed. *Yankees Under Sail.* Dublin, H.H.: Yankee, Inc., 1968.

Everyday Life through the Ages. New York: Reader's Digest Assoc., 1992.

Ferm, Vergilius. *Lightning Never Strikes Twice.* New York: Gramercy Publishing Co., 1987.

Fowler, William M. *Jack Tars & Commodores.* Boston: Houghton Mifflin Co., 1984.

Fowles, John. *Shipwreck.* Boston: Little, Brown and Co., 1975.

Freeman, F., and T. Roscoe. *Picture History of the U. S. Navy.* New York: Bonanza Books, 1956.

Garrett, Richard. *Voyage into Mystery.* London: Weidenfeld and Nicolson, 1987.

Gibson, Michael. *The Vikings.* New York: Wayland Publishers, 1972.1924.

Gribbin, J., J. Kington, et al. *The Weather Book.* Boston: Little, Brown & Co., 1982.

Gruppe, Henry E. *The Frigates.* Alexandria, Va: Time-Life Books, 1978.

Gunston, David. "The Man Who Lived in a Whale." *The Compass.* Spring 1972.

Henderson, R., and W. Kotch. *Heavy Weather Guide.* Annapolis, Md: Naval Institute Press, 1984.

History of the Great Lakes. Chicago: J. H. Beers & Company, 1899.

Humble, Richard. *The Explorers.* Alexandria, Va: Time-Life Books, 1978.

Kemp, Peter. *The History of Ships.* London: Orbis Publishing, 1978.

Kenney, Don H. *Ship Names: Origins and Usages during 45 Centuries.* Charlottesville, Va: University Press of Virginia, 1974.

Knox-Johnston, Robin. *The Twilight of Sail.* London: Sidgwick and Jackson, Ltd., 1978.

La Fay, Howard. *The Vikings.* Washington, D.C.: The National Geographic Society, 1972.

Laing, Alexander. *Seafaring America.* New York: American Heritage Pub. Co., Inc., 1974.

"Langley's Flying Ducthman." *Tailhook.* Fall 1989.

Leavitt, John F. *Wake of the Coasters.* Middletown, Conn.: Wesleyan University Press, 1970.

Lindquist, Lindy. "The Legend of Saint Nicholas." *The Compass.* Winter 1974.

Lorie, Peter. *Superstitions.* New York: Simon and Schuster, 1992.

Lovette, Lt. Cmdr. *Naval Customs, Traditions, and Usage.* Annapolis, Md.: U. S. Naval Institute, 1939.

Low, Charles P. "Cabin Boy on a China Clipper." In Snyder, F., ed. *Life Under Sail.* New York: The Macmillan Co., 1964.

Lubbock, Basil. *The Last of the Windjammers.* Boston: Charles E. Lauriat Co., 1929.

Ludlum, David M. *The American Weather Book.* Boston: Houghton Mifflin Co., 1982.

Maddocks, Melvin. *The Great Liners.* Alexandria, Va: Time-Life Books, 1978.

Magoun, Alexander F. *The Frigate Constitution and Other Historic Ships* (1928).Reprint. New York: Bonanza Books.

Maine, C. E. "The Atlantic's Sinister Triangle." In Canning, J., ed. *Fifty True Mysteries of the Sea.* New York: Stein and Day, 1980.

Maitland, Derek. *Setting Sails.* Hong Kong: South China Morning Post Ltd., 1981.

Malcolm, Robert S. "Navies of the Night." *The Compass.* Fall 1972.

Van Dervoort, J. W. *The Water World.* Chicago: Acme Publishing House, 1884.

Masefield, John. *Salt-Water Poems and Ballads.* New York: The Macmillan Co., 1912.

____. *The Wanderer of Liverpool.* New York: The Macmillan Co., 1930.

McDonell, Michael. "Lost Patrol." *Naval Aviation News.* June 1973.

Muilenburg, Peter. "Saga of a Seagoing Dog." *Reader's Digest.* Oct. 1992.

Mysteries of the Unexplained." New York: Reader's Digest Assoc., Inc., 1982.

Nordhoff, Charles. *Sailor Life on Man of War and Merchant Vessel.* New York: Dodd, Mead & Co., 1883.

Norton, Peter. *Ships' Figureheads.* Barre, Mass.: Barre Publishing, 1976.

Opie, I., and M. Tatem. *A Dictionary of Superstitions.* New York: Oxford University Press, 1992.

Rappoport, Dr. Angelo S. *Superstitions of Sailors.* Ann Arbor, Mich.: Gryphon Books, 1971.

Rawson, Eduardo. "Cape Horn Is the Terrible Test." *Cruising World,* December 1978.

Riesenberg, Felix. *Cape Horn.* New York: Dodd, Mead & Co., 1939.

Roberts, David. "The Iceman." *National Geographic.* June 1993.

Robinson, William. *Jack Nastyface.* Annapolis, Md.: Naval Institute Press, 1973.

Scammon, Charles M. *The Marine Mammals.* New York: Dover Publications, Inc., 1968.

Scandurra, Enrico. "The Maritime Republics: Medieval and Renaissance Ships in Italy." In Bass, G., ed. *A History of Seafaring.* New York: Walker and Co., 1972.

Schnepf, E. "Wilhelm Gustloff—The Worst Sea Tragedy in History."*Jinxed Ships & Doomed Voyages.* Vol. 2., 1990.

Secrets of the Seas. New York: Reader's Digest Assoc., 1972.

Sharper, Knowlson T. *The Origins of Popular Superstitions and Customs.* Detroit: Gale Research, 1968.

Shay, Frank. *An American Sailor's Treasury.* New York: Smithmark Publishers Inc., 1991.

Simpson, Jacqueline. *Everyday Life in the Viking Age.* New York: G. P. Putnam's Sons, 1967.

Snyder, Frank., ed. *Life Under Sail.* New York: The Macmillan Co., 1964.

Spectre, Peter H. *The Mariners Book of Days.* Brooklyn, Me: WoodenBoat Books, 1992.

"The Polynesian Mystery." In *Pacific Voyages: The Encyclopedia of Discovery and Exploration.* New York, Doublday and Co.,1971.

Thrower, W. R. *Life at Sea in the Age of Sail.* Sussex: Phillimore & Co., Ltd., 1972.

Viemeister, Peter E. *The Lightning Book.* New York: Doubleday & Co., 1961.

Waters, Harold. "Tiger Afloat." *The Compass.* 1975, no.3.

Webb, Wanda. "When Mary Met the Cape Horn Greybeards." In Heckman, R., ed. *Yankees Under Sail.* Dublin, N.H., 1968.

Wernick, Robert. *The Vikings.* Alexandria, Va: Time-Life Books, 1978.

Whipple, A. B. C. *Fighting Sail.* Alexandria, Va: Time-Life Books, 1978.

____. *Storm.* Alexandria, Va: Time-Life Books, 1982.

Williers, Alan. *The Way of a Ship.* New York: Charles Scribner's Sons, 1970.

Wilson, David. *The Vikings and Their Origins.* New York: McGraw-Hill Book Co., 1970.

Wirth, Rosalie. "The Unseen Skipper." *The Compass.* 1983, no. 3.

Woodcock, Robert. *Side Launch.* Toronto, Ont.: Summerhill Press, 1983.

Index

Benedict, Saint, helped drowning sailors, 225
Benjamin Morrel, American sealer searches for island, 158
Berge Istra, largest vessel ever lost, 248
Berkshire, England, 16
Bermuda called Isle of the Devils, 156
Bermuda psychiatric hospital named after St. Brendan, 156
Bermuda Triangle: characteristics of, 245; compared with Dragon's Triangle, 246; number of vessels believed lost in since 1800, 249; strange messages from, 260-61; malfunction of weather satellites above, 258; strange flight of B-24 in, 261; 3, 235
Bermudas, 3
berserkr, Old Norse term, defined, 318
Beuzec, Saint, calmed storms, 225
Bibles: considered Jonah's, anecdote, 166-67
billet instead of figurehead unlucky, 106
Billson, Cmdr. Marcus, recorded strange experience during flight, 262
bird attack omen, 219
birds, 18-27; related good or bad omens, 218
birthday of Cain, 73
Bisschop, Eric de, reports mermaid encounter, 200-01
Bittersweet, 206
Blachernes, Our Lady of, 223
Black Bird, 206
Black Cat, 206
Black Crow, 206
black neckerchief, 53
black rats, 13
Black Spread Eagle, 206
Black Watch, 206
black, foreboding signs of, 54
"Blackbeard," pirate, 230-31
Blaise, Saint, walked on water, 228
blood during building of a vessel, 37
blue sea, 54
bluebirds, 27
Bluenose, fishing schooner, 37
boarding a vessel, 33
boasting, 35-36
boatswain's pipe: origin of use; for piping aboard, 275
Bogoslof Island, changing appearance of, 158
Bombproof Belle, mascot, 17
bones from crab, 50

Bonnell, Caroline, *Titanic* survivor, 92
Bonnet, Maj. Stede, pirate, 229
Bonny, Anne, woman pirate, 233
boots nailed to mast, 50
Boreas, Greek north wind, 207
bores: phenomena of, largest bore, 277-78
Bosquez, dissects and examines mermaids in 1560, 198
boucaniers, 229
Bounty, popularity of tattooing of men on, 293-94
bowline, 172
"brain-fever," 338
Brander, Captain, dreams of *Wanderer*'s demise, 312
Brazilian malaga nuts, 50
breaking wood, 51
Breath, ketch, 18
Britannia survivors accompanied by dolphins, 56
Bronze Age, 2
Brown, Irwin, reports trench in sea, 258
Bruiser, 206
buccaneers, 229
building a vessel, 36-37
burial at night anecdote, 40
burial at sea, superstitions: 38-43; oldest ceremony; 38; of officer; 40, proper, improper; of poor Jack, 42
burial of Vikings, 42-43
burning the "dead horse," 296-97
buttons on sleeves, origin of, 53

Cabiri, Syrian legendary gods, 78
cackling hen, 29
"Calico Jack," 233
Callahan, Steven, survivor's dolphin story, 57-58
calling after someone aboard, 33
calm in Cape Horn described, 265
calming storms, 45-46
Calpean Star, sinking of, 21
Candlemas, 73
Canterbury, Saint Thomas of, 46
Canton, whaler, mysterious predicament on, 268-70
Cape Cod wreckers, 88
Cape Cod, 8
Cape Disappointment, foggiest area In United States, 336
Cape Fear, 12
Cape Horn: reputation of, estimate of wave heights, 264; fastest passage around, 265
Carmen, typhoon, enormous eye of, 334